THE FIRES OF ADVERSITY IN LATIN AMERICA

Neoliberalism, Globalization, and Free Trade

Faith N. Mishina

THE FIRES OF ADVERSITY IN LATIN AMERICA

Neoliberalism, Globalization, and Free Trade

Faith N. Mishina

COMMON GROUND RESEARCH NETWORKS 2017

First published in 2017
as part of the New Directions in the Humanities Book Imprint

Common Ground Research Networks
2001 South First Street, Suite 202
University of Illinois Research Park
Champaign, IL 61820 USA

Library of Congress Cataloging-in-Publication Data

Names: Mishina, Faith N., author.
Title: The fires of adversity in Latin America : neoliberalism,
  globalization, and free trade / Faith N. Mishina.
Description: Champaign, IL : Common Ground Research Networks, 2017. | Includes
  bibliographical references and index.
Identifiers: LCCN 2016032373 (print) | LCCN 2016044573 (ebook) | ISBN
  9781612299242 (hbk : alk. paper) | ISBN 9781612299259 (pbk : alk. paper) |
  ISBN 9781612299266 (pdf)
Subjects: LCSH: Capitalism--Political aspects--Latin America. |
  Neoliberalism--Latin America. | Free trade--Political aspects--Latin
  America. | Latin America--Foreign relations--United States. | Latin
  America--Foreign economic relations--United States. | Latin
  America--Economic policy. | Latin America--Politics and government.
Classification: LCC HC125 .M5495 2017 (print) | LCC HC125 (ebook) | DDC
  330.98--dc23
LC record available at https://lccn.loc.gov/2016032373

Cover Photo Credit: Phillip Kalantzis-Cope

Table of Contents

Forward

There is an astonishing ignorance about our Latin American neighbors that exists in the US population today. I marvel at the questions I receive from many university students: "How have we affected Latin America?" or "What do they think of us?" They are our neighbors, but we have been led to view them negatively and either as a threat for reasons of immigration, ideology, or perceived insignificance. Latin American news is clearly downplayed or omitted from our corporately controlled news media. They are our neighbors. Why do we ignore them? The answer to that question reveals a lot about ourselves.

Are they only important if they give us what we want? Since Latin America refused to ratify the free trade agreement (FTAA) with the United States in 2005, there has only been one significant political overture—President Obama's attempt to establish diplomatic ties with Cuba in 2015–16, an effort which was largely ignored by a Republican pro-business Congress.

There has been an even greater deliberate ignorance about our Latin American neighbors by US policy makers who, instead, bow to the demands of corporate America, their lobbyists, and the corporate push for profits in Latin America. Princeton polls have pointed out that American public opinion has no effect on American policy decisions whereas big donor opinion does. What is equally astonishing is the complete indifference on the part of US government policy for what we have imposed on our neighbors—military coups, invasions, genocides, and economic upheaval. Why do we not critically examine what we have caused? Why has there been so much silence around our past involvement in Latin America? Why is this knowledge restricted to small circles?

We have not seen their side of the story. It has ceased to exist; it has been deleted from our textbooks and from our media. Their populism and struggle for human rights was labeled "communism" and was swept under the rug, to be forgotten. One of my students has family in Guatemala. When his Indigenous mother found out that her son was critically studying the Guatemalan genocide, she was worried that Americans (US) might consider him a "communist." Over and over again, the label of "communism" was applied to their populist movements, an American (US) label that immediately shuts down discussion or any further examination. For Americans (US), the Latin American struggle for social justice was obliterated by a convenient label. The question is: convenient for whom?

In the attempt to clearly present the facts to my students, I began a serious investigation of the events and results of our corporations' involvement in Latin America. In the process, I have come to the firm realization that the brutal track record of US involvement in Latin America should become a public forum. There is a need in the United States for this type of discussion. Such a discussion might not only strengthen our humanity; it has to do with our own future. There is an ominous parallel of the past events in Latin America that is beginning to repeat itself in the US today. What is that connection?

One of my colleagues—a Chilean physicist—learned what I was teaching her students about the Chilean coup in 1973. She thanked me personally for "telling the truth" from the perspective of the majority of the Chilean people. She understood why most Americans knew almost nothing about what really happened because the Latin American events were never represented in the US by an unbiased media environment. Events were blatantly distorted to justify free market ideology. How could we not know about our participation in the torture, the internment camps, the *Kubark*, and US corporate involvement of incarcerating "subversives"? These issues were well reported in Europe and Latin America. Latin Americans felt that US multinational corporations saw Latin America as their corporate playground. By instigating such violence and illegal acts, US corporates were playing hardball to guarantee their profits at the expense of human lives…the *Desaparecidos.*

Reading the story of US involvement in Latin America is always a shock to my students. They cannot accept the breadth of the horrific events all at once. The details are myriad and important. They point to answers. America has a dark underbelly of corporate interests and investors with deep pockets who operate in as much autonomy as possible. Many of the accounts of their actions are either justified by an ideology that creates warring dualities (i.e., communism versus capitalism) or are complicated by conflicting information that serves a critical purpose—that of losing the public's interest and canceling out any argument. How long do we as Americans live with easy answers and manipulation, ignoring our underbelly? Apparently, until it hurts us.

In answer to my students' questions, I take them on a journey of the Latin American perspective through film, documentaries, and the declassified files of the CIA and the US government. I ask them to see all the facts before interpreting the bigger picture. I ask them to fit the pieces together to solve the puzzle. Using the Spanish metaphor of puppets manipulated by strings, I ask who the playing puppets are. Who is holding their strings? Whose money is being used?

A critical question always comes back to justice. Whose justice? My answer to my students is: Who has suffered the most? Is there a breakdown in human rights? Role-play! Walk a mile in each puppets' shoes. Then defend your answer with the facts.

It is my humble hope that this small book—presented partially from Latin American perspectives—makes the reader rethink the above questions. We should rethink why US policy did not care and the American public really did not recognized the Latin American experience of the past sixty-two years. Each chapter of this book concentrates on only one facet of a complex picture, of the fires of adversity that US corporate capitalism rained down on Latin America. Taken together like pieces of puzzle, the chapters point to answers. There are alarming patterns that emerge that need to be recognized and questioned.

American citizens were mostly blind, deaf, and dumb to these violent events in Latin America and to what the Latin Americans suffered at the hands of our multinational corporations. We are only just beginning to recognize the reality of some of these patterns as they are now hurting the average citizen of the United States.

CHAPTER 1

Introduction: The Fires of Adversity

There is a stark difference in the world-view of those who have lived through socially sanctioned atrocities and those who have not. This difference explains the silence of Latin Americans for the immediate years after thousands were disappeared in Latin America (1954–1990). The survivors of the disappeared experience and their families were silenced for decades by their pain and by laws protecting military and police officers who had participated in the atrocities. The fear of reprisal—assassination—for speaking out blocked the road to healing.

Such atrocities leave very deep scars and silent tongues. Language fails and cannot be organized to express the experience of torture without great cost to the survivors. Those that survived the torture and incarceration carried shame and were ostracized socially. The meaning of life and the value of self-identities were frequently shredded for such victims. The second half of the twentieth century was cataclysmic for many Latin American families who lost loved ones and for the survivors of such events.

Although there were many puppet-players that participated in the events of disappearing citizens, who were the puppet-masters? Today there are ominously clear reasons for the thousands of Disappeared in Latin America from 1954–1990.

Initiated by the United States, Operation Condor was an alliance with Latin American governments first in the Southern Cone and later in Central America, particularly during the decades of the 1970s and '80s. The primary objective of Operation Condor was to systematically exterminate left-winged progressives and dissidents who were "unacceptable citizens" (Garzón 1999). Latin America was to be cleansed of political progressives, socialists, union leaders, social democrats, Christian Democrats, nationalists, dissident generals, former presidents and congressional leaders—all of whom were strategically and indiscriminately branded as communists.

In true Nazi fashion, Latin America was to vilify its scapegoats and incarcerate them in numerous hidden detention centers echoing the Holocaust. This was a "political genocide" (Rozanski, 1998) because there was "no room for certain types of people" (Garzón 1999). Torture was taught at the US School of the Americas in Panama, using the CIA's manual on torture, the *Kubark* (1963). Many puppet-players have since been sentenced for their role in this oppression; however, the instigative role of the puppet-masters was left unchallenged and not investigated.

Responding to demands of many US multinational corporations—AT&T (formerly IT&T), Ford Foundation, Pfizer Chemical, Bank of America, Purina, and the corporations involved in extraction of minerals and copper, to name only a few—the US government was not supposed to tolerate communism or socialism. Socialism and communism could threaten North American corporate profits and investments in Latin America. Anti-communism was an obsession of corporate capitalists. The Dulles brothers, the E. H. Harriman bankers, the Rothschilds, the Rockefellers, the J.P. Morgan family, and the Walker-Bush family would push for wars against communism fought on every level by private corporations whose involvement, however, was conveniently paid for with public tax dollars or by the US military (Klein 2007, 14). In other words, the US government was a convenient front controlled by the elites of corporate capitalism.

Historically, Nazi Germany had protected these Western elites from Soviet communism. If one follows the money, it is well known today that many US corporations sold war materials, engines and fuel via Switzerland to sustain Nazi Germany during World War II while ironically, US servicemen died fighting the Nazis. The ideology of fascism was quietly favored by many US corporations and European elites who did not wish to suffer the fate of the Romanov Royal Family and their followers after the Russian Revolution. However, fascist ideas did not die with Hitler's defeat.

The US-supported military coups and conservative military governments in Latin America would generate right-winged strongmen—a condition that would reassure North American corporate profits and that would emulate fascism. In this fearful climate created by US corporate capitalism, internal Latin American elites and military officers of Argentina, Chile, Paraguay, Uruguay, Brazil, and Bolivia actively participated in the search for "subversives" by utilizing a sophisticated data base network supplied by US intelligence (McSherry 2005). It was US intelligence, then, that helped to identify the "unacceptable citizens." Colombia, Venezuela, Peru and Ecuador also took part by providing information on exiles or disappearing targeted individuals.

For the Latin American public, the fall-out from corporate capitalism's imposed years of terror was a nightmare: military coups, dirty wars, CIA propaganda and instruction on torture, thousands of Disappeared, social and economic upheaval. US economic influence also reactivated an old colonial characteristic of Latin America—the internal colonial structure of the business elites, a small percentage of the Latin American population. Alliance with US and Northern corporate interests against their own countrymen would greatly profit these elites.

Activating a very Spanish metaphor (from *Don Quixote de la Mancha*), the military puppet dictators were responding to the US's policy and money of "Shock and Awe" intervention. However, the US government was also a convenient puppet controlled by large corporate and banking interests in the United States. By the 1970s, these interests had morphed into the elite monolithic architecture of conservative think tanks, trade commissions, free trade agreements, associated banking institutions and a myriad of very influential interlocking business relationships.

A principle characteristic of both interior colonial elites and the external imperial elites is a blindness and deafness to any perspective that opposes unchecked capitalism. Unchecked corporate capitalism protects their wealth and their way of life. The enormous tragic fall-out of human lives as a result of their machinations is off the elites' radar and conveniently ignored.

Strong patterns emerge here: 1) The scapegoating of a part of society for genocide—socialists, progressives, and uncooperative thinkers, 2) the indiscriminate branding of the scapegoats as "communists," an "unacceptable citizenry," 3) the preference of corporate capitalism for strong men and right-winged governments, 4) the exponential increase in military involvement, 5) the use of public tax dollars and military lives to fund elite interests, and 6) a blindness and a deafness to large scale human tragedy so to protect the system that profits elite wealth.

Where the Latin American experience of the Disappeared echoed the extermination of the Jews in World War II, the motivations of US corporate capitalism also had an ugly comparison which needed to be disguised. Such an illegal agenda violated the Geneva Convention, the UN Charter and international law—US military entry into foreign nations without a declaration of war, torture of scapegoated citizens, kidnappings, assassinations, the manipulation of foreign elections, ad infinitum. The actions of the US government propelled by US corporations needed to be covert, hidden from US citizens, international courts and framed by deceptive arguments.

Deception destabilizes both perceptions and opinions. It unarms or delays any opposition. The use of deception is a deliberate tactic that operates on three levels. I.) The simple lies are one dimensional; however, if often repeated, simple lies can gradually supplant truth.

II.) The second dimension is a dual narrative of inversion, good versus evil. The dual narrative of inversion is bigger than a simple lie. It is a whole story that automatically justifies one position while vilifying the other side. More importantly, this type of narrative is used to quell critical judgment and to manipulate outcomes. It colors one side with evil intent while justifying the other side's presumed qualities. The North American public who still believed in the American Dream and who were raised on cartoons (such as the Joker and Batman), initially swallowed the good versus evil mantra for several decades.

Taken to the extreme, the narrative of inversion presents a beastly ideological struggle between two opposing opposites. A twentieth-century example would be the Cold War: communism versus capitalism. Each side considers the other a beast of destruction. The narrative of inversion dominated twentieth-century cartoons, advertising, and politics—including the narratives of two world wars. The human fall-out from these dual war-like stories was millions of lives lost. But the status quo and profits of corporate capitalism have been well protected by these dual stories. War could be considered a deliberate strategy by those who wish to protect their wealth and don't have to fight it. Moreover, for many US corporations tied to the US military industrial complex, World War II was very good business.

III.) When the dual stories are no longer enough to manipulate a more educated and war-exhausted public, the actions of elites who must hide their illegal or illicit agenda must be ensconced in overwhelming conflictual documentation to cancel out possible negative conclusions by the public. The agenda must become so confusing, so difficult to penetrate that the average citizen does not have the time to figure out that labyrinthine confusion is a deliberate tactic. Frequently into this three dimensional architecture of spin, the dual narrative of inversion can continue to be effective. Labyrinthine chaos destabilizes public opinion and increases fear, both of which encourage the re-effectiveness of the dual narrative of inversion.

An important advantage of a large architecture of deception is the disappearance of the perpetrators. An architecture of deception permits the creators of spin a place to hide. Planners of an agenda such as genocide like the anonymity, the plausible deniability and the protection of impunity. The public perceives the outcome as being so complex and overwhelming; thus, the events are impossible to stop. Those who originated the agenda cannot be found; however, they have activated the puppet players. The torture and disappearance of thousands of people is ironically mirrored by the prospering perpetrators who have vanished from public scrutiny. If a problem arises, the puppet players, not the puppet-masters, take the fall.

The Latin American who grasped this development was Gabriel García Márquez (Mishina 2016). As an experienced journalist and writer, he recognized that neoliberalism or corporate capitalism had morphed into a large covert three-dimensional architecture which hid US complicity and simultaneously overwhelmed the Latin American public with multiple interlocking events. The military coup in Chile activated García Márquez politically. He became a writer of labyrinths that would reflect the reality of what was happening in Latin America. The multifaceted program of Operation Condor became a pattern, the violent dawn of corporate Neoliberal agendas then (1973) and for the future.

Today, the control of all national sovereignty by an elite corporate class (guaranteed by their trade agreements) has come about, suggesting that some of the neoliberal fires of adversity that have happened in Latin America will come full circle globally. Free trade legalese guarantees multinational corporations the right to enter any country that has signed the agreements, and develop their resources even when the nation in question and its citizens fight that development. If there is too much resistance, the corporations will sue for billions of dollars. Any conflict is decided by ICSID's court, the International Centre for the Settlement of Investment Disputes, a judicial body controlled by big business that excludes any democratic checks and balances or outside witnesses. Corporate victory is almost always assured.

By signing these free trade agreements, Californians cannot prevent Nestlé from extracting water for profit from California's public forests. US citizens cannot prevent fracking in their national parks. Colombians cannot refuse the entry of the US multinational Tobie Mining and Energy in their national park to extract gold. Such mineral extraction is highly destructive of their Amazon region. For the corporate elites, the world has become their playground. Free trade agreements are contracts that subjugate the rights of all participating nations and cultures to the interests of wealthy corporations and their elites. Diverse peoples are to be homogenized for the convenience of corporate profits.

Globalization, a labyrinthine structure of trade agreements, banking institutions and their corporate elites, is overwhelmingly complex, but it protects and enriches the corporates' agenda and wealth. Given its history—US corporate involvement with Nazi Germany and in Latin America, the elite corporatist agenda points to violent repercussions for humanity. The corporate agenda's unchecked, "freed," and deregulated capitalism has consequences for world labor and humanity. It had terrible consequences for Latin America.

This book consists of eight researched investigations into different facets of the Monolith of corporate capitalism's involvement and control over Latin American natural resources, land, and economies. The aftermath of human suffering and the number of uprooted lives of Latin Americans have been enormous. To accept the general thesis of this first chapter—that of corporate accountability for massive destruction of humanity and its war on leftist populism—requires the strong documentation found in the following investigations (Chapters 2–9).

REFERENCES

Garzón, Baltazar. 1999. "Auto de procesamiento a militares argentines." Court case, November 2. Madrid. www.derechos.org.

Klein, Naomi. 2007. *The Shock Doctrine: The Rise of Disaster Capitalism*. New York: Picador.

McSherry, J. Patrice. 2005. *Predatory States: Operation Condor and Covert War in Latin America*. New York: Rowman & Littlefield Publishers, Inc.

Mishina, Faith. 2016. *Gabriel García Márquez's Subversive Agenda: Architectures of Deception to Discredit the Non-Ending Colonial Status Quo*. Urbana, IL: Common Ground Publishing.

Rozanski, Carlo. 1998. "Auto de la sala de lo penal de la Audiencia Nacional confirmando la jurisdicción de España para conocer de los crímenes de genocidio y terrorismo cometidos durante la dictadura argentina." Court case, November 4. Madrid. www.derechos.org.

CHAPTER 2

The Coup and the Genocide: The Ominous Strings of Corporate Puppet Masters—Washington, Allende, and Pinochet

In the twenty-first century, Latin American concerns for the atrocities committed under Pinochet's regime were reawakened by the arrest of Pinochet and the related legal controversies in the courts of Britain, Spain and Chile. This investigation analyzes the direct US involvement in Chile, in the '60s and the '70s. Behind the objective to bring down "communism"—a narrative fed to the US public to disguise the Neoliberal push for corporate profits—is the direct involvement of Dr. Milton Friedman, the father of the Neoliberal project, in Chile along with his "Chicago Boys." Chile was to be remade not only politically but also economically by imposing the neoliberal economic model. Washington's direct attempts to bring down President Allende highlight the brutal intensity that has characterized many Neoliberal projects when profits of corporations and their subsidiaries are threatened. Washington's open support for Pinochet is documented due to 24,000 declassified documents. Though Washington later claimed to have distanced itself from the atrocities committed by Pinochet's regime, Pinochet's atrocities only mirrored the egregious and illegal interference of the CIA and right-winged Neoliberal interests in Chile. The destruction of the democratically elected government of Allende and the substitution of a harsh right-winged military dictatorship to secure US corporate profits does not auger well for future Neoliberal projects.

Neoliberalism has long been understood as the corporate script that has authorized imperialism, social inequality, and the transfer of public wealth to private elites (privatization). This term was used and well understood for many years globally, but poorly grasped by American citizens. US citizenry were delayed in understanding the central tenants of neoliberalism and its effects because of the "shapeshifting nature of the ideology" that deliberately used so many different labels, changing its name and switching identities: globalization, free trade, Reaganomics, laissez-faire capitalism, corporate capitalism, and free market capitalism (Klein 2007, 17). Contributing to the confusion are the related words "conservative" (in politics) and "liberal" (in economics). Correlating two apparent opposites—conservative and liberal—as the same mind-set empties the word definitions of meaning. Distinct definitions lead to clarity; unclear definitions lead to muddled thinking. Such doublespeak and shapeshifting have been tools used to confuse the general American public.

This chapter argues that the free market capitalism as practiced in the second half of the twentieth century and the first sixteen years of the twenty-first century has been scripted by corporate agendas that favor profit over people. This "new" wave of "laissez-faire" capitalism, revived by Milton Friedman in the 1950s in the US and defined as Neoliberalism, is characterized by its aggressive political involvement. This strategic involvement is a direct reaction, on the one hand, to thirty-three years of Keynesian constraints (1935–1968) on wealth and corporate interests inside the US, and on the other, the unsustainable demand of corporate boards for continuously increasing profits. Since its practiced inception, however, the Neoliberal agenda has created an increasingly dysfunctional form of capitalism that has authorized imperialism, social inequality and large scale production with a dark side that exploits human rights and human labor. Chile (1964–1990) presents a classic example stripped and rebuilt by the corporate neoliberal narrative that imposed extreme forms of imperialism. This imposition included incarceration, torture, disappearance of citizens, the tearing apart of the fabric of social stability, and the creation of great social inequality, all for the purpose of maintaining US corporate investments and profits.

The advent of Neoliberalism (1944 Bretton Woods and 1948 the GATT) marks a major shift in intensity from the imperialism practiced in the earlier twentieth century. Under the neoliberal agenda, imperialism exponentially morphed in the second half of the twentieth century into extreme demonstrations of power. Chile lost its national sovereignty—it lost an elected democracy and it lost its economic system—so that corporate interests could impose a neoliberal economics that would favor US multinational corporations.

First applied outwardly to Latin America (1954–2007), the aggressive resource war waged by Neoliberal policies had devastating effects on Guatemala and the Southern Cone of Latin America. Chile, however, was a principle target as US mining giants feared losing their control of the profits from Chile's primary and abundant natural resource, copper. The Neoliberal Script for Chile enforced brutal political and economic reforms, blatantly violating human rights.

This chapter briefly reviews the neoliberal script that has authorized this heightened form of imperialism. This economic policy is then applied to the details of the neoliberal siege on Chile, a two-pronged attack, one that was political and the other, economic. The Chilean participants in this drama, Allende and Pinochet, were powerfully manipulated by corporatist demands. The former was assassinated, and the latter was supported by Washington's policies with the caveat that neoliberal economic policies be applied. Washington and its political policies, however, were also being manipulated by large US conservative think tanks whose corporate profits were their exclusive priority. The Chilean democracy, the Chilean president, the Chilean economy, Chilean sovereignty, and especially the Chilean people were all casualties in this neoliberal resource war.

NEOLIBERALISM: THE DEFINITION AND ITS PARADOX

There has been a serious division in global perspectives that arise from the word "Neoliberalism." It has been described as the "defining political, economic paradigm of our time" (McChesney 1998, 7). Neoliberalism is an economic theory with strong ideological roots that has spawned massive corporate production, reducing smaller competitors. In theory, neoliberalism defends the mythology of the "free market," a pure market control, cleansed of all government interruptions and trade barriers (deregulation). Theoretically, the market left to its own devices creates just the right number of products at the right prices and the right wages. In practice, it appears that neoliberal economic policies benefit massive corporations giving them advantageous control over their markets. While these policies profit the wealthy few, they have weakened and continue to reduce the quality of life for the poor and middle class citizenry of the world, that is, the majority of humanity.

The link between economics and politics has always been inextricably tied, and since 2008, much has been written about this link as corporate capitalists have deliberately and strategically striven to control the US political machine. Given this strong link between economics and politics, it is not a surprise that many people are confused by the term Neoliberalism.

Liberal in politics supports the poor and the middle-class citizens of the world; however, liberal in economics supports the exact opposite, that is, the wealthy and their corporate interests. Neoliberalism is an economic term whose policies favor the elites and the corporate push for profits. Freeing the market from government constraints favors large corporations in any competitive environment.

In the US, the term "neoliberalism" is rarely used and is frequently not understood. In the rest of the world, the term "neoliberalism" is much more familiar, and today is recognized as an economic policy that favors the corporate elites at the expense of the general populace. Since 2003, neoliberal policies have been openly scrutinized, criticized and in many cases, rejected on the world stage. A corresponding tactic of neoliberal corporatists has been to discard the term "neoliberalism" for "globalization" or "free trade." The mythology of the free market has been debunked; no one is fooled by the mythology anymore. However, because the terminology "neoliberalism" continues to be utilized in Latin America to express corporate capitalism's control of their resources, land, and cultures, the terminology is still applicable.

Neoliberalism is frequently defined by the following beliefs:

1. The rule of the market will free private enterprise from any government constraints, price controls, and union demands for wages or benefits. Free markets demand the deregulation of governmental and environmental controls on industry and corporations.
2. Privatization requires that all state-owned public assets should be sold to private investors. Privatization has had the effect of concentrating wealth in the hands of a small elite group and making the public pay more for its needs, that is, the transfer of public funds into privileged private hands.
3. Neoliberalism requires the reduction of public expenditure for social services such as education, health care, welfare, social security benefits and public works.
4. Neoliberalism rejects the concept of the "Public Good" or "Community". These concepts are replaced by "individual responsibility" and the implication that the poor are poor because they are lazy.

Using the American (US) vernacular, this neoliberal agenda means the big guy in the game of competition wins and can monopolize the market. Corporate power and policy-making strive to control the earth's resources and acquire the profits from these resources while eliminating the little guy who cannot compete on economies to scale.

A BRIEF HISTORICAL SUMMARY OF THE NEOLIBERAL AGENDA

Neo implies a new type of economic liberalism. The old economic liberalism was taken from Adam Smith's *The Wealth of Nations* (1776). It prevailed in the US until the Great Depression of 1929. As a result of the Great Depression, laissez-faire economics were debunked for an opposing economic theory by John Maynard Keynes (the Second New Deal in 1935) that promoted employment and the common good. Keynesian economics as practiced by President Roosevelt birthed a strong and prosperous middle class in the United States. However, under Keynesian economics, corporations in the US were experiencing shrinking profit rates that galvanized the big business sector into a major economic movement—with a new economic policy called Neoliberalism.

Neoliberal economic theory was first championed by Milton Friedman, a professor of economics at the Chicago School of Business. His department was known for its revolutionary fervor tied to the idea of pure market economics. He dreamed of de-patterning societies and returning them to the pure state of capitalism, divested of all controls on the market. (Klein 2007, 60). Thus, the mission of the Chicago School was one of purification—stripping away all constraints and government controls on market capitalism. Friedman saw the market as a pure science, a questionable assumption. Nevertheless, Friedman's vision of the market coincided perfectly with the interests of large US corporate think tanks and trade commissions (Heritage Foundation, Cato Institute, the American Enterprise Institute, The Council on Foreign Relations, The Trilateral Commission, etc.) who wished to encourage corporate capitalist expansion.

With the election of Republican Dwight Eisenhower (1953), the new president was reluctant to oppose a popular Keynesian support within the US, however, he was quickly swayed by influential conservative politicians and business cohorts to enforce neoliberal ideas abroad. John Foster Dulles was his Secretary of State and Allen Dulles was the head of the CIA. Both brothers saw the world politically in ideological black and white. Both had significant money invested into corporate interests that would stand to profit from American (US) intervention: J.P. Morgan & Company, the International Nickel Company, the Cuban Sugar Cane Corporation and the United Fruit Company. The US corporate agenda under Eisenhower applied the accusation of "communism" to oppose progressive movements in other countries that would restrict their trade and corporate profits. Under the Dulles brothers' political influence, the US military opposed two progressive movements by staging two successive coups—Iran (1953) and Guatemala (1954). In both countries, new governments were installed that would ensure access and profits for US corporate interests.

Nineteen years later, the plan to overthrow Allende exceeded this pattern; US corporate interests not only installed a compliant government but also a neoliberal economic system.

THE PUPPET MASTERS BEHIND THE
NEOLIBERAL PUSH TO CONTROL CHILE

The political and economic imperialism imposed on Chile (1964–1984) represents the height of the Neoliberal war against Latin American economic protectionism. The Chilean coup demonstrated imperialism on multiple levels: 1) academic imperialism, 2) CIA covert intervention, 3) the School of the Americas' teaching on torture to Latin American dictators and military leaders, 4) political intervention in Chilean elections, 5) economic strangulation to bring down President Allende's government, 6) the assassination of the Chilean president, 7) support of a military coup, 8) economic support of Pinochet's military dictatorship and finally, 9) the demand for Pinochet to immediately impose neoliberal economic policies. As Eduardo Galeano (1983) ironically put it in *The Days and Nights of Love and War*: "The theories of Milton Friedman gave him the Nobel Prize; they gave Chile General Pinochet."

In the 1950s and the 1960s, the Latin American countries of the Southern Cone were practicing "Developmentalism," that is, an economic practice that pursued in-country industrialization rather than a strong dependency or reliance on the importation of goods and resources. Local businesses were subsidized to keep out foreign imports; high tariffs protected their industries. The economic practices of Developmentalism were so successful in the Southern Cone that there were predictions that the class divide between the first and the third worlds would be reduced. Like Keynesian economics in the US, Developmentalism protected the poor and grew the middle class. Though far from Stalinism and Maoism, Developmentalism and Keynesian economics were both simplistically classified as "communism" and scripted as being "leftist" by Neoliberal conservatives with a dualistic black and white political map. Marxism was not the actual enemy that impeded their profits; the real enemy was the economic policies of Keynesians in the US, Developmentalists in Latin America and Social Democrats in Europe. The script, "communism," was a deliberate name tag used to vilify impediments to trade and corporate profits. The political binary vision of "communism" versus "capitalism" as favored by the Dulles brothers and McCarthy aided and abetted the corporatists' agenda.

In 1953, Albion Patterson, the Director of the US International Cooperation Administration in Chile (later known as USAID), and Theodore W. Schultz, chairman of the Department of Economics at the University of Chicago, met in Santiago, Chile. The purpose of the meeting was to discuss how to eradicate the progressive economics known as Developmentalism in Chile. Both agreed that the US needed to "influence" the economic education of Latin Americans.

Schultz's comment, "we want [Latin American countries] to work out their economic salvation by relating themselves to us and by using our way of achieving their economic development," was recorded in an interview with Juan Gabriel Valdés, in his book, *Pinochet's Economists: The Chicago School in Chile* (Valdés 1995, 89). That comment ironically points to the second half of an Orwellian quote from *Nineteen Eighty-Four*, "We shall squeeze you empty, and then, we shall fill you with ourselves." Orwell's words were prophetic.

Eradicating Developmentalism in Latin America was what the "Chile Project" was about. In 1956, 100 Chilean students were sent to the University of Chicago to pursue advanced degrees but their tuition and expenses were paid mostly by the US taxpayers and embellished by US conservative think tanks. This strategy was typically neoliberal; public funds were used for the benefit of private corporate interests. The Center for Latin American Economic Studies was created to instill neoliberal economic orthodoxy, a form of intellectual imperialism. By 1963, twelve of the thirteen full-time faculty members in Chile's Catholic University Economics Department were "Chicago Boys." Despite the "organized transfer of ideology from the U.S.," as Chile's foreign minister, Juan Gabriel Valdés (1995, 6), documents it, all three of Chile's political parties in the late 1960s pushed for nationalizing the country's largest source of revenue. The copper mines, Chile's principal resource, were controlled by US mining corporations which siphoned off most of the profits. The threat of Chilean nationalization of a very profitable US corporate revenue source galvanized US corporate interests into action.

In the 1960s the scope of the CIA's work expanded dramatically in Latin America (Weiner 2008, 322.) The covert operations of the Kennedys, particularly Bobby Kennedy who wielded great influence over the CIA, continued the strong man tactics practiced by the Dulles brothers under President Eisenhower. In 1962, President Kennedy approved a political-warfare program to subvert Salvador Allende's first run for the Chilean presidency in September of 1964. The CIA was the channel, and the agency pumped approximately $3 million into the political apparatus of Chile (Weiner, 2008, 355) to prevent Allende's election. Using South America's conservative Roman Catholic Church and certain trade unions manipulated by US corporate interests, President Johnson continued the covert anti-Allende program. The CIA successfully managed to infuse resistance to Allende in the Chilean military command and the national police. Frei's victory in Chile over Allende in the Chilean Presidential elections of 1964 was a triumph achieved "partly as the result of the good work of the CIA" (Weiner 2008, 355), an assessment delivered by Secretary of State Rusk to President Johnson in 1964.

By 1970, however, the leftist front-runner in the September elections was once again Salvador Allende. Helms, the director of the CIA, was insistent on US involvement; he strongly advised further covert action to prevent Allende's election. Consequently on March 1970, Secretary of State, Henry Kissinger, approved $135,000 for a program to defeat Allende on March 1970 and again, $165,000 in June 1970 (Weiner 2008, 355). Posters, leaflets, pamphlets, news stories, and editorials were written to equate the election of Allende with the destruction of the Chilean democracy. The object was to terrify the Chilean electorate. However, the US Ambassador to Chile, Korry, described the CIA's efforts as "propaganda." He stated "the idiots in the CIA who had helped create the campaign of terror should have been sacked immediately for not understanding Chile and Chileans. This was the kind of thing I had seen in 1948, in Italy!" (Centro de Estudios Públicos 1998).

On September 4, 1970, Salvador Allende won the Chilean presidency by a small margin. The CIA, whose involvement had backfired in fixing this election covertly and illegally, now backed the overt proposals for a military coup proffered by several large corporations. Kissinger immediately approved $250,000 more for political-warfare in Chile. In total, $1,950,000 was put into the anti-Allende program (Weiner 2008, 357) which consisted of two tracks. Track One was political-warfare, economic pressure, propaganda, and diplomatic hardball. Track Two was a military coup.

Upon hearing that Allende had been elected, Nixon ordered Richard Helms, the CIA director, "to make the [Chilean] economy scream" (declassified files: "Notes on Meeting with the President on Chile," 1970). Despite Allende's pledge to fairly compensate the US corporate sector in Chile due to the nationalization of the mines, most US multinationals rejected Allende's promise and ominously suspected that Allende's election was only the beginning of a possible Latin American trend. Secretary of State, Henry Kissinger, saw Allende's election as a global threat:

> The example of a successful elected Marxist government in Chile would surely have an impact on—and even precedent value for—other parts of the world, especially in Italy; the imitative spread of similar phenomena elsewhere would in turn significantly affect the world balance and our own position in it. (declassified: Memorandum to the President, 1970)

By 1968, 20 percent of US foreign investment was tied up in Latin America and US firms had 5,436 subsidiaries in the region producing staggering profits (Klein 2007, 28). Mining companies had invested $1 billion over the previous fifty years in Chile's copper mining industry—the largest in the world—but they had sent $7.2 billion home (Branford and Kucinski 1988, 40–52). For these reasons, corporate America was the impetus behind the US Republican Presidency that pushed for a coup against the Allende government.

The Ad Hoc Committee on Chile included members of the major US mining companies with holdings in Chile, representatives of the International Telephone and Telegraph Company (IT&T) which owned 70 percent of Chile's phone system, Purina, Bank of America and Pfizer Chemical. Nationalization was a threat to the profits of these companies. The primary objective of the committee was to cause the economic collapse of the Allende government, Track One. US loans to Chile were all blocked. Any purchases from Chile were delayed.

The most aggressive of the corporates was IT&T whose fear of nationalization of the Chilean telephone industry led them to plot with the CIA and the State Department to block Allende's election two years prior to his inauguration. A US Senate investigation, fueled by Jack Anderson, a syndicated journalist's articles based on IT&T's documents, discovered a major conspiracy in which IT&T officials had attempted to bribe Chilean forces opposed to Allende with $1 million (Subcommittee on Multinational Corporations 1973, 4, 18). The Senate report of June 1973 also uncovered further strategies planned by IT&T to undermine Allende after his election. Most notably, IT&T had composed a plan containing eighteen points that was delivered to Henry Kissinger and President Nixon. It called for a military coup.

Corporate America had scripted an extreme form of imperialism (US Senate, "Covert Action in Chile," 1975, 11, 15) despite the 1975 Senate Investigation's findings that, according to the Intelligence Reports, Allende posed no threat to democracy (United States Senate, Select Committee to Study Governmental Operations with Respect to Intelligence Activities 1975, 45). This Track Two component of Project FUBELT was highly compartmentalized; most members of the 40 Committee dedicated to undermining Allende's election were not even aware of Track Two's existence (Kornbluh 2003, 14). Corporate America had scripted the coup, and the legislative body of the US that holds the power to approve military action had been completely bypassed. The corporate puppet-masters' strings had outmaneuvered Washington's protocol and legislative control.

In Chile, "*los* Chicago Boys" in the Catholic University and in business were cultivated and funded by the CIA. Orlando Saenz, president of the National Association of Manufacturers, enlisted several Chicago Boys to create plans to remake Chile along neoliberal lines. The US Senate hearing also documented that

75 percent of the funds to create this opposition to Allende came directly from the CIA (United States Senate, Select Committee to Study Governmental Operations with Respect to Intelligence Activities 1975, 30). The plans developed by this opposition became known as "The Brick," and eight out of the ten responsible for the plans had studied neoliberal economics at the University of Chicago. In the plan, the military junta would kill Allende, and would then enforce a new neoliberal economy from scratch. Overnight, Chile would become a model, a clean slate, to enact neoliberal policies in the Southern Cone of Latin America. In this manner, the profits of the US corporate sector would be protected.

Of all the undercover interference by the CIA, the attempt to discredit "communism" in the ranks of the Chilean military was the most successful. General Schneider, a staunch defender of Chilean democracy, was assassinated. Thus, the CIA politically galvanized the enforcers of the coup—the Chilean military—while they simultaneously carried out Nixon's order to squeeze Chile's economy. The Chicago Boys scripted the new neoliberal economic program in Chile, and US corporate interests exerted economic control over the US executive branch to back the coup.

Immediately following the military coup and Allende's death, his cabinet was taken into captivity, and many influential prisoners were taken to the Dawson Island in the southern Strait of Magellan, a freezing parallel to a Siberian work camp (Klein 2007, 93). Approximately 13,500 civilians were imprisoned (Kornbluh 2003, 153–54). Thousands were gathered into the two football stadiums in Santiago, both the National Stadium and the smaller Chile Stadium in Santiago. Inside the National Stadium, prisoners were hooded, hundreds were executed while others were carted off as subversives to be tortured. Other prisoners were held in approximately twenty detention centers scattered throughout the nation. As reported by a CIA cable, "only a few [of these detention centers] were known to the general public" (Kornbluh 2003, 154). General Serfio Arellano Stark and his Caravan of Death, a roving death squad, undertook helicopter missions to the Northern provinces to seek out subversives (Klein 2007, 93). The numbers of the dead and missing are still contested because of the consistent attempts by Pinochet's regime to cover up the terror. However, respected journalists and authors, Jonathan Kandell, Leslie Bethell, and Rupert Corwell among others have estimated that, in total, more than 3,200 people were disappeared/executed, 80,000 were imprisoned, and 200,000 fled the country (Kandell 2006).

The Chicago Boys' Brick was approved by the General Officers of the Chilean Armed Forces. Its plan bore a striking resemblance to Milton Friedman's text, *Capitalism and Freedom*. Like Friedman's text, the Brick called for privatization, deregulation and cuts to social spending. For the first time, the Chicago Boys had a political climate—a dictatorship—that would not reject the application of their economic policies. All opposition was dead, incarcerated, or silent. It was the first all-out victory against Developmentalism in the American hemisphere. The political and economic agitation engendered by the corporatists' agenda had succeeded on a grandiose scale.

Great instability following counterrevolutions is a historical norm. Thus, within a brief timespan, Pinochet clinched his power by staging a coup within a coup to depose other military leaders who wished to return to Chile's historic democracy. Pinochet now controlled the power of the military, and he favored the free market vision of the Chicago Boys backed by the support of US corporate dollars. He enacted the Neoliberal agenda by eliminating price controls and trade barriers, by cutting government spending for all but the military and by privatizing state-owned companies. The threat of further nationalization of Chilean industries died. Profits for the multinational corporations increased. Nevertheless, Pinochet never privatized CODEX (also CODELCO), the state copper mine company nationalized by Allende. It was his card that gave the state a steady source of funds throughout the troubled decade following the coup (Piñera 2004, 296).

The neoliberal economic revolution was disastrous for the majority of Chileans. Within a year of the 1973 coup, inflation had reached 375 percent in Chile (Klein 2007, 97). Bread could no longer be afforded. Hundreds of working class Chileans lost their jobs because "free trade" was flooding the market with cheap imports. Unable to compete, many local businesses closed. Unemployment hit record levels. People starved. Meanwhile, Pinochet, urged on by Milton Friedman, cut public spending especially on health and education by 27 percent by 1975 (Constable and Valenzuela 1991, 172–73).

In reaction to the disastrous effects on the Chilean economy, the Chicago Boys blamed Pinochet for not implementing more neoliberal tactics. Pinochet was told to speedily enact more cuts and more privatization. His economic minister, De Castro, rapidly privatized almost 500 state-owned companies (Valdés 1995, 22). Known as the "piranhas," a small group of wealthy investors, many of whom were Chicago Boys, were making a killing and the northern foreign corporations saw profits rise. But the public outcry against excessive inflation and crippling unemployment drew attention. Within a year, Milton Friedman, the father of the neoliberal school at the University of Chicago flew to Santiago along with Arnold Harberger, head of the Latin American program at the same university, to confront Pinochet. Like the Chicago Boys, Friedman prescribed all market controls be removed. Chile needed to embrace the free market with even greater abandon, a form of "shock treatment" instead of "gradualism." Influenced by Milton Friedman, Pinochet complied, causing the Chilean economy to contract by an additional 15 percent while unemployment reached 20 percent (Valdés 1995, 23).

By 1982, the economy of Chile crashed; debt and hyperinflation exploded. Furthermore, unemployment had climbed to 30 percent. The only advantage Pinochet had was CODELCO, the copper mine that had been nationalized by Allende that Pinochet had not privatized. CODELCO produced 85 percent of Chile's export revenues and that kept the state in the only steady source of income it had during those years.

The "free market" economics of neoliberalism did not point to a liberated market but to a corporatist one, an alliance between a police state and large corporations that impoverished workers. By 1988, 45 percent of the Chilean population had fallen below the poverty line while the richest 10 percent enjoyed income increases of 83 percent (Klein 2007, 105). By 2007, the World Factbook at the CIA website noted that Chile was one of the most unequal societies in the world. Out of a comparison of 123 countries, Chile ranked 116th, that is, the eighth most unequal country on the list (Central Intelligence Agency 2007).

Though sold in the US as the "Chilean miracle," the neoliberal counterrevolution was no such miracle for the large majority of the Chilean people. Instead, a small elite, known as the Piranhas, had suddenly become very wealthy very quickly in a formula bankrolled by debt and then bailed out by public funds. This sequence of events appears to be a common result of neoliberal policies: 1) the transfer of wealth from the public to private hands, 2) private debt bailed out by public funds, 3) the striking rise of the small elite minority, 4) a problem of gross unemployment in the public sector, and 5) a marked growing income inequality. The "Chilean Miracle," a reference used by Milton Friedman, was another myth produced by free-market neoliberals that ignored the well-being of the large majority of the Chilean people.

For Chileans, the "economic miracle" was a war of the rich against the middle class and the poor. In Latin American politics, the terminology "rich versus poor" has colonial roots with privilege and imperialistic ties. García Márquez, in his famous journal article, "Chile, the Golpe and the Gringos" (García Márquez 1974), points out the intense political and economic polarization brought about by neoliberal policies. Orland Letelier, Allende's former Defense Minister, writing from exile in 1976 captures this dichotomy: "during the last three years [1973–1976] several billions of dollars were taken from the pockets of wage earners and placed in those of capitalists and landowners...the concentration of wealth is no accident" (Letelier 1976, 53). The Chilean crash of 82 served to further enhance the wealth of the Piranhas and the corporations.

Chile, the original laboratory of the neoliberal Chicago School, then, offers us a disturbing pattern of global economics under corporatist Neoliberal puppet masters. Corporatists' agendas have been especially evident in Indonesia, the Soviet Union, Argentina, Iraq, Bolivia, South Africa, and in the Asian crisis of 1997–1998, to name just a few examples. The application of neoliberal policy worldwide has had a black-lash in the twenty-first century. It is also a telling fact that the date of the attack on the World Trade Center (September 11, 2001), part of the neoliberal Washington Consensus apparatus that controls globalization, repeats the date of the coup against the first neoliberal laboratory, Chile, on September 11, 1973. Chile was the only country that was "rebuilt" on what neoliberals describe as a "clean slate." All political opposition had been incarcerated, tortured, silenced by fear, or killed.

Today in Chile and Latin America, there is an attempt to combine democracy and socialism, a combination that Salvador Allende was attempting to bring to Chile between 1970 and 1973. Popular opposition to privatization has become a defining issue; nationalization of mining sectors and natural resources has occurred to protect the public good. Land reforms have been passed, and there are new investments in education and health care. Latins have publicly turned their back on "free trade" because it shackled them. Their dream of economic equality is not dead, and the desire to close the "open veins of Latin America" to neoliberal "pillage" is strong (Galeano 2004). However even leftist presidents, though popular, are now beholden to a very active citizenry who remember. There is a strong memory of the pain of the last sixty years in Latin America. That pain resulted from what many Latins consider neoliberal and neocolonial enslavement.

Currently, there is also a deliberate rejection of US trade agreements in Latin America. A part of the Washington Consensus, the very powerful International Monetary Fund (IMF) of the '80s and the '90s, is no longer a controlling force in Latin America. Naomi Klein points out this rapid change: "In 2005, Latin America made up 80 percent of the IMF's total lending portfolio; in 2007, the continent represented just 1 percent—a sea change in only two years" (Klein 2007, 578).

In the US today, we are repeating some of the devastating social and economic patterns that Chile displayed under our own Neoliberal corporate puppet masters. But unlike the memories of Chileans, US citizens do not share powerful public memories of incarceration, torture, disappeared citizens, the assassination of a President for a replacement government, the loss of a social security system, the complete destruction of a democracy, and the gutting of an economic system by outside profiteers.

The economic and social patterns in Chile under US corporate neoliberal control after the 1973 coup are alarming. The principle events resulting from this neoliberal control have been 1) very large transfers of public wealth to the private hands of the few wealthy elites, 2) the exploding debt of elites buying public resources which led to an economic crash, 3) a rapidly rising income disparity between the super-rich and the large poor and dwindling middle class majorities, 4) the monopoly of Chilean wealth and natural resources in the hands of the wealthy few 5) a long difficult period of unemployment for workers, 5) the reduced sovereignty of the nation-state, and 6) a repeat of neocolonial control. This neoliberal pattern has become a global refrain since the Chilean coup in 1973.

REFERENCES

A Draconian Cure for Chile's Economic Ills. 1976. *Business Week*, January 12.

Anderson, Jack. 1970–1971. "The International Telephone and Telegraph Company and Chile." Senate Subcommittee on Multinational Corporations, Washington, D.C.

Bartels, Larry. 2008. *Unequal Democracy: The Political Economy of the New Gilded Age.* New York: Russell Sage.

Berryman, P. 1993. Report of the Chilean National Commission on Truth and Reconciliation. *University of Notre Dame Press.*

Bethell, Leslie. 1993. *Chile since Independence.* Cambridge, England: Cambridge University Press.

Branford, Sue, and Bernando Kucinski. 1988. *The Debt Squads: The US, the Banks, and Latin America.* London: Zed Books.

Central Intelligence Agency. 1970a. "A Secret Cable from Headquarters [Blueprint for Fomenting a Coup Climate]." September 27. www.gwu.edu/~nsarchiv.

———. 1970b. "Memorandum to the President." Subject: NSC Meeting, November 6—Chile, November 5, 1970. www.gwu.edu/~nsarchiv.

———. 1970c. "Notes on Meeting with the President on Chile." Declassified, September 15. www.gwu.edu/~nsarchiv.

———. 2007. "Field Listing—Distribution of Family Income—Gini Index." *World Factbook*. www.cia.gov.

Chomsky, Noam. 1999. *Profit over People: Neoliberalism and Global Order.* New York: Seven Stories Press.

Constable, Pamela, and Arturo Valenzuela. 1991. *A Nation of Enemies: Chile under Pinochet.* New York: W. W. Norton & Company.

Cornwell, R. 2006. "The General Willing to Kill His People to Win the Battle against Communism." *The Independent*, December 11.

Dworkin, P. 1981. "Chile's Brave New World of Reaganomics." *Fortune*, November 2.

Friedman, Milton. 1962. *Capitalism and Freedom.* Chicago: University of Chicago Press.

———. 1974. "Economic Miracles." *Newsweek*, January 21.

Friedman, M., and R. D. Friedman. 1998. *Two Lucky People: Memoirs*. Chicago: University of Chicago Press.

Galeano, Eduardo. 1978. *Days and Nights of Love and War*. Cuba: Casa de las Américas.

———. 2004. *Las venas abiertas de América Latina*. 76a ed. México: Siglo XXI.

García Márquez, Gabriel. 2008. "Chile, el golpe y los gringos." www.cubadebate.cu/opinion/2008/06/26/gabriel-garcía-marquez.

Gunder Frank, André. 1976. *Economic Genocide in Chile: Monetarist Theory versus Humanity.* Nottingham, UK: Spokesman Books.

Guzmán, P., dir. 1993. *Batalla de Chile.* First Run/Icarus Films.

———. 2004. *Salvador Allende.* First Run/Icarus Films.

———. 2001. *The Pinochet Case.* First Run/Icarus Films.

Hacker, Jacob, and Paul Pierson. 2010. *Winner-Take-All Politics: How Washington Made the Rich Richer—and Turned Its Back on the Middle Class.* New York: Simon and Schuster.

Kandell, Jonathan. 1976, March 21. Chile, Lab Test for a Theorist, *New York Times*.

———. 2006. "Augusto Pinochet, 92, Dictator Who Ruled by Terror in Chile, Dies." *The New York Times*, December 11.

Keynes, John Maynard, ed. 2004. *The End of Laissez-faire: The Economic Consequences of the Peace.* New York: Prometheus Books.

Kinzer, Stephen. 2006. *Overthrow: America's Century of Regime Change from Hawaii to Iraq*. New York: Times Books.

Klein, Naomi. 2007. *The Shock Doctrine: The Rise of Disaster Capitalism*. New York: Picador.

Kornbluh, Peter. 2003. *The Pinochet File: A Declassified Dossier on Atrocity and Accountability*. New York: New Press.

Letelier, O. 1976. "The Chicago Boys in Chile: Economic Freedom's Awful Toll." *The Nation*, August 28.

Lessig, Lawrence. 2011. *Republic, Lost: How Money Corrupts Congress—and a Plan to Stop It*. New York: Twelve.

McCarty, Nolan, and Keith Poole. 2006. *Polarized America: The Dance of Ideology and Unequal Riches*. Cambridge, Mass.: MIT Press.

McChesney, Robert W. 1998. "Introduction." *Profit over People: Neoliberalism and Global Order*. New York: Seven Stories Press.

Noah, Timothy. 2012. *The Great Divergence: America's Growing Inequality Crisis and What We Can Do about It*. New York: Bloomsbury Press.

Piñera, José. n.d. "The Chilean Model." *Economic Affairs*, 24–28.

———. 2004. "Wealth through Ownership: Creating Property Rights in Chilean Mining." *Cato Journal* 24 (Fall): 296.

Stiglitz, Joseph. 2012. *The Price of Inequality: How Today's Divided Society Endangers Our Future*. New York: W. W. Norton & Company.

Subcommittee on Multinational Corporations. 1973. "The International Telephone and Telegraph Company and Chile, 1970-71." *Report to the Committee on Foreign Relations United States Senate*, June 21.

United States Senate, Select Committee to Study Governmental Operations with Respect to Intelligence Activities. 1975. "Covert Action in Chile 1963-1973." December 18. Washington, D.C: US Government Printing Office.

Valdés, Juan Gabriel. 1995. *Pinochet's Economists: The Chicago School in Chile*. Cambridge: Cambridge University Press.

Weiner, Tim. 2008. *Legacy of Ashes: The History of the CIA*. New York: Anchor Books.

CHAPTER 3

Human Rights: "Chile, the Golpe and the Gringos" or the Power of Corporate Profits at the Expense of Human Lives

The laws of impunity and the Latin taboo that silenced the pain of the Dirty Wars are unraveled by the arrest of Pinochet (2000) and the legal controversies in the courts of Britain, Spain and Chile (2000–2006). Ignoring those taboos, the impunity laws and the waning of the political left in Latin America years before these events, García Márquez documented the violent beginnings of Neoliberalism in his Nobel Prize speech, *Clandestine, in Chile*, *The Autumn of the Patriarch*, and his journalism. This paper examines the violent political and economic events that occurred in Chile before and after Allende's death both in fact and in García Márquez's journal article, "Chile, the Golpe and the Gringos." García Márquez pointed to the ultimate complication of unchecked corporate power which destroyed human rights and consumed the lives of thousands of "desaparecidos" under Pinochet.

HUMAN RIGHTS IN LATIN AMERICA

The demand for human rights in Latin America reached resounding levels in 2011, suffered a number of backlashes in both 2011 and 2012, and then resumed a strong pace in 2013. The clamor for justice for those who were tortured, imprisoned, raped and disappeared during the years of the Latin American imposed military governments (1954–1990) has only increased with every discouraging backlash. In Latin America, this trend toward criminal prosecutions of abusers of human rights parallels similar trends elsewhere across the globe. Kathryn Sinkkink's recent book, *The Justice Cascade: How Human Rights Prosecutions Are Changing World Politics* (2011), makes numerous references to the expansion of norms favoring accountability for human rights violations and the realization of these norms through criminal prosecution.

Unlike the global tendency to prosecute these criminal violations in international tribunals, in Latin America the prosecution against violations of human rights has primarily been conducted in domestic criminal courts (Burt

2013, 102). This role of the courts, especially in Chile, from 1998 to the present has demonstrated an unprecedented shift toward human rights.

A number of key players in the struggle for human rights are the *Hijos de los Desaparecidos*, the Human Rights Watch, the Inter-American Court of Human Rights, the Inter-American Commission on Human Rights, the national courts, the Indigenous Peoples, and the accounts of persecuted judges. These groups have all become agents of publicity for the cause of Latin American human rights.

This twenty-first-century reality that demands accountability was not always so. Though human rights organizations emerged in Latin America in the 1980s in response to documented reports of grave violations, the public discussion of justice was effectively suppressed by taboos or threats, and legally enforced by impunity laws, for decades, to protect the military and police agents who participated in the abuse. Memories of the abuses were supposed to vanish like the Disappeared while crucial evidence was erased. Discussions of justice were repressed. Eduardo Galeano, a celebrated Uruguayan journalist and author, described his country under these years of repression as a "sanctuary of impunity" which threatened the families of the Disappeared and imposed years of silence.

Into this silence, fear and imposed shame, the biting words of García Márquez targeting US imperialism rang out in his Nobel Prize speech in Stockholm in 1982. Not only his novels but his articles implicated the impetus behind this suppression of rights. Before human rights really took hold in the 1980s, in Latin America, García Márquez was the harbinger for the violations of human rights, a supporter of the poor majority and an advocate for accountability. In the title of one well circulated journal article (1974), he summarized the connections between economic imperialism of the US and the brutal violation of human rights: "Chile, the Golpe, and the Gringos."

The impetus behind the push for Latin American military governments and the subsequent suppression of human rights (1954–1990) had two layers. The first layer was political and was born out of wealthy right-winged think tanks such as The American Enterprise Institute (1943) in the United States. With the strong conservative political influence of the Dulles brothers in the decade of the 1950s, these think tanks created the corporate narrative of anti-communism and the fear of socialist influence. For these think tanks, the cultivation of socialist objectives in Latin America had to be suppressed at all costs. Socialism was incorrectly equated with communism. The deeper layer, that is, the more powerful motive, was economic. Those who really feared socialism were the US corporate interests in Latin America which stood to lose large profits and their access to Latin

American natural resources. Thus, US corporate collaboration with small groups of Latin American business elites would be an on-going primary strategy so that profits for these Latin American elites would increase in proportion to their continued cooperation with large US corporations.

For purposes of clarification, the concepts of socialism, communism and capitalism need to be defined, not only from a theoretical perspective but also from the complications of place, time and culture. Naturally, these definitions will be very brief as these concepts could fill books. They are used here to understand the Chilean dilemma as orchestrated by US corporate interests.

Communism is an extreme form of socialism. It is common to find many countries that have dominant socialist political parties, but very few are truly communist. Even the US, whose government represents a staunch capitalist bulwark for business, has government programs that borrow from socialist—or in US terminology—democratic principles. However, in the US, it has been a frequent political tactic of conservatives to equate socialism with communism. The two concepts have stark differences. The most obvious distinction, apart from the skewed US perception, is that communism is a political system whereas socialism is primarily an economic system.

As an economic system, socialism can exist in various forms under a wide range of political systems. Where communism could be considered an "ideology," it is difficult to categorize socialism as such, given the very wide and distinct forms it has taken politically. Production in a socialist economy may be coordinated through either economic planning or markets. If economic planning is given a priority, there is an emphasis on profit being distributed to benefit society and the workforce. There are two types of property, personal property and public property. In a socialist system, all choices, including education, religion, employment and marriage are up to the individual while all health care and education are provided free to everyone. In contrast, in a communist political system, such choices are controlled by the state. All property is held "in common" by the state, and government is the only agent of change. All historical attempts to practice "pure communism" have created an oligarchical class; this contradicts the dictates of communist ideology that require a "classless" society.

Pure capitalism rejects the notion of the public good, demands a "free" market, deregulation and privatization of all property. All individuals must pay for their property, education, health and welfare. In the last forty years, there has been a strong impetus from Neoliberal interests to align US policies with pure capitalism. However, a critical eye could point out that instead of welfare for the general public, the US government has created a "corporate welfare," that is, benefits and tax breaks for the large corporate and banking interests. Welfare for the general public has been curtailed while welfare for a privileged public has been created. Thus, neoliberalism as practiced by the US favors the plutocracy and the oligarchs who control it. The extreme rise in income inequality in the US between the very wealthy and the working class in recent years demonstrates the neoliberal "liberty" to corrupt or buy the votes of US senators and congressmen. Capitalism that is bought out by big money interests will reduce the worker and undermine democratic principles. Such was the case of Chile from 1932–1970 and again, from 1973–2007 as this paper will present.

In terms of culture, the US has been a culture that espouses individualism. This underlying social expectation has encouraged US business practices allowing businesses an arena of dominance within the US. However, US business expectations operating in other sovereign nations have seldom been willing to compromise or work with the expectations of the host culture even though the resources in question belong to the host nation. The US multinational corporations operating in Chile in the decades following World War II not only violated Chilean cultural expectations but aggressively orchestrated the fall of Chile's democracy and undermined Chile's sovereignty.

The Latin American cultures are distinct, with strong communal expectations of social equality and living wages for workers. The Chilean culture is more collective in expectation, in part due to its long historical struggle with American imperialism which greatly profited US companies at the expense and misery of the Chilean worker. Given this bitter historical struggle, the "democratic" or "socialist" desire of the Chilean voting public elected a socialist president, Salvador Allende, in 1970, for a purpose. Voters wished to rid Chile of the "capitalist robber barons" who were making great profits from Chilean resources while keeping wages very low for Chilean workers and miners.

Lastly, as a clarification of the players in the Chilean dilemma, it is critical to note that US foreign policy has been strongly guided by ideology (Hunt 2009, 125). The power and the persistence of such ideologies were built upon attitudes about national greatness, racial superiority and strong resistance to political disorder or revolutions for business reasons. For twentieth-century policy makers—Harriman, Acheson, the Rockefellers, the Dulles brothers, the Bundys—who were disproportionately from elite Eastern, urban, Protestant backgrounds, ideology was a birthright (Hunt 2009, 150). Ideas such as geopolitics, containment of communism, a national mission of saving the world from totalitarianism, and a policy of aggressive development to encourage containment were woven together to create a powerful anti-communist ideology. For this generation of American policymakers coming out of World War II, the geopolitical world was divided into a chessboard, a war of binaries. This political ideology spawned the politics of the Cold War and the US policy of supporting fascist ideas such as dictators and strongmen like Pinochet.

Co-existing with the US political ideology of anti-communism was the economic ideology of Neoliberalism as developed by Milton Friedman of the Chicago School of Business in the 1950s. With free market deregulation and privatization of all public property, Friedman hoped to de-pattern societies and return them to a pure market state. It is ironic that this neoliberal ideology of deregulation and privatization gave Chile the 1982 economic crash and the US the 2008 crash. In both cases, these crashes devastated the working classes and enhanced the pockets of the very wealthy.

Today, the war-like binary positions of opposing ideologies are intellectually recognized as fallacies. But in 1970, Chile, under Allende, was perceived by US policy makers and corporations as an opposing ideological enemy in the geopolitical chessboard. It could be said that ideological stances have been convenient for US corporate and banking profits. Neoliberalism, as a free-market ideology, is still a deliberate tool used to bend American minds in order to cultivate and protect wealthy neoliberal interests. For these same interests, it is still convenient to equate socialism with their ideological enemy of communism. Several generations of corporately financed public relations in the US have deliberately demonized the term "socialism" while giving neoliberal ideas a near sacred aura (McChesney 1999). For this type of mentality, critical dialogue and cultural recognition of differences do not exist. The violence and terror of the Chilean coup were the intended results of the ideological push for free markets.

CORPORATE AMERICA SCRIPTS THE "*GOLPE*": HISTORICAL FACTS

By 1968, 20 percent of US foreign investment was tied up in Latin America and US firms had 5,436 subsidiaries in the region producing staggering profits (Klein 2007, 78). US mining companies had invested one million dollars over the previous fifty years in Chile's copper mining industry, the largest in the world, but these companies had sent $7.2 million home (Branford and Kucinski 1988, 40–52). International Telephone and Telegraph (IT&T) owned 70 percent of Chile's phone system. Pfizer Chemical, Purina, Bank of America, and Ford Foundation were also significant players in this resource war and the push for larger markets. The demand for resources and the profits from those resources, then, were at the heart of the sequence of events that led to blatant violations of human rights in Latin America in the second half of the twentieth century. The financial interests of US corporations were disguised by their very public narrative of anti-communism. The accusation of "communism" was used to oppose progressive movements in countries that would restrict US corporate access to resources and threaten their corporate profits. What these US companies feared most was nationalization of resources or industries which would force them to leave Latin America. Their anti-communist ideology cloaked their drive for profits. García Márquez, like Noam Chomsky, saw that the push for resources and their profits was far more important to these companies than the rights of the Latin American people. Ironically, these natural resources belonged to the Latin American people, not the US corporations.

García Márquez's article also targeted Chile. Why Chile? The copper from the Chilean mines was the most profitable of the US business interests in Latin America (Segarra 2013, 315). To protect these interests, "the Chile Project" was created. In 1956, 100 Chilean students were sent to the University of Chicago's Business and Economic Department, the home base of Milton Friedman and his Neoliberal corporatist agenda. The Chilean students were sent to the University of Chicago to pursue advanced degrees in business and economics but their tuition and fees were paid mostly by US taxpayers and embellished by US conservative think tanks. These "Chicago Boys" underwent an indoctrination of free market neoliberalism that would help protect US corporate interests and profits in Chile. The Center for Latin American Economic Studies was created to instill neoliberal economic orthodoxy, a form of academic imperialism. In the 1990s, Chile's foreign minister, Juan Gabriel Valdés, described this academic endeavor as an "organized transfer of ideology from the U.S."(Valdés 1995, 6). Despite these efforts and the influence of the Chicago Boys, all three of Chile's political parties in the late 1960s pushed for nationalizing the country's largest source of revenue—the copper mines—which were controlled by US mining giants. The populist anger against US corporations that extract Chile's resources mostly for corporate profits while reducing Chilean labor to meager salaries and poor working conditions had become a poignant political issue. This threat of Chilean nationalization of a very profitable revenue source activated US corporate interests.

On September 4, 1970, Salvador Allende, a socialist, won the Chilean Presidency. The US Secretary of State, Henry Kissinger, immediately approved $250,000 for political warfare in Chile (Weiner 2008, 357) to protect US corporate interests. In total, he approved of $1,950,000 to conduct the anti-Allende program which consisted of two tracts. Tract One was political-warfare, economic pressure, propaganda and diplomatic hardball. Tract Two was a military coup (Weiner 2008, 358). The politics of the executive division of the US government bowed to the corporates' demand for profits.

The most aggressive of the corporates was IT&T whose fear of nationalization of the Chilean telephone industry had led them to plot with the CIA and the State Department to block Allende's election two years prior to his inauguration. A controversial US Senate investigation was instigated by Jack Anderson, a syndicated journalist. His articles, based on IT&T's documents, discovered a major conspiracy in which IT&T officials had attempted to bribe Chilean forces opposed to Allende to act for $1 million (Klein 2007, 79). The Senate report in June of 1973 also uncovered further strategies planned by IT&T to undermine Allende after his election. Most notably, IT&T had composed a plan containing eighteen points which was delivered to Henry Kissinger and President Nixon (Klein 2007, 80). It called for a military coup. Corporate America was scripting an extreme form of imperialism. García Márquez's title connected the dots: "Chile, the Golpe, and the Gringos."

What followed in Chile activated García Márquez politically. Though Neoliberalism was not yet publicly recognized, García Márquez understood that the imperialistic intervention of the US had morphed exponentially into a multifaceted program. The program consisted of 1) academic imperialism, 2) CIA covert intervention, 3) the School of the Americas' teaching on torture, and the application of the CIA's 1963 manual on torture, the *Kubark*, to political prisoners, 4) political intervention in Chilean elections, 5) economic strangulation to bring down President Allende's government, 6) support of a military coup, 7) economic support of Pinochet's military dictatorship, and finally, 8) the demands to immediately impose neoliberal economic policies that benefited US corporate interests. Milton Friedman, head professor at the Chicago School of Business and the recognized father of neoliberalism, visited Chile with the objective to instruct Pinochet on the economic plan for Chile. His Chicago Boys implemented "The Brick"—a plan that bore a striking resemblance to Milton Friedman's text, *Capitalism and Freedom*—and this plan would favor US corporate interests. This multifaceted program provoked the violent dawn of the corporate Neoliberal agenda.

THE "GOLPE'S" HUMAN RIGHTS VIOLATIONS: HISTORICAL FACTS

Immediately following the military coup and Allende's death, his cabinet was taken into captivity, and many influential prisoners were taken to the Dawson Island in the Southern Strait of Magellan, a freezing parallel to a Siberian work camp (Klein 2007, 93). Approximately 13,500 civilians were imprisoned

(Kornbluh 2003, 153–54). Thousands were gathered into the two football stadiums in Santiago. Inside the National Stadium, prisoners were hooded, hundreds were executed while others were carted off as subversives to be tortured. General Sergio Arellano Stark and his Caravan of Death, a roving death squad, undertook helicopter missions to the Northern provinces to seek out "subversives," those opposed to the new military government (Klein 2007, 93). Although the numbers are contested because of the consistent attempts by Pinochet's regime to cover up the terror, respective journalists and authors (Kandell, Bethell, and Corwell) have estimated that, in total, more than 3,200 people were disappeared/executed, 80,000 were imprisoned, and 200,000 fled the country (Kandell 2006).

Thus, the massive violation of human rights in Chile was set in motion by a military coup or *golpe* which was orchestrated by and for the interests of US corporate investments. García Márquez's title of his article, "Chile, the Golpe and the Gringos" points to those who were responsible while twenty-nine years later, Noam Chomsky's book title, *Profits over People*, summarizes the reasons. It is not surprising then, that Chile, one of the Latin American nations with the richest mineral resources, endured one of the longest periods of military suppression of all the Latin American military dictatorships (1973–1990).

THE PLAYERS AND THEIR PROGRAM: GARCÍA MÁRQUEZ'S INTERPRETATION

In his article on Chile, García Márquez described a dinner (1969) in which three Pentagon generals met with a number of Chilean generals and one Chilean Admiral to discuss what would happen if Salvador Allende, the Socialist Candidate for the Chilean Presidency, won the election in 1970. Within a few paragraphs, García Márquez mentioned the Contingency Plan of IT&T (the military coup), the names of the Chilean officers, US officials, and agencies. The Chilean officers were catalogued: Colonel Gerardo López-Angulo, General Toro Mazote (the Director of the Chilean School of Aviation), General Ernesto Baeza (Director of Chilean National Security), Admiral Arturo Troncoso, General Augusto Pinochet (the president of the military Junta), General Javier Palacios (involved in the final clash with Salvador Allende), General Gustavo Leigh (who bombed the presidential palace), and General Sergio Figueroa of the Air Brigade. These were major Chilean officers who were politically cultivated by the CIA to oppose President Allende. Also mentioned were the Defense Agency of the Pentagon, Secretary of State Henry Kissinger, US President Richard Nixon, the

National Security Council and Operation Unitas (the collaboration of US and Chilean joint military exercises in the Pacific).

In paragraph nine, García Márquez emphasized that Chile was not chosen by chance, but because it was going to become the second socialist republic in the continent after Cuba. For this reason, the US purpose was not only to create obstacles for the government of Salvador Allende but to repeat the blatant imperialism, a military coup imposed on Brazil in order to preserve US investments. Nevertheless, the Contingency Plan could not immediately be put into practice as the plan had solicited 200 visas for a supposed choral group to enter Chile. This group, as García Márquez ironically pointed out, included "admirals who couldn't even sing." The coral group was denied entry by the Chilean government. Thus, the Contingency Plan for an immediate military coup was delayed.

In the course of the first year of Allende's Unidad Popular, García Márquez reported that forty-seven businesses were nationalized as well as more than half the system of credits. García Márquez mentions the agrarian reform of 2,400,000 hectares of active land. The "chilenization" of copper had already begun under the former government of Eduardo Frei as many Chileans had for years believed that the US companies were exploiting their resources. But the Popular Unity government of Allende recovered the copper exploited by the US companies from the Anaconda and Kennecott mines in one legal act. In 1973, Allende's government made public the calculation that, within their last fifteen years (1958–1973), the two companies had made earnings in excess of $80 million, earnings that were not benefitting the Chilean public as they should but primarily contributing to US corporate profits.

In retaliation for Allende's election in 1970, the US response was economic sanctions, a loan embargo, and the involvement of the CIA in strikes and propaganda. These measures, in the words of President Nixon, were to make the Chilean economy "scream" (declassified files: "Notes on Meeting with the President on Chile, September 15, 1970, www.gwu.edu/~nsarchiv). Despite the strikes and the rising inflation, Allende was reelected in 1973 by a larger vote (44 percent) than his first victory (36 percent). On the 11th of September, after three years of delay, the original Contingency Plan discussed at the Pentagon dinner for the Chilean generals was enacted. It was not, however, a conventional coup, but a devastating operation of a war to uproot an unfavorable government and plant a regimen politically favorable to the economic demands of the US multinational corporations in Chile.

García Márquez denigrated the myth of legalism and the docility of the Chilean army as an invention that served the interest of a small Chilean upper class, the elites. The Latin American relationship of the military to political elites was a colonial reality for centuries; Latin American history documents this relationship. By revisiting numerous historical events in which the Chilean military terrorized its own people, García Márquez emphasized the brutality with which the Chilean military resolved strikes, plagues and carried out mass burials. This military was trained by 300 years of intense warfare with the hostile Indigenous Araucanos. Thus, the severe massacres and slaughter of those that resisted in the 1973 military coup should have been expected. In addition, the impetus for many of the violations of human rights, the practices of terror, torture and interrogation, came from the efforts of the CIA and the School of the Americas' teachings on torture (the *Kubark*), funded mostly by unaware US taxpayers. This strategic support behind the Chilean military coupled with the virulent anti-communist rhetoric pushed by the CIA spawned brutal violations of human rights.

"A Social Cataclysm"

Again, pointing to Chilean history, García Márquez acquaints his reader with the great disillusionment of the Chilean mine workers in 1932. With the mines under foreign control, even the push for profits kept the miners in squalid working conditions with meager salaries. The desperation of the mine workers finally led them to support socialism. When the first socialist government of Chile (1932) attempted the nationalization of copper to the great enthusiasm of the miners, the experience only lasted for thirteen tumultuous days. Thus, the violence of the 1973 military coup was to put an end once and for all to the needs and aspirations of mine workers in Chile. Corporate capitalism crushed labor. Pablo Neruda, the great Chilean poet and Nobel Prize winner whose literary works celebrated the dignity of the Chilean workers' struggle, was said to have died from heartbreak (September 23, 1973) directly following the violent 1973 military coup of September 11th. According to García Márquez, so did the human dignity and human rights of many Chilean workers.

In another major point in his article, García Márquez underscores the terrible polarization that was forced on the country. There were extreme divisions and confrontations of social classes brought on by the CIA anti-communist rhetoric and reinforced by the CIA's monetary support of multiple strikes causing scarcity of food products and fear. The truckers' strike (el Paro Patronal) that paralyzed the country, cutting off supplies of bread, milk, and oil, was financed by the CIA.

Divisive polarization appeared to be a strategic tactic of corporate neoliberal interests to divide and conquer creating what García Márquez refers to as a strategy of political chess. Thousands of Chileans fell into poverty from unemployment from the neoliberal policies enacted under Pinochet while the elites, known as the Piranhas, profited greatly from their cooperation with US corporations. Within a year of the 1973 coup, inflation had reached 375 percent in Chile (Klein 2007, 97). Reports from André Gunder Frank, one of Milton Friedman's students, documented much higher inflation rates on food necessities. Hundreds of working class Chileans lost their jobs as "free trade" was flooding the market with cheap imports from foreign production. Many local businesses closed in the onslaught of such competition, and unemployment hit record levels. Pinochet, urged on by Milton Friedman, cut public spending especially on health and education by 27 percent by 1975 (Constable and Valenzuela 1995, 172–73). By 1982, Chile suffered a financial crash in which the loans taken out by the elites to buy up Chilean resources had to be bailed out by public funds, a forerunner of the events of 2008 and 2009. By 1988, 45 percent of the Chilean population had fallen below the poverty line while the richest 10 percent enjoyed income increases of 83 percent (Constable and Valenzuela 1995, 219). Milton Friedman's reference to the "Chilean Miracle" was considered to be neoliberal doublespeak that excluded the great majority of the Chilean population. The great disparity in income created a very unequal society; the analysis is noted in the World Factbook on the CIA website. By 2007, Chile was considered one of the most unequal societies in the world, ranking 116th out of 123 countries. The end result was as García Márquez had predicted in his 1974 article: Chile in the seventies underwent "a social cataclysm without historical precedent."

THE FALL OF THE RULE OF LAW

Lastly, García Márquez disputes the CIA's account of the death of Allende as a suicide. He describes General Javier Palacios and his unit's last encounter with President Salvador Allende. Allende died in a volley of gunfire, and all the officers in a rite of caste fired on his fallen body. One subordinate destroyed his face with the butt of a rifle. A photograph exists of a dead Allende made by Juan Enrique Lira, a photographer, who was present for the newspaper, the *Mercurio*. Allende, who sought social and progressive change for his country by legal, nonviolent means, succumbed to the violence of power, neoliberal money and corporate control. The concepts of human rights and democratic legality ceased to exist in Chile for many years thereafter.

García Márquez's reaction to the military coup in Chile is well documented. Greatly angered by the coup, he felt that the Chilean people should not allow themselves to be governed by a "gang of criminals in the pay of North American imperialism (Martin 2010, 363)." But the sheer level of brutal violence unleashed by the coup and the shock value of "rounding up thirty thousand alleged left-wing activists" had terrified the Chilean populace.

García Márquez remained the most politically consistent of the major Latin American writers. In Latin America where colonialism has lasted for centuries, it has been the men of letters who have critiqued the "Official History" which was written by the colonial elites. "Though the Soviet Union was not the socialism García Márquez wanted, from the Latin American standpoint, García Márquez considered it essential as a bulwark against [the violence of] such U.S. hegemony and imperialism." For him, this was a "rational appraisal of reality" to help fend off more possible violence during the period of the Cold War (Martin 2010, 362).

So in a political act of solidarity with the Chilean people, García Márquez announced he would write no more novels until the military junta led by General Pinochet in Chile fell from power. Instead, he founded a liberal journal, *Alternativa*, which before long was selling 40,000 copies, an unheard of figure (Martin 2010, 165) for his conservative country of Colombia. This journal included the first of two articles by García Márquez, one under the headline, "Chile, the Golpe and the Gringos." This article achieved worldwide distribution by March of 1974. His early voice of protest against the violation of human rights, against imperialism and the corporate violence of the "Gringos" repeated his former satirical protest against the United Fruit Company in his hometown of Aracataca, Colombia. The "Gringos" in their unlawful intervention into Chilean sovereignty were those responsible for provoking the coup. They spawned a grim record of human right's violations and record dispossession of the Chilean workers' wealth. Orlando Letelier, Allende's former Defense Minister, writing from exile in 1976 summarized this great social cataclysm in Chile to which García Márquez referred in 1973: "during the last three years [1973–1976] several billions of dollars were taken from the pockets of wage earners and placed in those of capitalists and landowners….the concentration of wealth is no accident" (53).

Today, the Chilean coup stands out as an extreme case, a precedent of the fall of law, democracy and elections to the wealthy forces of neoliberal corporate power, a case whose echo is being repeated in varying forms all over the globe and even in the US proper today. It appears that corporate wealth, power and its strategy of massive econo-production are above the law. Even the courts cannot always re-allocate the costs of corporate violations, sustained at the price of human rights violations.

That corporates remain above the law has been substantiated over and over again by recent legal cases. One such case is *Aguinda v. Texaco*, where 30,000 plaintiffs in the Ecuadorian Amazon claimed that Texaco perpetrated environmental and human health damage through deliberate oil spills and polluted water in the Amazon tributaries. This case went on for years (1993–2011). The courts found Chevron-Texaco liable for $18.2 billion of damage in favor of the Indigenous Ecuadorians. However, Chevron "declared the judgment to be 'illegitimate and unenforceable' and said they would not pay" (Keefe 2012).

These court cases reflect shades of the extreme case of Chile in which corporate power appears to be above international law and the law of governments. In the Chilean coup, these large US corporations were the puppet-masters whose strings controlled Washington and Pinochet. Allende and the majority of the Chilean people were the disposable pawns.

LATIN AMERICA TODAY

In Latin America today, human rights organizations are frequently bringing Latin American citizens into confrontation with powerful corporate, economic, and political interests. These confrontations are a result not only of violations but of the economic development policies that have left the quality of the lives of many Latin American citizens greatly reduced. The power of corporate profits in Latin America has usually been at the expense of human rights—human life, human health and the human environment. In the case of the Chilean coup, the battle for corporate access and profits made a mockery of the law and the rights of human life. Chile was the classic example, stripped and rebuilt by the corporate neoliberal narrative that imposed extreme forms of imperialism. The Chilean population suffered incarceration, torture, disappearance of citizens, the tearing apart of the fabric of social and economic stability, and the creation of great social inequality, all for the underlying purpose of maintaining neoliberal, corporate investments and profits.

In the twenty-first century, Latin Americans are strongly rejecting US and multinational corporations that impose neoliberal policy. The financial and political institutions of the Washington Consensus such as The International Monetary Fund, The World Trade Center, and The World Bank have largely been abandoned. Naomi Klein, in her book, *The Shock Doctrine*, documents this rejection: "In 2005, Latin America made up 80 percent of the International Monetary Fund's total lending portfolio; in 2007, the continent represented just

1 percent—a sea change in only two years" (Klein 2007, 578). Latin Americans' dream of economic equality is still very much alive, but, using a paraphrase of Eduardo Galeano's book title, their desire to close the "open veins of Latin America" to corporate neoliberal "pillage" is strong. García Márquez (1928–2014), one of the first prophetic voices that spoke out very clearly against this pillage in "Chile, the Golpe and the Gringos," lived through the long decades of suppressed justice, taboos and impunity to see this day.

References

Abbas, Alma. 2010. *Liberalism and Human Suffering: Materialist Reflections on Politics, Ethics, and Aesthetics.* New York: Palgrave Macmillan.

Anderson, Jack. 1970–1971. "The International Telephone and Telegraph Company and Chile." Senate Subcommittee on Multinational Corporations, Washington, D.C., 4, 18.

Burt, Jo-Marie. 2013. "The New Accountability Agenda in Latin America: The Promise and Perils of Human Rights Prosecutions." *Sustaining Human Rights in the Twenty-First Century: Strategies from Latin America*, 101–41. Washington, D.C.: Woodrow Wilson Center Press.

Branford, Sue, and Bernando Kucinski. 1988. *Debt Squads: The U.S., the Banks, and Latin America.* London: Zed Books.

Bremer, Ian. 2011. *The End of the Free Market: Who Wins the War between States and Corporations?* New York: Portfolio/Penguin.

Central Intelligence Agency. *Notes on Meeting with the President on Chile,* September 15, 1970. Declassified. www.gwu.edu/~nsarchiv.

———. "Field Listing—Distribution of Family Income—Gini Index," *World Factbook 2007.* www.cia.gov.

Collins, Catherine. 2010. "Human Rights Trials in Chile during and after the 'Pinochet Years.'" *International Journal of Transitional Justice* 4: 67–86.

Constable, Pamela, and Arturo Valenzuela. 1995. *A Nation of Enemies: Chile under Pinochet.* New York: W.W. Norton & Co.

Friedman, Milton. 1982. *Capitalism and Freedom.* Chicago: University of Chicago Press.

Galeano, Eduardo. 1978. *Days and Nights of Love and War.* Cuba: Casa de las Américas.

———. 1980. *Las venas abiertas de la América Latina.* España: Siglo XXI de España Editores S.A.

García Márquez, Gabriel. 1987. *Clandestine in Chile: The Adventures of Miguel Littín.* New York: New York Review Books.

———. 1999. *El otoño del Patriarca.* Barcelona, Spain: Random House Mondadori, S.A.

———. 2008. "Chile, el golpe y los gringos." www.cubadebate.cu/opinion/2008 /06/26/gabriel-garcía-marquez.

Gunder Frank, André. 1976. *Economic Genocide in Chile: Monetarist Theory versus Humanity.* Nottingham: UK: Spokesman Books.

Guzmán, Patricio. 1978. *The Battle of Chile.* First Run/Icarus Films

———. 2001. *The Pinochet Case.* First Run/Icarus Films.

———. 2004. *Salvador Allende.* First Run/Icarus Films

Hunt, Michael. 2009. *Ideology and U.S. Foreign Policy.* New Haven, CT: Yale University Press.

Kandell, Jonathan. 1976. "Chile, Lab Test for a Theorist." *The New York Times,* March 21.

Keefe, Patrick Radden. 2012. "Reversal of Fortune." *New Yorker,* January 4. http://www.newyorker.com/reporting/2012/01/09/120109fa_fact-keefe.

Klein, Naomi. 2007. *The Shock Doctrine: The Rise of Disaster Capitalism.* New York: Picador.

Kornbluh, Peter. 2003. *The Pinochet File: A Declassified Dossier on Atrocity and Accountability.* New York: The New Press.

Letelier, Orlando. 1976. "The Chicago Boys in Chile: Economic Freedom's Awful Toll." *The Nation,* August 28.

Lutz, Ellen, and Kathryn Sikkink. 2001. The Justice Cascade: The Evolution and Impact of Foreign Human Rights Trials in Latin America. *Chicago Journal of International Law* 2: 1–34.

McChesney, Robert. 1999. "Introduction." *Profit over People: Neoliberalism and Global Order.* New York: Seven Stories Press.

Martin, Gerald. 2010. *Gabriel García Márquez: A Life.* New York: Vintage Books.

Roht-Arriaza, Naomi. 2005. *The Pinochet Effect: Transnational Justice in the Age of Human Rights.* Philadelphia: University of Pennsylvania Press.

Segarra, Monique. 2013. "Challenging Neoliberalism and Development." *Sustaining Human Rights in the Twenty-First Century: Strategies from Latin America.* Washington, D.C.: Woodrow Wilson Center Press.

Sinkkink, Kathryn. 2011. *The Justice Cascade: How Human Rights Prosecutions Are Changing World Politics.* New York: W.W. Norton.

Valdés, Juan Gabriel. 1995. *Pinochet's Economists: The Chicago School in Chile.* Cambridge: Cambridge University Press.

Verdugo, Patricia. 2001. *Chile, Pinochet, and the Caravan of Death.* Boulder, CO: Lynne Reinner.

Weiner, Tim. 2008. *Legacy of Ashes: The History of the CIA.* New York: Anchor Books.

Wilde, Alexander. 2013. "Human Rights in Two Latin American Democracies." *Sustaining Human Rights in the Twenty-First Century: Strategies from Latin America.* Washington, D.C.: Woodrow Wilson Center Press.

CHAPTER 4

Torture: The Power of Metaphor in the Reprogramming and Controlling of the Mind

According to accepted statistics of human rights and related NGOs, 30,000 Argentineans were tortured and disappeared under the Military Junta. Among the survivors of the experience, they document that memory is perhaps the greatest tool of resistance, and the use of metaphor, the greatest weapon to regain lost memory. As there are very few accounts of Argentinean torturees who have consented to publishing their painful experiences, primarily due to fear of retaliation or shame, this chapter combines Argentina's historical experience with Argentina's author, Luisa Valenzuela's account of a torturee. The novella, "The Exchange of Arms," presents a complex metaphor woven from simple metaphors of Western psychiatry and politics. Multiple levels of metaphor—the body and mind as machine, the "care-giver" as re-programmer and ironically, the patient condition as a war for mind control—are imposed on a political prisoner. These inverted metaphors of emptying and controlling the mind aid the practice of torture. Most of the Latin American military governments in Operation Condor were taught these metaphors as practiced by the CIA in the School of the Americas. The CIA manual, *The Kubark Counterintelligence Interrogation* handbook, used in the second half of the twentieth century, maximized the metaphor of reprogramming the human machine. Luisa Valenzuela's novella portrays the condition of a prisoner who has lost her memory due to the trauma of torture and the attempt to reprogram her mind. Her resistance using opposing metaphors of health and her personal feelings—the body as a plant, the body as a deep well of protected water for rebirth—captures the battle for mind control between the colonel "re-programmer" and the prisoner "patient." These juxtaposed positions form a strategic dance, exchanging weapons. From an Argentine perspective, the political metaphor for mind control, taken to its extremes by the *Kubark*, is portrayed as a tool of inversion not only to degrade human health but to control the human condition politically and economically.

Interest in human rights has become an important centerpiece of Argentine politics since Nestor Kirchner, the predecessor and late husband of President Cristina Fernández de Kirchner, overturned the impunity laws (Gilbert 2013, 12). On March 5, 2013, the trials of the "Dirty War" began in Buenos Aires to examine the human rights abuses during Operation Condor, a secret, decade-long (in Argentina) campaign by six allied military governments quietly led by the US. The purpose of Operation Condor was multi-tracked but governed by the primary objective to exterminate socialist and communist interests in the Southern Cone of South America. In the spirit of the recent trials, this article will examine one Argentine author's story about such human rights abuses under the historical conditions of Operation Condor.

Luisa Valenzuela's dense short story, "Exchange of Arms," is set against the period of the Argentine Dirty War in the early 1980s. The story revolves around a political prisoner, a "desaparecida" who has been tortured to the point of losing her memory. She is a kept prisoner of a Colonel who is using her as an experiment in brain washing as well as a victim of sexual abuse. This imprisonment contrasts the residue of the CIA's persistent experiments in human brainwashing with the astounding abilities the human brain has to survive even in situations when enduring torture seems inconceivable.

Thus the themes inherent in this short story are layered with an historical foundation. The US involvement in its support of the Dirty War by way of Operation Condor, the actions of the CIA and the forced imposition of Milton Friedman's neoliberal ideology all create the background conditions for this story. The protagonist is a tortured *desaparecida* whose haunting metaphors map her "forgotten" identity, leading her to a critical moment of recognition and decision. This investigation explores both the underlying background of the US involvement that contributed to the conditions of this story and the prisoner's experience of resistance. By examining her metaphoric landscape, she recovers episodes of memory and self-identity. The short story introduces the only war such a prisoner could wage, a war of metaphors—the prisoner's embodied metaphors which fill her consciousness, leading her back to health and memory versus the imposed metaphor of brainwashing which empties and reprograms the human machine. Her so called "insurgency" is not entirely obliterated, but can only continue the pattern of resistance on a metaphorical level.

THE METAPHOR OF REPROGRAMMING THE HUMAN MACHINE:
"WE SHALL SQUEEZE YOU EMPTY, AND THEN WE SHALL FILL
YOU WITH OURSELVES." GEORGE ORWELL, *NINETEEN EIGHTY-FOUR*

Torture, or in the language of the CIA, "coercive interrogation" is not only a tool used to enforce undesirable policies on resistant peoples; it is also a demonstration of the effectiveness of shock and awe, the Machiavellian principle of applying numerous injuries all at once. Intense disorientation is used to crumble the resistance of the mind. A violent gulf between prisoners and their capacities to make sense of the world is deliberately created. In this state of overwhelming disorientation, most incarcerated victims cannot hold back information or confessions that their interrogators are demanding. The prisoners are so regressed that they are incapable of thinking rationally to protect themselves. The CIA's *Kubark* manual that was declassified in the 1990s describes this state:

> There is an interval—which may be extremely brief—of suspended animation, a kind of   psychological shock or paralysis. It is caused by a traumatic or sub-tramatic experience which explodes, as it were, the world that is familiar to the subject as well as his image of himself within that world. Experienced interrogators recognize this effect when it appears and know that at this moment the source is far more open to suggestion, far likelier to comply, than he was just before he experienced the shock. (CIA 1963)

Prisoners do not always respond to this state with regression. Dr. Ewen Cameron, an American psychiatrist residing in Canada, attracted the CIA's attention in the 1950s because of his experimentation with patients. He believed that he needed to obliterate the minds of his patients, emptying them of their identity and their thoughts before he could rebuild them with new narratives. In his estimation, a prisoner's memory turned out to be the greatest tool of resistance. Thus, the first step in this disorientation theory was a de-patterning to erase the mind, creating a blank slate. Side effects of this ECT or electric shock therapy resulted not only in regression but also in amnesia. This type of amnesia is the probable state of the female prisoner in Valenzuela's story.

Applying these special interrogation techniques of Cameron's which also included drugs, chemicals and isolation, the CIA referred to this project of creating prisoners with erased minds as Project Bluebird. Later the name was changed to Project Artichoke4, and finally it was renamed MK Ultra in 1953. For more than ten years, $25 million was spent on research for MK Ultra in the hopes of discovering groundbreaking ways to break prisoners suspected of being communists (Klein 2007, 39). This was a more widespread phenomenon than the public was ever aware of as eighty institutions were involved in the program, including forty-four universities and twelve hospitals (Klein 2007, 39). Brainwashing was a fear that was real in the '50s as American GIs who were taken captive in Korea were apparently willing to go before cameras denouncing US imperialism (McCoy 2005, 218).

In 1957, Cameron got his first grant from the CIA through a front organization called the Society for the Investigation of Human Ecology. (Weinstein 1990, 122; Marks 1979, 133). By 1960, Cameron reported in a paper that there were "two major factors" that allowed humans to "maintain a time and space image" (Cameron 1960, 27, 1961, 231). These images permitted humans to know where they were as well as who they were, and these factors were 1) a continued sensory input and 2) one's memory. Cameron annihilated memory with electric shock. He controlled the sensory input by isolation.

In the 1990s, due to a threat of a lawsuit by The Baltimore Sun, the CIA finally acquiesced, surrendering to Senate investigations as well as public pressure a handbook called *Kubark Counterintelligence Interrogation.* The handbook was a 128-page manual on the "interrogation of resistant sources" based heavily on the research commissioned by MK Ultra and Dr. Ewen Cameron's work (Klein 2007, 47). The manual was dated 1963 and claimed that if the techniques were used properly, they would take a resistant prisoner and "destroy his capacity to resist by the destruction of memory and the restriction of his or her sensory input" (Klein 2007, 47).

Though approved by successive administrations in Washington, US participation in the Latin American dirty wars was conducted secretly for obvious reasons. Clearly violating the Geneva Conventions as well as the US Army's own Uniform Code of Military Justice, the US participation in torture could not be seen as overt. So from the 1970s on, the role favored by American agents was that of a mentor or a trainer, not a direct interrogator. "Testimony from Central American torture survivors of the seventies and eighties is littered with references to mysterious English-speaking men walking in and out of cells, proposing questions or offering tips" (Klein 2007, 50). Much of this advisory capacity was also clearly a function of the School of the Americas, first in Panama and later in Texas, when the School had to be moved because of strong Latin American popular opposition.

REPROGRAMMING THE COUNTRY:
THE INVERTED METAPHOR CONTINUED

The background to the Argentine Dirty War and treatment of prisoners is not just influenced by forms of torture to deprogram or reduce "communism" but the background also includes other forms of reprogramming by disorientation. For several decades, the US State Department presented the dirty wars in the Southern Cone as dangerous confrontations between the military and guerrillas in which Latin American military forces, backed by the CIA, needed US economic and military aid. Likewise, the juntas of the Southern Cone clearly expounded their reactionary intent to recreate their respective societies, justifying themselves on the grounds that they were fighting a war against dangerous Marxist terrorists. In Argentina, the Junta presented the Montoneros, a left-winged guerrilla group, as such a dangerous threat to national security that the Junta had no other option but to create a military state and crush them by force. However, the Montoneros were completely dismantled in the first six months of the Junta dictatorship, and the dictatorship went on to last for seven years in Argentina. In this time, the Junta "disappeared" tens of thousands of citizens after the Montoneros were crushed. Numerous organizations estimate that 30,000 were disappeared in Argentina.

In 2006, an Argentine judge of the federal court, Carlos Rozanski, found the Buenos Aires Police Commissioner, Etchecolatz, guilty of "political genocide." Etchecolatz was guilty of trying to eliminate "those citizens that did not fit the model determined by the repressors to be suitable for the new order being established in the country." ("Auto de la Sala de lo Penal de la Audiencia Nacional confirmando la jurisdicción de España para conocer de los crímenes de genocidio y terrorismo cometidos durante la dictadura argentina," Madrid, Nov. 4, 1998, www.derechos.org.) In 1999, Spanish Judge, Baltazar Garzón, who issued a warrant of arrest for Chile's Pinochet, described the Argentine Junta. He wrote that the intention of the Junta was "to establish a new order, like Hitler hoped to achieve in Germany, in which there was no room for certain types of people" (Garzón 1999).

Political genocide then, like torture and memory loss, is a cruel metaphor for reprogramming only on a much larger scale. Valenzuela's protagonist was one of those targeted as an unnecessary commodity for the Argentine nation. She was used as a guinea pig in the experiments to reprogram the "human machine." Though the story is fiction, Valenzuela is writing about a very real and traumatic series of events that produced the approximately 30,000 desaparecidos. Because it is fiction, it could be published in 1985, years before the impunity laws allowed this frank portrayal of political genocide in Argentina.

Lastly, the idea of economic change being launched like a surprise military attack (the US military Doctrine of Shock and Awe) is a reoccurring theme in the Southern Cone of the Americas in the 70s and 80s. That economic shock or crisis was also the mantra of Milton Friedman whose Chicago Boys tried to install neoliberalism all at once: eliminating food subsidies, canceling price controls, creating large hikes in resources and energy, making deep cuts to government spending, allowing unrestricted imports, and downsizing state companies for purposes of privatization. These efforts brought about very high numbers of unemployment, inflation, and the selling of public assets to private US and multinational corporations.

Even more significant than the US political influence, were the US corporate interests in Latin America in the 1960s, the '70s and the '80s. By 1968, 20 percent of total US foreign investment was tied up in Latin America (Klein 2007, 78). Right wing corporate think tanks which espoused neoliberal trade policies such as The Heritage Foundation and Cato were funded by large corporate interests such as General Mills, Getty Oil, Firestone Tire and Rubber Company, Pepsi Co., General Motors, and Bechtel (Friedman and Friedman 1998, 603).

The Ford Foundation was the primary donor for the University of Chicago's Program of Latin American Economic Research and Training. This foundation undergirded some of the educational costs of hundreds of Latino Chicago Boys to promote the neoliberal agenda. Consequently, the Ford Foundation was probably one of the leading sources of funding for the dissemination of Milton Friedman's economic ideology throughout Latin America. In the 1970s, the Southern Cone became a laboratory for his economic model. The Argentine "Death-mobiles" were green Ford Falcons donated to the Junta by the Ford Foundation to round up dissenters, union leaders and intellectuals that opposed the Junta's political control and its new economic policies.

In March 1975, Milton Friedman and Arnold Harberger, a professor at the Chicago School of Economics, flew to Santiago, Chile, to back up his Chicago Boys and their attempts to install neoliberal policies under Pinochet. Friedman had already collaborated with the Brazilian military junta, flying to Brazil in 1973. In Uruguay, the generals of their military coup of 1973 had already invited Arnold Harberger and his Chicago Boys to their country. So when Milton Friedman collaborated with the Argentine Junta in 1976, shortly after their coup overthrowing the government of Isabel Perón, the neoliberal pattern was becoming the rule in the Southern Cone.

In Argentina, this conservative policy that favored the US and multinational corporations, the landed gentry and the elites, was seen as a war upon the workers. It was a rolling back of forty years of gains by the Argentine workers under the politics of the Perons. Martínez de Hoz, Argentina's new minister of the economy under the Junta, immediately installed the Chicago Boy's agenda. He lifted price controls which caused food prices to skyrocket, he allowed privatization, lifting all restrictions on foreign ownership thus permitting hundreds of state companies to be bought. This, of course, bought him strong friends and powerful influences in Washington. Argentine workers were no longer protected as strikes were banned, and employers could now fire workers at will. However, a year after the coup, poverty in Argentina became rampant, the doors of many factories were closed, and wage losses were around 40 percent (McCaughan and Galeano 2002, 299). This type of chaos or crisis that Milton Friedman called the "opportunity" for real change was paralyzing for most Argentineans. Before the coup, Argentina had known an unemployment rate of 4.2 percent and only 9 percent fell below the poverty line (McCaughan and Galeano 2002, 299). Thus the change was dramatic, economically painful and very disorienting for most of Argentine citizenry.

The economic chaos that befell much of the Southern Cone because of neoliberal policies became prevalent throughout the decades of the '70s and '80s. The political change to military governments created gaps where the normal requirement of consensus was no longer applicable, bringing about the economic overturn, and a return to the politics favoring the colonial elites. Thus, it was the combination of the three destabilizing changes—political transformation, economic upheaval and the enforced use of terror, torture, and disappearance— that created tremendous instability in the lower and middle classes.

THE BORGIAN "*MISE EN ABÎME*": A METAPHOR OF CONSUMPTION

This moment of historical upheaval is the backdrop for Luisa Valenzuela's story, "El Cambio de Armas" (The Exchange of Weapons). Like the prisoner who can break under torture as the Kubark pointed out, Argentine society, was also reeling from the disorientation of immense change that was particularly harsh for the majority of Argentineans. The experience of the prisoner in Valenzuela's tale could also be a metaphor for the state of the Argentine society under the Junta and the neoliberal US corporate influence. The metaphors from this short tale could be layered like a progression of Russian dolls, one inside the other. The metaphor of the disoriented prisoner is swallowed up by the metaphor of the disorientation of the nation which is swallowed up by the disorientation of the nations in the Southern Cone. The labyrinth of chaos and violence in the Southern Cone is swallowed up by the bigger labyrinth of powerful right-winged interests in the US—the multinationals seeking access to South American resources, the right-winged foundations who wish to destroy communism in the Western Hemisphere, and the elites in South America who not only sell to US corporations but who also sell out their countrymen. On the broadest scale, reflecting a vision of the Argentine master writer, Jorge Luis Borges, the events in Valenzuela's tale are sustained by an ugly metaphor of consumption by moneyed interests. These interests consumed the lives of hundreds of the Disappeared, *los Desaparecidos*.

THE POWER OF THE METAPHOR BEFORE
IT WAS INVERTED: A TOOL FOR HEALING

The wielding of metaphor is perhaps one of man's most fruitful potentialities as José Ortega y Gasset has acknowledged. When we connect with our symbolic domains of experience, in this case, the metaphoric domain, we also connect with patterns that have deep personal significance or patterns that have strongly affected us.

Using a cognitive linguistic framework which was established in the '80s by Lakeoff and Johnson, metaphors not only occur in language but primarily in thought. This theory of metaphor then means that people actually understand the world by metaphors (Kövecses 1986, 2). They are not only spoken, but they are used to understand and explain experiences. When one has to understand something intangible such as time, the inner life, emotions, intrigues or mental constructs, the metaphors used to translate these intangibles become crucially important, mapping a whole raft of components into an image. The image helps people grasp the totality.

In the cognitive linguistic view of metaphor, metaphoric theory is complex. Metaphors have components. They have a variety of parts that interact with each other. A metaphor makes a jump from a *source* that is more physical to a *target* that is more abstract. Thus a labyrinth is a physical construct—a source—that is very confusing usually for the purpose of hiding violence and motives. The labyrinth's target is power. The deceptive architecture of the labyrinth is used to acquire power, restricting opposition and concealing the hands that reach for that power. This type of metaphor could be considered a "complex metaphor" as well as a universal one, as the deceptive reach for power is very much a part of human history.

Frequently metaphors reflect an embodied human experience (Köveces 1986, 101). Metaphorically, affection is described as warmth, an embodied experience of the loving embrace of a parent. This metaphor, according to Köveces, is a "primary metaphor."

Both primary and complex metaphors reveal another way of perceiving ourselves. When the metaphors we use are self-analyzed, they sometimes begin to evolve, a process that can lead to either a re-organization or a transformation of one's metaphoric landscape. This is the experience of the prisoner in Luisa Valenzuela's short story as she accumulates and processes her metaphors throughout the narrative. These metaphors carry great meaning for her. Her metaphoric thought processes are all she really has of herself as her memory "was erased." The reader sees this progression which appears to lead to self-awareness and perhaps, a transformed prisoner at the end of the story. Lawley and Tompkins (2003, 8) succinctly sum up this phenomenon: "Metaphor[s] can heal, transform and enrich lives."

THE DISPLACEMENT OF THE METAPHOR OF CONTAINMENT: FROM HIS ALIEN METAPHOR OF CONTAINMENT TO HER CONTAINMENT METAPHORS OF SELF-PROTECTION

In "Cambio de Armas," Valenzuela delineates the prisoner's past and her journey to memory in sixteen short chapters. Each chapter is labeled symbolically. The prisoner's environment is a locked apartment, contrived to create the narrative desired by the Colonel who holds her captive. Thus her "sensory input" is strictly controlled. Her memory and, therefore, her identity appear to have been erased. The Colonel imposes upon her physical control by drugs and sexual violence (Valenzuela 1998, 121–23). He has tamed her like a horse; she was his guinea pig (Valenzuela 1998, 145). He has deliberately left false keys on the shelf, testing her for resistance, to see if she will try to escape. The "so-called Laura" senses the keys will not work and refuses the temptation to try them. Her own psyche is still damaged. Yet, somehow she knows resistance causes pain, and her brain has adapted a mode of self-preservation.

Shutting down specific aspects of itself—in this case its memory—the brain defends itself against harmful physiological effects of this torture and abuse. Suspended in a fog of metaphors, symbols and scattered incomplete thoughts, the woman prisoner struggles to recover some aspect of her identity, an intangible entity. When the focus of understanding is on intangible entities, such as mental processes, emotions, and personal identity, the metaphors the "so-called Laura" uses become her keys to what has been shut down, contained within herself, but not completely erased. Not only does the human mind understand the world by metaphor, but throughout this tale, the prisoner creates a metaphoric landscape that maps and embodies her experience of suffering. By visiting and revisiting these metaphors, the reader and prisoner try to construct a past which corresponds to the way the prisoner perceives herself. As this self-modeling continues, a surprising phenomenon occurs—the prisoner begins to generate strong flashes of memory. This restructuring combined with the shock of the Colonel's rejection of her at the end of the story appear to provoke a developmental spiral, a transformation. Her metaphoric landscape implodes bringing her back to an apparent consciousness. This journey to consciousness is briefly summarized.

The contrasts between the metaphors used by the Colonel and those used by the woman prisoner are in contention in this short narrative. The metaphor of the emptied container is not infrequent in psychology, and as previously stated, metaphors of containment embody the experience of suffering as a prisoner. The Colonel believes he has emptied her and erased her memory, a desired effect of reprogramming the human machine. Thus, the prisoner is an emptied container (the elusive target) and she is contained in a locked apartment (the concrete source). The locked apartment is the controlled environment with deliberate details that are meant to reconstruct an identity that the Colonel wishes to impose on his prisoner. He is reprogramming her.

But this empty container, the target, that is the "so-called Laura," is not entirely empty; it contains the weapons of words. She knows nothing about herself, yet she can participate in the social contract that is language. Her first moment of strength is the awareness that she can control language and therefore, her thoughts. Laura perceives her empty container (the apartment) differently than the Colonel: "the so-called door" that is locked, materializes in her personal metaphor of containment. She perceives that this door divides her container, that is, her body/mind experience. She somehow knows her memory is a "crouched defensive form" behind the door. He sees her as an empty container; she sees herself as a divided container that represents a divided self. She also perceives "his side" of the container as alien.

"The Picture" is her false identity as a woman wed to the Colonel. This is the Colonel's imposed identity on her; it details his narrative in a single image. This metaphor of her false identity is one of his weapons. Yet, her identification is not at all with the picture but with a plant that is green and that grows. She is that city plant that is alive, though the flower is dying. She resists, then, by seeing herself in a healing metaphor of life that grows even though she has lost "her flower."

The double nature of the "so-called keys" has been apparent since the beginning. The woman prisoner is aware of the false keys that are a trap, and the real keys that unlock the door, are only carried by the Colonel and his men. The keys symbolize the Colonel's weapons; they contain the "so-called Laura." But in the language of the prisoner who grasps at metaphors as an expression of meaning, the keys morph into other objects in the story. The keys are the false wedding picture, the drugs that are used to control Laura, the window handle that the Colonel keeps in his pocket so to contain her. Throughout the story, the keys are a metaphor for all the devices used to maintain the "so-called Laura" in subjugation and containment. The keys (concrete source) are initially metaphors for the Colonel's weapons (concrete sources) used against Laura's mind (the abstract target). As the story progresses, the "so-called Laura" reverses the trajectory of the keys: She uses her metaphoric mind (abstract target) as her own keys to resist the Colonel's weapons (concrete sources).

She calls the Colonel the nameless one; she calls him many different names, because he represents many different men and the treatment they have inflicted on her. In her mind, he is the same as nothing. Deliberately using overhead mirrors, he sexually abuses her, an abuse repeated in the mirrors. She sees the many images of a subjugated shattered identity that is completely controlled. This abused empty container that is Laura is interrogated by "The Colleagues" and is entertainment for the Colonel's men in the sadomasochistic show, "The Peephole." Their act of witnessing her continued subjugation, her howling and her whimpering, is proof to them that she has been brainwashed. The Colonel appears successful in his attempt to empty and reprogram her. She is his prize machine under his control.

Yet Laura resists by her words and her thoughts in her reverse trajectory. Her mind (the abstract target) is the empty window pane (the concrete source) that looks out on an empty stained wall (the extended source) which is her body (the extended target) with its big scar down her back. She is willing herself to see. Though her identity has been erased, her internal voices still howl. Her desire to see (herself as the window) and her identification with life (herself as the plant) point to her reach for health and growth.

With this shift in her thoughts, the alien container that is the apartment has morphed. Her container has now become a deep well within her. Her well has been "so mistreated." Though it is a metaphor of containment, because it embodies Laura, it is also a metaphor of drowning and rebirth. In the water there is an "almost drowned" animal with claws (Valenzuela 1998, 129–30). The walls of the well reverberate with flashes of memory: the vision of the Colonel through the crosshairs of a gun, the sudden knowledge that she had a lover and he is dead, and the awareness evoked by the specific words that "she has been a disappeared person for so long" (Valenzuela 1998, 136). This metaphor of the inner well points to a possibility of "rebirth" of her memory and identity.

In memory recall, some symbols serve as a detonator. Two such symbols evoke strong reactions from the prisoner—the riding crop and her gun. The riding crop elicits a reaction of terror out of Laura, a probable association with a tool of torture, an instrument used to physically torture prisoners. Her gun is also used by the Colonel to evoke her memories. The days of the Junta are now numbered, and the Colonel wants her to come out of her "pretty dream." He is deliberately trying to jolt her memory by giving her the gun. When she won't touch the weapon, he assumes that she truly has been reprogrammed.

What he has not counted on is the resistance of a prisoner to face reality when that reality has been very harsh. Laura reacts true to the Stockholm syndrome, that is, she begs her captor for protection. Rejecting her advances, the Colonel insults Laura, calling her an animal and garbage. He reiterates his intention to abandon her, getting up to go out the door. Laura responds in fear, terror, anger and sudden recognition. He has torn her door open, and the probable transformation process is seismic. Her crouched figure of memory and identity on the other side of the door is exposed. The formerly brainwashed and passive prisoner suddenly reclaims her original intent to assassinate the Colonel. She picks up her weapon and points it at the source of all her pain. The short story ends before the shot is heard.

The Exchange of Weapons portrays a war of the Colonel's concrete weapons—the locked apartment, the wedding picture, the keys, the drugs, the mirrors, the peephole, the riding crop, her gun—all of which target her mind. He emptied her mind to fill it with himself and his narrative. The prisoner's weapons of resistance that reach for her lost identity are transformative metaphors—the door dividing the self, the plant demonstrating her desire to live, the window representing her desire to see and the well, protecting the rebirth of memory. The war is between the Colonel's use of concrete weapons and the prisoner's abstract metaphors that resist his alien definition of her. The repeated attempts to erase the prisoner's mind, the target, are obstructed by the prisoner's reach for language weapons, metaphors of resistance and health. The appearance of the gun returned to her by the Colonel is one of the detonators that provokes the rush of memory and her descent into the concrete reality to grasp the loaded gun. The short story closes on a suggested exchange: his concrete death for imposing on her the death of her identity, her intangible essence.

The Colonel's reprogramming of the prisoner reflects the hardline powers behind Neoliberalism to politically and economically erase and recreate the politics as well as the economy of the Southern Cone of Latin America in the '70s and the '80s. This erasure and restructuring would realign these Latin American nations not only in accordance with the vision of Milton Friedman and his Chicago Boys, but also to the benefit of the wealthy US and multinational corporations. The North American multinational corporations had guaranteed their access to Latin American natural resources and the continuation of their profits at the expense of 30,000 *desaparecidos*, not to mention the survivors of torture and their families.

The body of the prisoner and her terror is the body of the Argentine nation and the collective terror of many families of the disappeared. The rape and subjugation of the prisoner was also the rape and subjugation of the Argentine pueblo when certain people did not fit the "perceived ideals" of the ruling Junta or the multinational corporations which outwardly encouraged and helped to finance the "restructuring of the country."

In cases of such extreme containment and torture, the only weapons available to combat such traumatic experiences are the weapons of words, thoughts and the interior metaphors that map the body's response to health. These metaphors are the embodied weapons that evolve, resisting a death of self, provoking a renewal and a restoration of memory. They reflect the astounding abilities tied to language that the human brain holds to resist torture, death and reprogramming, a counter reaction that the Colonel and the Junta did not foresee. As for the US corporate boards and their involvement, it appears that they do not care as they enjoy impunity.

REFERENCES

Cameron, Ewen. 1960. "Production of Differential Amnesia as a Factor in the Treatment of Schizophrenia." *Comprehensive Psychiatry* 1 (1) : 27.

Cameron, Ewen, et al. 1961. "Sensory Deprivation: Effects upon the Functioning Human in Space Systems." *Symposium on Psycho-Physiological Aspects of Space Flight*, edited by Bernard F. Flaherty, 231. New York: Colombia University Press.

Central Intelligence Agency. 1963. *Kubark Counterintelligence Interrogation.* https://www.uscrow.org/downloads/Survival%20Public%20Domain /Kubark_Counterintelligence_Interrogation_torture_manual1963.pdf.

Cordones-Cook, Juanamaría. 1992. *Poética de transgresión en la novelística de Luisa Valenzuela.* New York: Peter Lang, Inc.

Craig, Linda. 2005. *Juan Carlos Onetti, Manuel Puig and Luisa Valenzuela: Marginality and Gender*. Rochester, New York: Tamesis.

Friedman, Milton, and Rose D. Friedman. 1998. *Two Lucky People: Memoirs*. Chicago: University of Chicago Press.

Garzón, Baltazar. 1999. "Auto de procesamiento a militares argentinos. Madrid, November 2. www.derechos.org

Geary, James. 2011. *I Is an Other: The Secret Life of Metaphor and How It Shapes the Way We See the World*. New York: Harper Perennial.

Gilbert, Jonathan. 2013. "Dirty War Trials Begin." *The Christian Science Monitor Weekly*, March 18.

Klein, Naomi. 2007. *Shock Doctrine: The Rise of Disaster Capitalism*. New York: Picador.

Köveces, Zoltán. 1986. *Metaphors of Anger, Pride, and Love: A Lexical Approach*. Philadelphia: John Benjamins Publishing Company.

———. 2002. *Metaphor: A Practical Introduction*. New York and Oxford: Oxford University Press.

———. 2007. *Metaphor in Culture*. Cambridge: Cambridge University Press.

Lakoff, George. 1993. "The Contemporary Theory of Metaphor." In *Metaphor and Thought*, edited by A. Ortony, 202–51, Cambridge: Cambridge University Press.

Lakoff, George, and Mark Johnson. 1980. *Metaphors We Live By*. Chicago: University of Chicago Press.

Lawley, James, and Penny Tompkins. 2003. *Metaphors in Mind: Transformation through Symbolic Modeling*. London: The Developing Company.

Marks, John D. 1979. *The Search for the Manchurian Candidate: The CIA and Mind Control*. New York: Times Books.

Magnarelli, Sharon. 1988. *Reflections/Refractions: Reading Luisa Valenzuela*. New York: Peter Lang.

McCaughan, Michael, and Eduardo Galeano. 2002. *True Crimes: Rodolfo Walsh, the Life and Times of a Radical Intellectual*. UK: Latin American Bureau.

McCoy, Alfred W. 2005. "Cruel Science: CIA Torture and Foreign Policy." *New England Journal of Public Policy*. 19 (2): 218.

Medeiros-Lichem, María Teresa. 2002. *Reading the Feminine Voice in Latin American Women's Fiction: From Teresa de la Parra to Elena Poniatowska and Luisa Valenzuela*. New York and Oxford: Peter Lang.

Ortega y Gasset, José. 1968. *The Dehumanization of Art and Other Essays on Art, Culture and Literature.* Princeton, NJ: Princeton Paperbacks.

Rozanski, Carlo. 1998. "Auto de la sala de lo penal de la Audiencia Nacional confirmando la jurisdicción de España para conocer de los crímenes de genocidio y terrorismo cometidos durante la dictadura argentina." Madrid, November 4. www.derechos.org.

Valenzuela, Luisa. 1998. *Cambio de armas.* Hanover, VT: Ediciones Del Norte.

Weinstein, Harvey M. 1990. *Psychiatry and the CIA: Victims of Mind Control.* Washington, D.C.: American Psychiatric Press.

CHAPTER 5

Toxic Pollution: The Latin American Indigenous Perspective in Three Recent Court Cases— Environmental Rights Are Human Rights

Since 1990, unrelenting social mobilization in Latin America has vigorously opposed the environmental degradation that the combination of powerful multinational corporations and complicit state officials have permitted in the past. The pollution generated by mining and oil interests has become a dire threat to the health and cultural survival of many Indigenous groups. Consequently, in Latin America, environmental rights—the right to clean air, water and land—have recently become a principle category in the struggle for human rights. Landmark court cases have launched biting critiques against the neoliberal policies that have encouraged environmental contamination of Indigenous lands. The inability of nation states to control or alter corporate exploitation of resources has led to the ultimate question of ownership of these resources. The Indigenous perspective insists that environmental rights are also human rights, that a degraded ecosystem also destroys human health and cultural sustainability. Environmental rights are social rights, to be held for the benefit of all and not to be destroyed for the benefit of the wealthy few. Having suffered environmental dispossession, Latin American Indigenous groups are now demanding guarantees of environmental justice, accountability for environmental pollution and a vested interest in the ownership of the land.

NEOLIBERAL RESOURCE ACQUISITION VERSUS THE ECONOMIC, SOCIAL AND CULTURAL RIGHTS OF GLOBAL SOCIETIES:

In a book chapter, Henry Carey talks about our divided global society in which our global politics are increasingly shaped by civil society (Carey 2013, 267). The principal actors of this global civil society are nongovernmental organizations (NGOs). Such NGOs include human rights monitors, Indigenous groups, trade lobbyists, public relations advisers, research institutes, humanitarian relief providers, corruption whistleblowers, and numerous websites. Carey points out their influence has become so predominant that in reaction to this influence, sovereign states, egged on by corporate interests, have attempted to check this trend since 2001. Consequently since 2001, global civil society has polarized into two opposing Transnational Advocacy Networks (TANS) which Carey labels the southern progressive camp and the northern neoliberal camp. Human rights have been extended to include Economic, Social and Cultural Rights (ESCRs) in the global southern progressive camp while an economically more powerful northern coalition of international institutions, corporations and NGOs with business and trade interests have tried to constrain the progressive coalition.

The main theatre for these confrontations between the Transnational Advocacy Networks (TANS) is at the United Nations or in the courts. Despite all the recent advances in Economic, Social and Cultural Rights (ESCRs) in the past two decades, the northern neoliberal coalition maintains the new definitions are primarily soft law, and thus can be conveniently ignored. However, in the southern progressive Transnational Advocacy Network, Economic, Social and Cultural Rights have been found justifiable by nation states in domestic courts. Moreover, the judgment from these court cases appears to have expanded the soft law norms in the UN.

Today, in India, Brazil, Argentina, Chile, Ecuador and the European Union, many Economic, Social and Cultural Rights have passed into hard law, becoming part of their constitutions. These ESCRs represent issues of cultural autonomy, health, assess to water, food and housing, social security, education and employment (Carey 2013, 276). The newest addition to these rights is the problem of environmental rights that is intricately connected to the rights of health, clean water and land that has not already been ruined by toxic dumping.

The drama between the interests of these two TANS—the northern neoliberal corporations and their conservative think tanks versus the southern progressive NGOs—can be illustrated by several Latin American influential courts cases. These cases were brought on by Latin American Indigenous claims that their health, their crops and their cultural sustainability have been badly compromised by repetitive toxic oil spills, degraded watersheds, poisoned soils from oil and mining extraction, and foreign ownership of their water sources.

The lack of constraints on corporations in twentieth-century Latin America led to higher corporate profits and consequently, an acceleration of the resource war. For decades in the twentieth century, a small percentage of elites who controlled the governments in South America continued to encourage foreign direct investment in mining and oil. Their association with North American corporations enriched their earnings at the expense of the Latin American majority, and particularly, the Indigenous populations. The elites aligned themselves with resource development and were encouraged by the neoliberal corporate push behind the imposed military governments in the second half of the twentieth century. After the military coups, the father of Neoliberalism, Milton Friedman, visited Latin America multiple times to instruct the military dictators on the tenants of neoliberal development in order to benefit North American corporations. Military officials who were part of the national elites supported such cooperation for reasons of remuneration. Economic statistics point to the fact that the Latin American elites rode the US corporate neoliberal bandwagon. By 1988, fifteen years after the Chilean coup, the elite—the richest 10 percent of Chileans had seen their incomes increase by 83 percent (Klein 2007, 105). Meanwhile the middle class shrank; 45 percent of the Chilean population had fallen below the poverty line because of the neoliberal policies enacted to benefit corporate investment. From 1954 to 2016, neoliberal policies elevated the incomes of the elites, lowered the living standard of the majority of South Americans while foreign oil and mining interests polluted Indigenous lands, endangering their survival.

MINING: THE CASE OF PASCUA LAMA

Mining in Latin America has been the primary target of the western nations' push for resources since the Conquista. Silver and gold fueled the colonial Spanish *Metropoli*, institutionalized labor exploitation in the Americas, and have been at the center of western imperialistic ventures since 1492. (Columbus' Diary documents the search for gold). The acceleration of investment in mining in the latter part of the twentieth century was generated by the rising prices of minerals on the world market and an increased demand by emerging nations.

In the 1990s, the environmental costs of mining were also linked to human health that became a highly controversial issue. Mining extraction and processing require large volumes of water (Segarra 2013, 312). Toxins such as dioxin and heavy metals poison rivers and watersheds used for drinking, fishing, and agriculture (Franks 2009). Mining sites have tremendous impacts on cultural societies who live near the sites as once sustainable environments become toxic. "Moreover, when a mine is played out, its closure must be monitored over time to prevent further contamination, a process that requires significant company and state oversight" (Fields 2009, 536–39).

By 2011, the Observatorio de Conflictos Mineros en America Latina registered more than 155 community controversies (Segarra 2013, 314). This success of the social and cultural mobilization against mining pollution has provoked angry responses from the mining companies involved, including underhanded criminal behavior. Private contractors hired by mining interests have employed strong-man tactics of threats and assassinations. Barrick Gold, a Canadian company operating the Pascua Lama open pit mine project, is under investigation by human rights groups and the United Nations for violence and intimidation (Corpwatch 2007).

Consequently, Barrick Gold has provoked multiple legal suits by Indigenous groups against its pit mines at the Pascua Lama site. Part of the growing Canadian investment in mineral exploitation, Barrick Gold was able to obtain a mining concession at the Pascua Lama site in 1994, which straddles the border of Chile and Argentina. The boundaries of the mines fall 75 percent in Chilean territory and 25 percent in Argentinean land. Situated at a height of 15,000 feet in the Andes, access to the mining area is through Indigenous lands and communities.

Desert ecosystems in the high Andes are sensitive. The contamination of water and soils as a result of the Pascua Lama mines have threatened the livelihoods and the cultural traditions of the Indigenous groups on both sides of the border. Located at a region that is at the headwaters of several rivers and glaciers, the Barrick Gold concession is situated so that mining interests have access to water. However, the glaciers and the rivers form the watershed for the Huasco Valley, a fertile region where more than 70,000 people are involved in agricultural production (Segarra 2013, 317). In 2004, Barrick Gold produced a plan to move or alter the glaciers that fall within its concession (Franks 2009). At that point, the original protests of the Indigenous groups and agriculturalists became a very heated national controversy.

Gold and silver mines pose large threats to water and soil as they generate acid mine drainage, and the potential dumping of arsenic, cyanide and mercury from trucks. Any pollution generated by spills would have profound impacts on both local agricultural communities and Indigenous groups downstream within the watershed (Corpwatch 2007).

Historically, before the 1970s, the larger mines in Chile were owned by foreign corporations. But the great profits earned by the US foreign control of the mines were at the expense of the Chilean mine workers who received meager pay and could not rely on secure work. The issue was such a sore point for mine workers that twice they voted for socialistic governments. The first pro-socialist election took place in 1932 and then again in 1970 with the hopes that the government would nationalize the mines and create more favorable working conditions and salaries for the mine workers. After the military coup, encouraged by US corporations (IT&T scripted the eighteen-point military coup), Pinochet returned many industries expropriated by Allende to these corporations. However, he maintained one exception under the Chilean government, the copper mines in Northern Chile (Klein 2007, 80, 104).

When Pinochet left the Chilean government in 1990, the Concertación government that replaced him began to consider environmental protection as an important priority. The National Commission on the Environment, la Comisión Nacional del Medio Ambiente (CONAMA) was created in 1990. By 1994, a new law, la Ley de Bases Generales del Medio Ambiente became effective allowing CONAMA to manage and protect human health and the environment (Carruthers 2001, 343–58). However, despite the fact that the Chilean state is the legal owner of subsoil mineral rights, production and the processes of production are owned and run by private investors and CODELCO, the National Copper Corporation of Chile. The Chilean government leases concessions to these companies in return for royalty fees, which are reported to be low, between 4 and 5 percent (Craze and Orihuela 2010). The role of the Chilean government is to regulate the balance between exploitation of resources and an environmentally sustainable resource management. The government's role is backed by Article 19.8 of the Chilean Constitution which states that a Chilean "has the right to live in an environment free from contamination." "It is the state's duty to guard against infringement of this right and to oversee the conservation of nature" (Embassy of Chile, http://www.chile-usa.org/ecologye.htm).

In 2006, the then future president, Michelle Bachelet promised to place the glaciers off limits to Barrick Gold, restricting the company's access to the glaciers. However, despite the risks of potential spills and acid mine drainage, the Chilean state signed off on Barrick Gold's mining projects in 2006, before Bachelet was installed in office.

Within short order, by 2007, opponents of the Pascua Lama mine filed lawsuits in Chile and sought the help of international human rights' NGOs such as the Inter-American Commission on Human Rights. The Diaguita Agricultural communities of the Huasco-Altinos insisted that the Chilean state had allowed Barrick Gold to continue with the development without consulting the local Indigenous and agricultural communities. As the mining site is located in the midst of ancestral Indigenous lands, the mining project would destroy Indigenous health, their land-oriented customs and their environment. Moreover, the state of Chile is constitutionally obligated to disallow environmental violations of human rights. For the Diaguita Agricultural Communities, the state's involvement with the corporation, Barrick Gold, was not politically transparent, and thus the claims of the agricultural and Indigenous communities were ignored. In Report No.

141/09 and the Protest-Barrick of April 28, 2010, the Diaguita Agricultural Communities stated: "The Pascua Lama project, as occupying part of our ancestral territory, takes away from us the possibility of protecting our natural and cultural heritage" (Protest Barrick, April 2010).

Galvanized by the outcry, Barrick Gold invested in a sweeping public relations campaign. Arguing that the impact statements for the mine were examined and passed by both Chilean and Argentinian agencies, the company promised to be a "good corporate neighbor" (Segarra 2013, 319). The PR from the company insisted that there would be strong economic advantages for the communities as well as development. Moreover, there would be additional job creation. There would be a "rising tide that would lift all boats," the classic neoliberal argument for corporate involvement. In an attempt to display corporate social responsibility and generate positive public opinion, Barrick Gold provided an immediate response for earthquake assistance in 2010.

Forgetting Barrick Gold's poor reputation in other countries, the Chilean and Argentinian states responded to the soaring price of gold in 2011 and the obvious potential revenues that would dispel all hesitation in the matter. Despite the presence of economic, social, and cultural rights in hard law form, particularly in Chile, corporate development overrode the Indigenous demand to safeguard their heritage.

Consequently, the debate about ownership of the environment and the state's role in protecting the environment is even more heated today. Many petitioners and NGOs point out that the wealth and clout of many multinational corporations such as Barrick Gold are both greater and stronger than the state. The use of corruption or economic remuneration to ensure the dominance of corporate neoliberal agendas appears to be an ongoing threat to environmental rights. This corruption continues despite the fact that a state's constitution establishes that a person "has the right to live in an environment free from contamination" (Article 19.8 of the Chilean Constitution). In summary, even hard law appears to be an insufficient deterrence when state actors who are associated with the elites see increased revenues. Hard law is not enough to prevent environmental dispossession nor uphold economic, social, and cultural rights.

OIL: THE ECUADORIAN CHEVRON TEXACO DEBACLE

The production and extraction of oil in Latin America have historically been regulated by US and multinational corporations (MNCs), sometimes in partnership with locally owned oil companies. The technologies and the capital have typically come from the multinational corporations.

Oil was originally discovered in the Amazon Basin of Ecuador in the 1960s. Perceived as a marginal area, the state of Ecuador promoted expansion into the Amazon with plans to develop this resource base. The Corporación Estatal Petrolera Ecuatoriana, later known as Petroecuador, sought out multinational corporations (MNCs) to provide the technology, expertise and investment capital. By 1967, Texaco had ferreted out the first major oil reserve in the Ecuadorian Amazon. Classified as the *tierras baldías* or the *tierras salvajes* (the barren or savage wastelands), the Amazon was to become the source of black gold for the state of Ecuador. By 1972, a trans-Andean pipeline was finished that connected the Amazon to the Pacific ports. Shortly thereafter, Ecuador joined OPEC as a smaller producer. Unhampered by environmental legislation because of the neoliberal push behind the controlling military governments (1972–1979 in Ecuador), oil extraction boomed, and oil became the principle resource for development.

In the 1980s two diverse agendas became apparent. The falling oil prices and the 1982 debt crisis only led to increased oil extraction to make up shortfalls. On the other hand, Indigenous critiques of the damage to their ancestral lands festered to critical levels. By the 1990s, these critiques had become very politically active protest networks. Additional criticism pointed to the very uneven distribution of oil revenues in addition to the contamination of environments. Texaco was taking home huge profits while damaging the health, the environment and the livelihoods of Indigenous Ecuadorians.

The 1990s only saw heightened controversy over oil production. The oil sector in Ecuador underwent increased production, specifically because of state liberalization and the rising prices of crude. In 1992, President Sixto Durán Ballén in his inauguration speech, promised to provide greater incentives for multinational oil investment. He withdrew Ecuador from OPEC with the intention of raising the production quota of oil higher than OPEC's production quota for Ecuador. Consequently, production of oil jumped from 275,000 to 373,000 barrels a day (Sawyer 2004, 95). President Sixto Durán Ballén and his elites were sending a clear message to global capital; his government would embrace the free market economy with no restrictions. By 1994, the revenues from oil made up approximately half the state's budget and half of the revenues were used to pay Ecuador's international debt.

However, while foreign investment surged under the neoliberal rules of the '90s, so did legal action from the Indigenous groups on whose lands exploration and extraction of oil was taking place. The continued increase of the oil industries' production led to major displacements of local and Indigenous groups, threatening cultural integrity and survival (Franks 2009). The changes that President Sixto Durán Ballén was introducing provoked the seventh round of talks (la Séptima Ronda) between Indigenous groups and the state. As several decades of experience with Texaco had proved, oil companies were experts at disavowing any responsibility for the social and environmental degradation. Placing state resources in the hands of multinational corporations appeared to be a mistake that spelled environmental disaster.

The environmentally negative by-products of oil extraction are numerous. Large quantities of wastes and toxic elements are generated by oil production and extraction. Spills and toxic dumping have been frequent, polluting both the land and watersheds. Moreover, natural gas is a by-product of oil production, and until recently, much of this by-product had been burned as waste. This procedure of burning or flaring the natural gas led to acid rain, greenhouses gases, ground level ozone, soot, and dioxin (Kimerling 2013, 44–115). Consequently, oil companies and corresponding state involvement have come under intense criticism by human and environmental rights groups in Latin America.

Adding to this grim picture of environmental pollution, hired security agents and oil interests have provoked direct violence against communities or Indigenous groups living next to oil production sites. Oil companies have thus come under a landslide of legal suits and increasing scrutiny. In one case, a legal battle in Ecuador's Amazonian territory (the Oriente), 30,000 plaintiffs of mostly Indigenous communities, launched a decades-long suit against Texaco for toxically dumping in the Amazonian tributaries. The Indigenous groups' hunter-gatherer lifestyles were bound to the rivers as well as the rainforest. The history of oil spills, water pollution and exposure to toxic wastes by the multinational corporations galvanized Indigenous groups—the Amazonian Indian Confederation (CONFENIE) and the Confederation of Indigenous Nationalities of Ecuador (CONAIE).

Texaco, the principle oil operator, had concessions of almost a million acres in the Oriente from1967 to 1990, initially with Gulf Oil and in the later years with Petroecuador (Kimerling 2013, 44–115). As there were strong ties between Ecuador's legal system and Petroecuador, the Indigenous groups did not believe they would receive a fair trial in Ecuador (Black 2004, 142–64). Consequently, a group of Ecuadorian and US lawyers worked together to prepare numerous lawsuits against Texaco in the United States.

This class action suit of 30,000 plaintiffs, *Aguinda versus Texaco*, applied the Alien Tort Claims Act. The suit claimed that Texaco provoked degradation of human health and environmental damage through twenty years of oil spills and deliberate dumping of toxic materials to cut costs. They used untreated waste water and unlined waste pits, leaching toxins both into the watershed and the land (Kimerling 2013, 44–115; Sawyer 2004). By launching this lawsuit in the US, the plaintiffs and their lawyers strove to introduce the case to an international audience, emphasizing the linked nature of human rights and environmental rights. Large multinational corporations obviously needed regulatory controls, or, as in the case of *Aguinda versus Texaco*, they would contaminate areas the size of the state of Rhode Island. One of the head lawyers in the case emphasized the sheer size of the contaminated area and the backlash of cancer for an Indigenous population that was economically marginalized.

For eight years from 1993 to 2001, the suit continued in the US courts. Texaco's lawyers made a strategic argument to send the case back to Ecuador as the US courts were not the appropriate venue for a legal dispute that took place in Ecuador. The case was sent back to Ecuador on the judicial stipulation that Chevron Texaco would then have to abide by the ruling of the Ecuadorian court, or the US would enforce their judgment (Black 2004, 142–64). Texaco's hope was to return the case to Ecuador because the case would die given the previous ties between the Ecuadorian judicial system and the elites controlling Petroecuador. But the political and legal situation in Ecuador had changed greatly in those eight years.

From 1996 to 2003, Indigenous groups had become politically influential in Ecuador, ousting several elected presidents who would not address their concerns. By 1998, Indigenous power became hard law by definition as the Constitution of Ecuador now recognized Indigenous rights and their environment as being critical to their autonomy and cultural heritage. Combined with the strong discontent of all Ecuadorians against all neoliberal interests of both the Multinational Corporations and the IMF, the Indigenous indignation led to the election of a leftist president, Rafael Correa. Correa promised to establish the state's management over natural resources and to increase democracy. In 2008, the 1998 Constitution was rewritten to prioritize Indigenous concerns, their rights to their ancestral lands and the defense of their cultural heritage by environmental protection. Moreover, Correa's administration tightened control over the hydrocarbon sector, reversing the neoliberal lack of constraints. The concessions and royalty shares of the oil companies were decreased. The oil companies were reined in by the new Ecuadorian government seeking better environmental control and higher returns.

It was in this political atmosphere that the *Aguinda versus Texaco* trial resumed in Ecuador.

Chevron Texaco challenged all data and deliberately dragged out the proceedings, raising issues that had been resolved, failing to produce documentation, raising the ire of the Ecuadorian courts. *The Washington Times*, in 2009, reported that Chevron Texaco solicited trade sanctions against the Ecuadorian government to add muscle to their case. Meanwhile, President Correa openly supported the plaintiff's case and pursued fraud charges against former Ecuadorian officials who had tried to release Chevron Texaco from any further claims.

The extreme controversy surrounding the case became legendary. The lawyers for the Ecuadorian plaintiffs openly claimed that the courts had the ability to redistribute some of the costs of globalization. Chevron Texaco, for its part, tried to discredit not only the plaintiffs, but the plaintiff's lawyers and even the judge. It also launched federal action against the plaintiff's lawyers for conspiracy against the company and a claim against the government of Ecuador for the "biased" position of the Ecuadorian government. The company perceived this was high stakes poker for the future of all Multinational Corporations. The confrontation of one of the most powerful Multinational Corporations and the marginalized Indigenous populations of the world became a drama that drew international interest.

In 2011, the Ecuadorian court found Chevron Texaco liable for $18.2 billion. Human rights activists, Indigenous groups and environmental NGOs celebrated the decision. However, Chevron Texaco "declared the judgment to be illegitimate and unenforceable and said that the company that had no assets in Ecuador, would not pay" (Keefe 2012). Furthermore, the threat given by the US judge— that Chevron Texaco would then have to abide by the ruling of the Ecuadorian court, or the US would enforce the Ecuadorian court's judgment—never was applied. Thus, the case is considered to be over. Those who seek legal justice for human and environmental rights have almost an impossible task to go up against the world's most powerful and wealthy corporations. Though the Indigenous groups were backed by hard law, the Constitution of Ecuador, hard law was not enough. It appears that multinational corporations have a blatant disregard for the law when it works against their favor, and can operate flagrantly above and outside of the law of nation-states.

WATER WARS: LATIN AMERICA, THE BOLIVIAN UPRISING AND BECHTEL'S SUIT

In 1995, Ismail Serageldin, vice president of the World Bank, made a much-quoted prediction about the future of water: "If the wars of this century were fought over oil, the wars of the next century will be fought over water" (Shiva 2002, 1). Water is a life force that in parts of the world is seen as sacred, tied to the sacredness of life itself. Food and water are the necessities of life, but even food cannot be cultivated without water. In Bolivia, water is perceived as the sacred gift of *Pachamama* to be held in common for all. This viewpoint of the sacred Commons clashes with the North's commodification of water for profit, with its value only as a raw material.

The World Bank has played a principal role in the commodification of water and estimates that the potential water market lies at $1 trillion (Barlow 2001, 15.) In its edition of May of 2000, *Fortune* magazine points out that the most profitable industry for investors is water. Privatization projects of water funded by the World Bank are designated as "public-private partnerships," a deliberately misleading label. While it suggests public participation and accountability, it does not disclose the fact that public funds are used to privatize public goods.

Public-private partnerships have flourished under the guise of soliciting private capital and reducing public-sector employment. In a study done for the World Bank in 1995, public systems worldwide employ five to ten employees per 1,000 water connections. In contrast, private companies employ two to three employees per 1,000 water connections (Shiva 2002, 91). Thus, the privatization of water demands a reduction of staff and points to the lack of accountability in the public sector of utilities. However, there is no evidence that private companies are any more accountable. In fact, it appears that privatization of water lacks a track record of success and demonstrates a high record of failures, such as the privatization of water in Mexico City in the last decade of the twentieth century.

In addition, private water companies have often violated operational standards and promoted price gouging. When Suez Lyonnaise des Eaux took over the contract for privatization in Chile, they demanded a 35 percent profit (Shiva 2002, 92). In Buenos Aires, the public utility sector provider, Obras Sanitarias de la Nación, was reduced from 7,600 employees to 4,000 in 1993. However, while employment in the water service went down, the price of water increased by 13.5 percent the first year (Idelevitch and Ringkeg 1995, 9).

Though very unpopular with regional residents, the privatization of water continues. Nations around the world who carry debt and ties to the World Bank and the International Monetary Fund are forced to privatize their water. A lending condition of the World Bank and the IMF is often a demand to deregulate public water utilities. The World Trade Center pushes for water privatization by means of free-trade rules found in the GATS (the General Agreement on Trade in Services). A critical point of GATS is that governments may not oppose corporations because of cultural issues in their WTO negotiations. GATS eliminates government restrictions and permits private companies to sue countries who refuse free-market entry. Governments are not allowed to discriminate between local service providers and foreign corporations. Neither is favoritism permitted for community nonprofit organizations against large corporations. Thus, GATS rules openly favor the large multinational corporations who have the resources to make the best offer.

In 1999, in the most famous of the water wars, the case of Bolivia, the World Bank imposed the privatization of Cochabamba's water, Bolivia's third largest city. Situated in an arid region of Bolivia, Cochabamba is also a center for many Indigenous communities. Cochabamba's municipal water service, Servicio Municipal del Agua Potable y Alcantarillado (SEMAPA) was forced to accept a concession to International Water, a subsidiary of Bechtel (Barlow 2001, 54). Consequently, a Drinking Water and Sanitation Law was passed in October of the same year which permitted a privatization of the water supply.

Within a short period, water bills jumped 60–90 percent, and in some cases, doubled. These increases forced some of the poorest families in South America to choose between food and water. Bechtel insisted that the price hikes were minimal—only a 10 percent increase—and that many residents had increased their water usage. Jim Schultz rebuts this claim with copies of actual water bills. A typical case was that of Germán Jaldín, a Cochabamba resident, whose bill documented the unsustainable rise in the price of water. In December of 1999, his bill was eighty-two Bolivianos (about $13.67) for thirty-five cubic meters of water. After Bechtel's rate hikes, in January, his water bill jumped to 157.60 Bolivianos or ($26.27) for the use of thirty-eight cubic meters of water. "This means that while his water use increased by less than 10%, his water bill from Bechtel jumped by more than 90%" (CorpWatch 2003). Jaldín was classified "R-3," that is, just above the very poorest, with a kitchen tap and shower. R-3 households are headed by workers who earn $60 to $80 per month, and as such, they are unable to cope with such increases (CorpWatch 2003).

By January of 2000, a citizen's alliance that consisted of different Indigenous groups had coalesced. This alliance, La Coordinadora de Defensa del Agua y de la Vida (The Coalition in Defense of Water and Life), worked to engage the Bolivian population. The initial mass mobilization in protest of the privatization of water and the jump in water prices managed to shut down Cochabamba for four days. Within several short weeks, millions of Indigenous Bolivians marched on the city, stopping all transportation and holding a general strike. The protesters demanded protection of universal water rights, the termination of the water contract with Bechtel, and the participation of the Bolivian population in setting up a public water service. For them, "Water is the Gift of *Pachamama* and Not a Merchandise," as their signs indicated. For the Indigenous communities, water was part of the "commons," the centerpiece of Indigenous belief. Water was life, and a foreign corporation had denied them the right to life. Protests against the commodification of water and the inability to pay such high prices for water continued for several months. These protests gathered steam when Indigenous Bolivians were even jailed for trying to collect rainwater.

In reaction to these protests, the Bolivian government initially stated that the price hike would be reversed. However, that was never done as the obstacles of GATS and the contractual agreement with Bechtel explicitly did not allow for cultural perceptions to interfere. Bechtel Corporation held the threat of suit over the government's head. In April of 2000, the government, through martial law, attempted to shut down the water protests. Violence flared; protesters were injured, media personnel were locked up and their messages were censored. Activists grew more numerous in response to the government's support of Bechtel. The situation in Cochabamba became a flagrant water war.

Within ten days, the people were victorious; Bechtel left Bolivia. The government was forced to turn over the water company (SEMAPA) to the people. La Coordinadora held numerous public meetings to establish a democratic control, a water democracy. Bechtel threatened to sue the government of Bolivia. The Bolivian government, in the anxiety to show good faith to its contractual obligations with Bechtel, continued to threaten participants of La Coordinadora.

Vandana Shiva, in her book, *Water Wars, Privatization, Pollution and Profit*, concludes that giant water projects benefit the powerful and dispossess the weak (Shiva 2002, 87). She mentions Suez Lyonnaise des Eaux, Vivendi Environment, Biwater, Thames Water, Coca Cola's Bon Agua/Dasani, Pepsi's Aquafina, Bechtel and Cascal as some of these water projects. Privatization is couched in neoliberal rhetoric about the disappearing role of the state. Policies imposed by the World Bank, the IMF, the World Trade Center, and GATS are creating a sweeping culture of corporate states with rules shaped entirely by corporate elites. No input from NGOs, cultural groups, local governments, or national governments is allowed (Shiva 2002, 94). Corporate trade rights, granted by trade agreements such as NAFTA and GATS, apply to corporate water ownership and control. Every level of government, including regional and local, is now forced to adhere to rules to which it did not negotiate or agree. Policy-making for water rights is no longer in the hands of local or national governments but in the grip of large Multinational Corporations (Shiva 2002, 97). The erosion of water rights has become a global phenomenon.

Eighteen months after Bechtel was forced to leave Bolivia, the multinational corporation and its co-investor, Abengoa of Spain, filed a $50 million legal suit against Bolivia. Bechtel sought $25 million in damages and $25 million in lost profits. The case was filed before the International Centre for Settlement of Investment Disputes (ICSID), the World Bank trade court, located in New York. The ICSID process bars the public and media from being present at its proceedings or even allowing disclosures of who is testifying. The secrecy and the exclusivity of such proceedings favor multinational corporations and their investors. For four years following the filing of this suit, NGOs and citizen groups on five continents waged a global campaign against Bechtel, demanding that the corporation drop the case. Groups from forty-three nations endorsed a legal petition to the World Bank insisting that the court case be opened to public participation (Earthjustice 2006, 2). Bechtel was strongly criticized on the world stage and only managed to earn a very negative notoriety in the international media.

Jim Shultz, the executive director of the Democracy Center in Cochabamba, Bolivia, and a leader in the global effort to back the Bolivian people, felt vindicated. "This is the first time that a major corporation like Bechtel has had to back down from a major trade case as the result of global citizen pressure" (Earthjustice 2006, 2). He added that this case should be a signal to multinational corporations who consider similar legal actions. They might have "to defend those actions in the court of global public opinion, not just behind closed doors at the World Bank" (Earthjustice 2006, 2). Sarah Anderson who works for the Institute for Policy Studies in Washington, D.C., points out the need "to build on this momentum to press for new trade and investment rules that promote democracy and sustainable development rather than the narrow interests of large corporations" (Earthjustice 2006, 3).

The Indigenous Bolivians, by their very active will and participation, have redefined and inverted the relationship of a citizen to the state, and in the process, managed to capture global sympathy for their struggle against Bechtel. This case has demonstrated that privatization is not always an inevitable reality; it can be circumvented by a highly participatory democratic will.

CORPORATE STRATEGIES AND TACTICS

Corporations adapt rapidly to challenges posed by critics. They are usually highly adept at responding to the strategies and tactics of their critics, which require activists to engage in continual strategic innovation.

Stuart Kirsch, in his book, *Mining Capitalism* (2014), has classified the three phases of corporate response to public criticism (182–87).

Phase I is "Denial" that the critique is valid. The goal is to avoid any engagement that would erode corporate profitability or threaten continuing operations. The key strategy of Phase I is to provoke the proliferation of doubt. This phase appears to be the most profitable position for corporations to occupy as it buys them time to continue their procedures. In the suit, *Aguinda versus Texaco*, Chevron-Texaco clung to the strategy of proliferating doubt not only against the accusations of environmental contamination but against the validity of all the plaintiffs, the judges and the jurors, drawing out the suit for eighteen years (1993–2011).

Phase II occurs when the problems become too large for corporations to deny, particularly when the critique of the corporate activity has scientific validity or ethical merit. In order to limit accommodation or payment of compensation, this phase might be labeled "Tactics of Deception."

One such tactic is to develop monitoring or accountability that avoids significant structural change or cost. In such cases, activists are recruited, many times with financial compensation, to join corporate boards, thus reducing their voice as well as their ability and motivation to bring about change.

A second tactic commonly employed is to divide and conquer. In the Pascua Lama case, this tactic was used to buy off one Indigenous group against another, and in the subsequent disputes between the groups, the corporation once again bought more time to continue their operations.

The third and most powerful tactic that has been used significantly by corporate resistance is to co-opt the discourse of their critics, inverting their position from a destroyer of the environment to a participant of growth and sustainability. However, the result of an inverted discourse is to empty out the meaning of a term such as "sustainability" (Negri 1999, 9). In this manner, the term "sustainability" undergoes continual re-definition, each time to lessen its meaning and its effect on corporate behavior. Inverted discourse eventually nullifies all argument; it robs those opposing the corporate behavior of their major weapon—meaningful language. There are no longer two opposing arguments and two opposing camps. Both camps are reduced to occupying the same controversial ground, a tactic employed to confuse the public. Some of this inverted language used by corporations even extends to oxymoron, such as the claim of "clean coal" to falsely reassure the public. Inverted language is a powerful weapon used to conceal intractable problems, to whitewash dirty conflicts and to nullify the language of the opposing critic. Using co-opted discourse, Barrick Gold, in the case of Pascua Lama, sought to whitewash its public image.

Phase III occurs when the problems facing a corporation become financially and socially too great to manage such as in the case of Bechtel. Phase III is usually the last resort for corporations. The threat of a complete loss of legitimacy usually motivates a corporation either to participation in a regulatory process or to a suit. However, the costs of this remediation are typically born by public dollars. Armed by trade agreements like GATS which favor corporate interests, Bechtel sued the Bolivian government. However, in Bechtel's suit against the government of Bolivia for contractual violation, this case supplied the only winning stroke against corporate agendas—the overwhelming engagement of the NGOs, the media, and the global public against the corporation of Bechtel. This engagement against Bechtel threatened to completely rob its legitimacy in the very public and global eyes of the world. This case represents the rare and stunning success of a less powerful country and its culturally marginalized Indigenous population against a highly influential corporate giant.

CONCLUSION

In the attempt to control corporate pollution and/or environmental dispossession, the Southern Progressive Transnational Advocacy Networks have pushed for recognition of economic, social, and cultural rights. These rights have been eliminated from large trade treaties such as GATS or from loans orchestrated by the IMF or the World Bank.

In the past two decades, environmental rights have been recognized by many countries and the United Nations as a legitimate part of Economic, Social and Cultural Rights. The Neoliberal Northern Transnational Advocacy Networks have easily ignored this "soft law" and more alarmingly, have totally disregarded "hard law" that restricts corporate activity as found in the constitutions of governments. In two cases, Barrick Gold in the Pascua Lama region between Chile and Argentina and *Aguinda versus Texaco* in Ecuador, "hard law" posed no deterrent to either corporation. Barrick Gold used economic remuneration of elites to ensure the dominance of the corporation's agenda over "hard law." Chevron Texaco baldly stated that the court's decision against Chevron Texaco imposing payment of $18.2 billion for the destruction of a large section of the Ecuadorian

Amazon was "unenforceable." The wealth and clout of large multinational corporations have become both greater and more powerful than sovereign states. For corporate purposes, law is a convenient imposition to gain corporate benefits, however, law can be ignored when fines are levied against corporations. Multinational corporations are now above or outside of the law. However, this reality eventually leaves a very bad impression of multinational corporations in the public's eye.

Due to the information age of the internet, Bechtel's case against Bolivia was broadcast on five continents raising awareness and the ire of the public against Bechtel and its co-investor, Abengoa. This campaign on the part of citizen groups and NGOs to de-legitimize Bechtel's suit against the Bolivian government was highly successful. A bad impression of Bechtel was spread on the world stage, greatly reducing the profits and the stock of the corporation. The public has not only the power to wage a negative public relations campaign on the internet but can also refuse to buy a corporation's product. The power of an informed public has stepped into the position vacated by governments weakened or controlled by corporate demands and their trade deals.

Bechtel's suit against the Bolivian government has demonstrated that corporate will is not always an inevitable reality given the average citizen's connectedness to information. This case has also been an alarm signal to multinational corporations. It appears likely that this case may have created an impetus for the recent corporate demands on the US Federal Communications Commission (FCC) and the net restrictions against the public inserted into the Trans Pacific Partnership agreement. Corporate wealth seeks to restrict open access to the internet in part to reduce the potential power of public awareness and intervention against corporate agendas.

REFERENCES

Barlow, Maude. 2001. *Blue Gold: The Global Water Crisis and the Commodification of the World's Water Supply.* San Francisco: International Forum on Globalization.

Black, Elizabeth C. 2004. "Litigation as a Tool for Development: The Environment, Human Rights, and the Case of Texaco in Ecuador." *Journal of Public and International Affairs* 15 (1):142–64.

Boyle, Alan, and Michael Anderson, eds. 1998. *Human Rights Approaches to Environmental Protection.* New York: Oxford University Press.

Carey, Henry. 2013. "The Longue Durée of NGOs Promoting and Monitoring Economic, Social and Cultural Rights in a Divided Global Civil Society." In *Sustaining Human Rights in the Twenty-First Century: Strategies from Latin America*, 267–302. Washington, D.C.: Woodrow Wilson Center Press.

Carruthers, David. 2001. "Environmental Politics in Chile: Legacies of Dictatorship and Democracy." *The Third World Quarterly* 22 (3): 343–58.

Corpwatch. 2003. "Bechtel's Water Wars." Report May 1. http://www.corpwatch.org/article.php?id=6670.

———. 2007. "Barrick's Dirty Secrets." Report May 1. http://www.corpwatch.org/article.php?id=14466.

Craze, Matt, and Rodrigo Orihuela. 2010. "Chile May Rise Mining Taxes to Fund Reconstruction (Update 2)." *Bloomberg*, March 19.

Earthjustice. 2006. "Bechtel Surrenders in Bolivia Water Revolt Case." http://earthjustice.org/news/press/2006/bechtel-surrenders-in-bolivia-water-revolt-case.

Fields, Scott. 2006. "The Price of Gold in Chile." *Environmental Health Perspective* 114 (9): 536–39.

Franks, Daniel. 2009. "Avoiding Mine-Community Conflict: From Dialogue to Shared Futures." In Jacques Wiertz and Chris Moran, *Environmine 2009: Proceedings of the First International Seminar on Environmental Issues in the Mining Industry*. Santiago, Chile, September 30–October 2.

Idelovitch, Emanuel, and Klas Ringskog. 1995. "Private Sector Participation in Water Supply and Sanitation in Latin America." World Bank. https://www.wsp.org/sites/wsp.org/files/publications/multi_page10.pdf.

Joseph, Sarah. 2012. "Protracted Lawfare: The Tale of Chevron Texaco in the Amazon." *Journal of Human Rights and the Environment* 3 (1): 70–91.

Keefe, Patrick Radden. 2012. "Reversal of Fortune." *The New Yorker*, January 4, 2012.

Kimerling, Judith. 2006. "Indigenous Peoples and the Oil Frontier in Amazonia: The Case of Ecuador, Chevron Texaco and *Aguinda v. Ecuador*." *International Law and Politics* 38: 413–664.

———. 2013. "Oil, Contact, and Conservation in the Amazon: Indigenous Huaorani, Chevron and Yasuni." *Colorado Journal of International Environmental Law and Policy* 24 (1): 44–115.

Kirsch, Stuart. 2014. *Mining Capitalism: The Relationship between Corporations and Their Critics.* Oakland, CA: University of California Press.

Klein, Naomi. 2007. *The Shock Doctrine: The Rise of Disaster Capitalism.* New York: Picador.

Liverman, Diana, and Silvina Vilas. 2006. "Neoliberalism and the Environment in Latin America." *Annual Review of Environment and Resources* 31: 327–63.

Negri, Antonio. 1999. "The Specter's Smile." In *Ghostly Demarcations: A Symposium on Jacques Derrida's Specters of Marx*, edited by Michael Sprinkler, 5–16. New York: Verso.

Protest Barrick and "Report No 141/09. http://www.oas.org/en/iachr/defenders /default.asp.

Sawyer, Suzana. 2004. *Crude Chronicles: Indigenous Politics, Multinational Oil and Neo-Liberalism in Ecuador: American Encounters/Global Interactions.* Durham, NC: Duke University Press.

Segarra, Monique. 2013. "Challenging Neoliberalism and Development: Human Rights and the Environment in Latin America." In *Sustaining Human Rights in the Twenty-First Century: Strategies from Latin America*, 303–40. Washington, D.C.: Woodrow Wilson Center Press.

Shiva, Vandana. 2002. *Water Wars: Privatization, Pollution and Profit.* Cambridge, MA: South End Press.

The Democracy Center. Bolivia Investigations: The Water Revolt. http://democracyctr.org/bolivia/investigations/bolivia-investigations-the -water-revolt.

Yashar, Deborah J. 2005. *Contesting Citizenship in Latin America: The Rise of Indigenous Movements and the Post-liberal Challenge.* New York: Cambridge University Press.

CHAPTER 6

Internal Colonial Aftermath: "Silenced Memory" and "The Eye That Cries"—The On-Going Narrative of *Dos Demonios*

In the last two decades, through the very persistent efforts of nongovernmental organizations for human rights, the expectation of economic, social, and cultural rights has become hard law, constitutionally recognized, in a number of Latin American nations. However, economic, social, and cultural rights have only been rubber-stamped and not actively recognized as human rights in Guatemala and Peru. There has been consistent resistance to the reconstruction of these nations' recent political histories of massacres, torture, genocide, and racial discrimination. The 1999 Guatemalan Truth Commission for Historical Clarification's report was entitled "Memory of Silence," a poignant title, expressing the Indigenous lack of voice. Peru's Truth and Reconciliation Commission's monument included a representation of the Indigenous Goddess, *Pachamama*, entitled "The Eye That Cries." Reactions to both Truth Commissions and the Peruvian monument have hardened the old colonial line, raising once again the political architecture and narratives of "*Dos Demonios*" in Guatemala and Peru.

THE POLITICS OF MEMORY

For Latin American countries faced with their public's demand to reevaluate the recent violent histories of their Dirty Wars, truth commissions have been the most widespread official response to this pressure by the public and nongovernmental organizations (Hite 2013, 344). The hope has been to build a public consensus, heal injustices by acknowledgment and accountability, and thus create a political present that is more governable. In order to restore citizens' trust, a state must demonstrate that it is a respecter of justice.

Where robust justice has taken root in several Latin American nations in the past twenty years, there is a parallel of reduced authoritarian platforms in their governments. "The process of restoring democracy in Latin America has advanced parallel to the fight against Human Rights' abuses" (Thompson 2013, 86).

Argentina and Chile represent this fortunate development where accountability for the crimes of torture, genocide and blatant violations of human rights have been and are being addressed in their national courts. The extreme suppression of human rights under the right-winged military juntas of these two nations was so offensive to families of victims and nongovernmental organizations that the impunity laws protecting the authoritarian forces for their inhumane actions have been struck down. The demand for justice and accountability appears to succeed where democracy and democratic principles are encouraged.

In contrast, where powerful militaries and authoritarian elite structures of privilege still prevail, the demands to maintain impunity have been accompanied by threats of violence or the assassination of national actors fighting for human rights. Any formal peace agreements that have been painstakingly worked out have been consistently dismantled by military and elite groups who have resorted to violence rather than ceding any authoritarian power.

This contradiction has been particularly true of Guatemala and Peru. The political realities of these two nations reflect this on-going struggle against relentless, authoritarian control. Consequently, the reconstruction of horrific events that took place under their military and civilian governments during the second half of the twentieth century is a process fraught with debate. Whose truth should be emphasized and which truths should be downplayed provoke deep emotions. The collective and historical recounting of memory has reverted to a divisive politics of memory.

When democracies are practicing oligarchies under such authoritarian or elite control, justice and accountability for human rights violations are frequently sham exercises destined to fail. In such cases, the citizens' distrust of the oligarchy deepens the divide between the minority ruling elite class and the poorer majority, retreading the old colonial path that led to rightist suppression of human rights and leftist insurgencies. This condition of duality was first labeled "*Dos Demonios*" in Argentina, but broadly describes the stalemate initially created by colonialism's lasting effects that point to the great difficulty of shedding a colonial past with its racist implications. In both Guatemala and Peru, Indigenous people made up the bulk of victims of the dirty wars involving right-winged military or security forces and left-winged guerrillas. In Guatemala, Indigenous populations make up greater than 60 percent of the population; in Peru, the Indigenous Pueblos constitute more than 45 percent of Peruvians.

The racist implications cannot be ignored. Both Guatemala and Peru were historically home to great Indigenous nations, the Mayan and the Incan civilizations. Today, there are estimated to be more than 40 million Latin Americans who define themselves as Indigenous peoples (Reid, 2009, 223). Approximately 90 percent of them live in just five Latin American countries: Guatemala, Bolivia, Peru, Ecuador, and Mexico. These Indigenous groups make up some of the most disadvantaged people in their respective regions, with less education, poorer health, and worse living conditions than those who are not Indigenous (Psacharopoulos and Patrinos, 1994). In both Peru and Guatemala, there still remain influential elements of a caste society with a racist white elite that has strong ties to the military (Reid 2009, 217).

THE RISE OF THE POLITICS OF ETHNIC IDENTITY

In the past several decades, a growing politics of ethnic identity has proliferated in Latin America for the first time in centuries. Race and racial discrimination have become explicit and urgent issues to be tackled (Reid 2009). For South American Indigenous groups, the effects of globalization have mirrored the upheaval of the Conquista. The traumatic effects of globalization have especially affected Bolivia and Ecuador. Neoliberal interests in oil (the Chevron-Texaco debacle), mines (Pascua Lama) and water privatization (the Bolivian water wars) have threatened Indigenous lands and the sustainability of Indigenous cultures. In Bolivia and Ecuador, corporate neoliberal interests provoked massive protests and accelerated significant political organization of Indigenous groups: CONAIE (Confederación de Nacionalidades Indígenas de Ecuador), CONFENIAE (Confederación de Nacionalidades Indígenas de la Amazonía Ecuatoriana) and COICA (Coordinadora de las Organizaciones Indígenas de la Cuenca Amazónica). These Indigenous confederations have undergone steep learning curves in few decades to become effective political actors. They have recognized that the economic clout of the world's largest multinational corporations eclipses the sovereignty and resources of their nation-states. Consequently, these Indigenous confederations and their NGO actors are now exerting pressure on the financial institutions that invest, guarantee loans and provide risk insurance to multinational corporations.

In Peru and Guatemala, the International Maya League, COPMAGUA (Coordinación de Organizaciones del Pueblo Maya de Guatemala), CONIC (Coordinación de Organizaciones Nacionales Indígenas y Campesinos), and COPPIP (Coordinadora Permanente de Los Pueblos Indígenas de Perú) have not had the same impact. They have worked to educate their populations; however, these less political Indigenous groups are confronted with state environments that are hostile and frequently have overridden Indigenous demands by threats or violence.

The colonial divide of elites, military, and white racists versus Indigenous *campesinos* is an old rigid mindset that rejects any economic, social, or cultural concessions to Indigenous considerations. Thus, the failure of the Peruvian and Guatemalan governments to allow more of their people to share in the benefits of growth points to the continuation of extreme inequalities, a centuries-long neglected problem. The political instability in both of these countries in the second half of the twentieth century was a result of the extreme inequalities, a condition that provokes outbreaks of "*Dos Demonios.*"

GUATEMALA: 1950–2014 (CIVIL WAR 1960–1996)

In light of the CIA declassified material amalgamated by Nick Cullather (2006) and the analyses by Piero Gleijeses (2006), much more is known today about what happened in Guatemala before, during, and after the US-sponsored military coup of 1954.

President Jacobo Arbenz Guzmán was the second of two presidents who governed Guatemala during the country's "democratic spring," which lasted from 1944 to 1954 (Kinzer 2006, 129). In 1952, President Arbenz's Agrarian Reform Law was the crowning achievement of Guatemala's democratic revolution. The land reform underscored his attempt to convert Guatemala from a dependent nation with a semicolonial economy into an economically independent nation. Since the Conquista, Guatemala had endured an unbalanced system of land ownership that was at the root of the problem of poverty in Guatemala. The consideration of land reform was in the air; Mexico had just initiated the breakdown of large haciendas in 1948. Arbenz's new Guatemalan government planned to redistribute all uncultivated lands on estates larger than 672 acres, but would compensate owners with the land's tax value (Kinzer 2006, 133). Though the majority of Guatemalans strongly supported Arbenz's agenda, his reforms challenged the power and the autonomy of the giant US-backed company in Guatemala, United Fruit (also strategically recognized as "La Fruit" or "American Fruit" by Latin Americans).

United Fruit perceived the Agrarian Reform Law as a direct challenge because the company controlled more than one-fifth of Guatemala's arable land, but cultivated less than 15 percent of it. When Arbenz subjected the company to these new regulations and taxation, the company howled in protest, charging that the Guatemalan government was communistic (Kinzer 2006, 129). No real evidence ever backed the American fear of Soviet involvement in Guatemala nor was there any substantial evidence that Arbenz was leading Guatemala toward Communism. Communists never held more than four out of sixty-one seats in the National Assembly and no communist ever sat in Arbenz's cabinet. Arbenz's friend, Fortuny, was communist, however, he was not in a government post. He only shared Arbenz's belief that the old colonial structure of Guatemala needed to be dismantled.

The accusation of "communistic" also revealed the complete ignorance by wealthy US Republicans of the realities and depravity of conditions that the majority of Guatemalans suffered. Indigenous peoples revere the land. Owning plots of ground to cultivate food was their only escape from *encomienda*-like circumstances of working on the large corporately run haciendas. As Louis Halle, a State Department official asserted, Guatemala was in desperate need of social reform, and its government was "nationalist and anti-Yanqui" but not pro-communist (Kinzer 2006, 140–41). He perceived the entire crisis was brought about by United Fruit, and the moniker of "communism" was convenient to protect United Fruit's interests.

John Foster Dulles, the corporate lawyer for United Fruit as well as the US Secretary of State, was driven by two interests—the rights of multinational corporations and an ideological hatred of communism. These new regulations in Guatemala cut into the profitability of United Fruit and reduced its uncultivated land. Regulation was a new experience for United Fruit as it had prospered for the first half of the twentieth century in Guatemala in the privileged capacity of paying no taxes nor coping with any legal regulations.

The requirements of Arbenz's reforms provoked the first instance of an American corporation waging a propaganda campaign to undermine a president of a foreign country so to protect its profits. (United Fruit's actions later became the precedent for another corporation, IT&T, to script the eighteen points of the Chilean coup in 1972.) The coup in Guatemala was conceived in top secrecy; only a few men knew about the coup to prevent any objections.

It is significant that eight influential US statesmen and bankers held blocks of stock and/or were board members of United Fruit: 1) Alan Dulles—CIA director, 2) John Moors Cabot—assistant secretary of state for inter-American affairs, 3) Thomas Dudley Cabot—director of international security affairs in the State Department, 4) General Robert Cutler—head of the National Security Council and former chairman of the United Fruit Board, 5) John J. McCloy—the president of the International Bank for Reconstruction and Development, 6) Walter Bedell Smith—undersecretary of state, 7) Robert Hill—American ambassador to Costa

Rica, and 8) John Foster Dulles, the corporate lawyer for United Fruit and the US Secretary of State. Few private companies have ever been as closely interwoven with the US government as United Fruit was during the mid-1950s (Kinzer 2006, 129–30).

Largely ignorant of the colonial realities of Guatemalan life, US politicians and officials opposed Arbenz, cataloging as "communism" every manifestation of nationalism, and all desires for social progress or progressive reforms for Guatemala. Thus, President Eisenhower and John Foster Dulles, Secretary of State, ordered that Arbenz be overthrown. The project was named Operation Success and was funded by $4.5 million US tax dollars.

Piero Gleijeses points out that from January 1953 to June 1954, 500,000 people (one-sixth of Guatemala's population) received the land they desperately needed to survive as a result of the Agrarian Reform Law. "For the first time in the history of Guatemala, the Indigenous were offered land rather than being robbed of it" (Gleijeses 2006, xxiv). But since Arbenz's overthrow and the abrupt removal of the new Indigenous occupants from the land they had just received, the elite class, and the military have ruled Guatemala. The thirty-six-year-old civil war, from 1960 to1996, had as its justification the removal of communist guerrillas. The army undertook what the CIA called "its extralegal terror campaign"—a wave of "kidnappings, torture, and summary executions" (CIA 1966c) of thousands of Indigenous peasants in order to eliminate a handful of guerrillas (Gleijeses 2006, xxvi). The culture of fear, as old as the Conquista in Guatemala, once again became a widespread contagion. The anti-Communist paranoia of the United States was supremely indifferent to the fate of the Guatemalan people as it continued to arm the Guatemalan military. The result was tragic for Guatemalans, especially the Indigenous peoples. In addition, any Guatemalan civilian presidents, reinstated after 1986 have not tried nor been capable of challenging the army or the elite landowners to help the Indigenous majority.

After the end of the civil war in 1996, the power of the Guatemalan Army was such that it was able to broker an amnesty that would exclude most serious crimes for charges of genocide against Indigenous communities. There has only been minimal progress in two human rights cases in the national courts: 1) Four former Guatemalan soldiers received a sentence of life imprisonment for the horrific massacre at the community of Dos Erres. 2) The arrest of General Héctor Mario López Fuentes in 2011 for events that happened in 1982 and 1983 fell under the charges of genocide (Hayner 2013, 156). In a county where the number of Disappeared has been estimated to be 200,000, these two cases represent a very minimal effort by Guatemala's courts to restore demands for justice. Consequently, there has only been a slow and often halting advancement toward accountability of the widespread atrocities that occurred under Guatemala's military governments and its military controlled civilian governments (1960–1996). The rigid demands for the military's protection against prosecution have formed an on-going political position of entrenchment that has not changed.

In 1994, the Guatemalan military allowed for a truth commission. However, it was to be a truth commission that would be "just like Chile, truth, but no trials" in the words of Mario Enriquez, the Guatemalan defense minister (Hayner 2001, 86). In 1994, Chile had not yet come to the stage of accountability for which it is now known. In addition, the Guatemalan military was insistent that the truth commission could not name those responsible for the violence and killings.

By 1996, Guatemala's Amnesty Law had been hammered out by the political spectrum of the Church, the Guatemala Military—the nongovernmental organizations for human rights, the Indigenous groups and the political elite. The Amnesty Law underscored the primary influential stronghold of the military as the law only reinforced the military's demand for impunity.

However in 1998, the Comisión para el Esclarecimiento Histórico (CEH), the Guatemalan Truth Commission for Historical Clarification, which included anthropologists, historians, social workers and diplomats, reached their own conclusions. Their report was far more than the Guatemalan military had bargained for; it was a report that uncovered the traumatic history of inequality, racism, and cultural prejudice. The CEH members had accumulated more than 8,000 testimonies, both from their interviews and the interviews of human rights and Indigenous groups. Using a truth-telling model of the careful documentation of victims' stories, this effort was recognized as a restorative measure to help heal the personal experiences of those who endured violence. This model was a project of the Guatemalan Catholic Church, known as "The Recovery of Historical Memory." The military's reaction was instantaneous. Two days after the report was released, in April of 1998, the project's director, Bishop Juan Gerardi, was assassinated. The assassination only underscored the levels of violence and atrocities practiced by both the military and the elites.

The full released report of the Guatemalan Truth Commission for Historical Clarification (CEH) established evidence of the military and security forces systematic abuse and massacres of the Indigenous peoples in the *altiplano*, the Guatemalan highlands. For the thirty-six years that Guatemala underwent a "dirty war" run by its military and perpetuated against the Indigenous peoples, the CEH found that greater than 93 percent of the 200,000 killings were civilians who were murdered by the military. The remaining 7 percent were killed by leftist guerrillas (Sieder 2001, 164–65; Commission for Historical Clarification, 2010).

The Guatemalan Truth Commission also found that General Efraín Ríos Montt, with his scorched earth policies of 1981–1983, had provoked a genocide (Hite 2013, 347). Genocide had not been a term included in the 1996 Amnesty Law, a fact that left the Guatemalan military in a precarious legal position. General Ríos Montt was accused of crimes against humanity in connection with the killing of 1,771 Indigenous Mayans during his rule in 1982–1983 and the forced displacement of 29,000 Indigenous Guatemalans as part of his scorched earth policies (*BBC News* 2013). His seventeen months in power are believed to have been one of the most violent periods of the war.

General Efraín Ríos Montt, however, returned unscathed to the political limelight when he ran for president in 2003, despite a constitutional rule that no one who had overthrown a Guatemalan government could stand for the presidency (*BBC News* 2015). The Guatemalan Constitution and the rule of law had thus far never appeared to constrain the Guatemalan military. Ríos Montt again returned to public office in 2007 as a member of the Guatemalan Congress, an office that secured him immunity from prosecution over war crimes allegations. When his immunity expired in 2012, within two weeks of leaving office, he was formally charged with genocide and crimes against humanity. On May 10, 2013, the general was found guilty of both charges, but his conviction was later overturned on technicalities. On January 5, 2015, the retrial of General Ríos Montt was suspended. The on-going power and clout of the Guatemalan military has been able to suspend acknowledgment and accountability for crimes against humanity, making a sham of the courts and the Indigenous Guatemalans' need for justice. This very recent turn of events continues to underscore the unchanging nature of Guatemala's authoritarian power structure.

The Commission for Historical Clarification's report was poignantly labeled *Memory of Silence*, alluding to the racist mentality and colonial violence that for years has silenced the Indigenous peoples of Guatemala. This pattern of exclusion is reflected in restricted economic access, in social relationships and cultural sensitivities still prevalent in the country today. Historically, Guatemala's independence from Spain merely replaced the power of the *Metropoli* with elite colonialists. Thus, internal colonialism overtook the governing role of external imperialism. The newly independent state of Guatemala (1821) maintained the authoritarian and patriarchal structure in its institutions to protect and privilege the European colonial elite. The Commission cited that racist precepts and violent practices directed by the state have perpetually targeted the Indigenous Mayans as well as those who have fought for greater social justice in Guatemala.

From a Guatemalan perspective, Pietro Gleijeses describes his country as living with an on-going culture of fear (1988, xxiii). It remains the "fabric of Guatemalan society" (Gleijeses 2006, xxxv). As the CIA itself once admitted, "the Guatemalan upper class and officer corps were adamantly opposed to even the most elemental progress and reform that would alleviate the miserable poverty of most Guatemalans (CIA 1968a). Pietro Gleijeses points out that Guatemala has defied any reasonable hopes for the Indigenous masses since 1954:

> It still has the most regressive fiscal system and the most unequal land ownership pattern in Latin America. Its army, victorious on the battlefield, has evolved into an all-powerful mafia, stretching its tentacles into drug-trafficking, kidnapping, and smuggling. And its civilian presidents have shown no inclination to challenge the army and the upper class, to fight for social reform, or to clamp down on corruption. (Gleijeses 2006, xxxvi)

Thus the analysis, "Memory of Silence," from the Commission for Historical Clarification (2010), represents a poignant rewriting of Guatemala's history. It explains the Indigenous lack of voice by the "historical dynamic of exclusion," a result of Guatemala's "colonial genealogy of violence" (Commission for Historical Clarification 2010).

PERU: DIRTY WAR 1980–2000

Although Peru has the significant historical distinction of the famous widespread rebellion of *Tupac Amaru* in the 1780s, Indigenous movements have not emerged on a national or even regional scale in contemporary Peru, as in Ecuador and Bolivia (Yashar 2005, 240). Peru's colonial and demographic characteristics are common to conditions in Ecuador and Bolivia. Nevertheless, Peru has not experienced the level of contemporary Indigenous political activity as demonstrated by its neighbors in the Andean corridor.

Peru, like Ecuador and Bolivia, has an estimated Indigenous population of 35–40 percent. A precise census is an almost an impossibility given the remote regions of the Amazon and Andes as well as the cultural unwillingness of some tribes to participate in a census. For historical reasons, many Indigenous people are hesitant to identify themselves publicly as native (Degregori 1995; de-la-

Cadena 2000). Peruvian Indigenous groups are separated into two distinct ecological zones—the Amazon and the Andes. The largest majority of Indigenous Peruvians lives in the Andes while the greatest diversity of Indigenous groups is found in the Amazon.

In the 1920s, ethnic, communal principles were included in the Peruvian Constitution, granting a mechanism for Indigenous communities to acquire legal recognition. This addition to the Peruvian Constitution permitted some Indigenous communities the right to communal landholdings, thus institutionalizing a legal, physical space for Indigenous identity. It did not, however, impose any political or social organization on these Indigenous groups until 1968 when General Juan Velasco Alvarado (1968–1975) initiated a revolutionary land reform with his military coup. The peasant uprisings and the great land inequalities had laid the groundwork for Velasco's military coup and his land reforms.

Velasco's redistribution of land decimated the *latifundia* and the privileged class of landowners of big haciendas. By the later 1970s, there were virtually no more haciendas in Peru (McClintock 1989, 62). This radical land reform was augmented by the 1970 Statute on Peasant Communities in which the Indigenous were redefined as peasants. The intent was to undermine their ethnic identification and restructure the Incan ideas of the *ayllu* and *varayoh* with a new administrative framework. Under these pressures of assimilation and the growing pejorative association with the word "Indian," many Indigenous no longer admitted their Indigenous heritage openly. These efforts of cultural assimilation to reframe Indigenous identities were only partially successful.

A part that was not successful was situated in the Andes where a different type of land association was established—the SAIS—as opposed to the associations near the coast—the CAPs. In the Andes, the majority of peoples affected by the SAIS system were Indigenous, whereas in the CAPs associations by the coast, Indigenous and peasant communities were scarce.

When the haciendas were broken down, the SAIS model largely excluded the highland communities of the Andes because the land was distributed first and foremost to permanent workers on the haciendas (Yashar 2005, 244). This very uneven distribution of land excluding many Indigenous groups only served to create tensions with the Indigenous, who took part in the cooperative SAIS. Thus, the land reform, a potential solution to Indigenous poverty and their geographic isolation, only served to create tension between beneficiaries of the land and those who received considerably less. The reform, then, did not foster the internal organization of Indigenous communities. Rather, it degraded the organizational capacities of Indigenous communities in Peru.

By 1975, Morales Bermúdez dismantled many of these communal policies with a neoliberal regime that favored economic policies such as privatizing cooperatives and privileging the role of the individual over the communities. Succeeding presidents, Alan García, and Alberto Fujimori, further privatized land markets, reversing the inviolability of Indigenous community lands and eliminating all price supports and subsidies to agriculture.

Consequently, in the 1980s, the unrest, the lack of solutions and the strong control by both the elites and the military fostered conditions for *Dos Demonios*. Two Marxist groups sprang up—the *Sendero Luminoso* (the Shining Path) and the smaller MRTA (*Movimiento Revolucionario de Tupac Amaru*). Commonly and incorrectly portrayed as an Indigenous movement, in reality the *Sendero Luminoso* did not promote the Indigenous ethnic claim, and many of the Indigenous communities were victims of the *Sendero Luminoso*'s violence. The *Sendero Luminoso*, with its Maoist rhetoric and structure, promoted violence against both the Peruvian government for what was perceived as a failure of governance for the poor *campesino* and against Indigenous communities for their resistance. The Marxist structures of both groups intentionally set out to undermine Indigenous communal systems as they did not tolerate alternative forms of organization.

The resulting dirty war pitted the Peruvian military primarily against the *Sendero Luminoso*, posing insurmountable obstacles for any other Indigenous political organization as it would be seen in the light of the *Sendero Luminoso*. By July 1991, the state of emergency that arose from the war included eighty-five provinces in sixteen of Peru's twenty-four departments which included more than half the national population and 40 percent of the territory (Roberts and Peceny 1997, 198). In the zones of conflict, the military became the governing authority, and elected officials were replaced by military control (Mauceri 1997, 34). With civil liberties nonexistent and serious human rights abuses abounding, violence was mostly perpetrated by the Peruvian Military and the *Sendero Luminoso* with participation from death squads, insurgencies, drug traffickers and *rondas campesinas* or civilian paramilitary patrols (Roberts and Peceny 1997, 192). In the intensity of the war, civilian government was replaced by the military, and constitutional guarantees and the rule of law broke down (Roberts and Peceny 1997, 195). When Fujimori's backers responded with a coup against the current government in 1992, even the civilian courts were shut down. The military's response was increased power and impunity.

In 1992, because of the capture of the leader of *Sendero Luminoso*, Abimael Gúzman, as well as several leaders from the MRTA, the leftist guerrilla movement lost most of its intensity (Degregori 1997). The military was soon able to bring about the end of the very brutal civil war.

After Fujimori's right-winged coup in 1992, a new constitution was signed into law on December 31, 1993, Peru's fifth constitution in the twentieth century. This Constitution replaced the 1979 Constitution, guaranteeing greater powers to the President and reducing the bicameral Congress of 240 members to a unicameral Congress of 120 members. This same Constitution opened the doors for dispossession of Indigenous lands by concessions of oil, gas, mining, tourism and logging, especially in the Amazon. The 1993 Constitution repealed the "inalienable, indefeasible and inviolable" nature of the Indigenous lands as put forth in the 1979 Peruvian Constitution. These lands of the native peoples became "negotiable in accordance with the market economy." The 1993 Constitution and the 1995 Ley de Tierras (Law 26505) created deep fears amongst Indigenous groups in Peru of losing their patrimony, their community-held lands.

The upshot of the Peruvian failed land reform and two decades of civil war violence was that any political associational space for Indigenous communities and any trans-community networking among Indigenous groups in Peru were destroyed (Yashar 2005, 246–47). The conditions under which the Indigenous political groups of Ecuador and Bolivia became widespread thus contrasted greatly with the Indigenous plight in Peru.

The task of the Peruvian Truth and Reconciliation Commission (Commission 2003) was truly complex and clearly approached the Argentinian argument of "*Dos Demonios*." This architecture reiterated the conflict of both right-winged and left-winged extremists which forced both military action and counter-violence. Few Indigenous groups joined the Shining Path (*Sendero Luminoso*) and participated in the slayings. Under attack, Indigenous Peruvian groups created self-defense communities, sometimes against the military but mostly against the onslaught of the Shining Path. Infrequently, Indigenous groups collaborated with the State against the Shining Path. Thus the task of the Peruvian Truth and Reconciliation Commission (the CVR) was a difficult one, distinguishing among a range of different situations. According to the CVR, both national and local politicians were guilty of abuses of violence and repression during the armed conflict from 1980 to 1993. In response to their findings, under a pro-Fujimori Congress (1995), two amnesty laws were passed in Peru that protected all state actors from human rights violations.

From 1993 to 2000, the Truth Commission continued to investigate President Fujimori's growing abuse of power after the defeat of the guerrilla movement. By 2000, Fujimori was forced out of office. A watershed moment came in 2001 with the Inter-American Court of Human Rights found the Peruvian state responsible for the 1991 massacre in the Barrios Altos case. In this massacre, fifteen Peruvian citizens, including an eight-year-old child, were murdered by a state-sponsored death squad. The Inter-American Court also declared that the amnesty laws passed by a pro-Fujimori Congress violated the American Convention on Human Rights and were, therefore, void.

The Peruvian Truth and Reconciliation Commission (CVR) submitted a final nine-volume report in 2003, implicating the spectrum of perpetrators that included local and national officials, political parties, vigilante groups, state security forces and the Shining Path guerrillas. Attempting to foster reconciliation by exacting documentation on two decades of conflict, the CVR scrutinized the communities that had been most affected by the violence. There were nationally televised public hearings and strong recommendations for reforms to prevent further societal breakdowns. Many anthropologists and nongovernmental organizations were instrumental in documenting the testimonies of the Indigenous. Mass graves were dug up to verify claims.

Nevertheless, the momentum built up by the Peru's Truth and Reconciliation Commission and the Inter-American Court of Human Rights was tempered by the persistent refusals by both government and military officials to provide access to necessary information in order to advance criminal investigations. Under President Alan Garcia (2006–2011), there was a hostile political reaction to human rights prosecutions of state actors. Most of the cases committed by the *Sendero Luminoso* had already been prosecuted; the cases of state-sponsored abuses were dragged out, and most were acquitted. Of the 2,880 complaints of human rights violations in Peru, less than one percent of the cases have been sentenced, and the majority have been acquittals (14In).

As in Guatemala, the response to the Truth Commission's report resulted in escalating criticism. Targeting Peru's urban middle class, the Commission described the marginalization of rural areas and, in particular, the racism against the Indigenous communities. By implicating the failure of political leaders and political parties, the report emphasized the human rights abuses by both the guerrillas and the Peruvian military. Commentators and critics from both sides ridiculed the Commission, stating that the number of dead (69,000) was excessive. The Truth Commission had only 20,000 complete documented cases of individuals (Ball et al. 2003). Leftists objected to the claim that governmental

security forces were only reacting to Shining Path's violence; they claimed that
the Peruvian government had failed the people. Rightists condemned the Truth
Commission for stirring up more discord and defended the military. They argued
that the guerrillas were implicated in greater than 50 percent of the human rights
crimes. It is to be noted, however, that the number of human rights crimes
committed by state-sponsored actors has been suppressed by the Peruvian Justice
system. Despite the heated responses to the Truth Commission, its report has
provoked intense dialog, activated think tanks, and advocacy groups.

"THE EYE THAT CRIES" MONUMENT

"The Eye That Cries," is located in a park—el Campo de Marte (The Field of
Mars, the Roman god of war), in a district of Lima named Jesus María. It was
created by Lika Mutal, a Dutch-born sculptor who has lived in Peru for more than
forty years. She cites that her inspiration for the memorial was the 2003 exhibit,
"Yuyanapaq: To Remember," a devastating and haunting display of 200
documentary photographs, organized by the Peruvian Truth Commission (Hite
2007, 121). The photographs portray a running account of the *Sendero
Luminoso*'s conflict throughout the decade of the 1980s ending with the
senderistas' offensive against Lima in 1989. The images of conflict, destruction,
death, and mourning reflect the enormity of the trauma.

Lika deliberately sculpted the ancestral Goddess, *Pachamama*, from an
ancient pre-Inca stone that she found, using a second rock in the sculpture as an
eye from which a trickle of water runs continuously. Her intent was to create a
sense of eternal victimization. Around "The Eye" is a path containing 42,000
rocks, polished smooth by sea water of which 27,000 are inscribed with victims'
names, ages and the years of death or disappearances, all in alphabetical order
(Hite 2007, 122). The labyrinthine walk created by the stones is meant to be a
path of contemplation, forgiveness, cleansing and reconciliation (Mutal 2008,
41).

Nevertheless, the very existence of this monument, like the history of Peru, is
fraught with a reactionary politics of anger and hatred, an on-going demonstration
of the intractable nature of "*Dos Demonios*," the two sides of a political divide
bent on either the submission or the destruction of the other.

In 2006, the Inter-American Court of Human Rights rendered a decision
against the government of Peru for its military action (1999) against the Miguel
Castro Castro Penitentiary that housed female *senderistas*. The Peruvian military
and security forces bombed and dynamited their cells, killing forty-one inmates,
as well as torturing and beating pregnant prisoners. The Intra-American Court of

Human Rights determined that the Peruvian government should pay the families of the dead inmates as well as add their names to the list of victims commemorated by "The Eye That Cries." Many Peruvians outraged that terrorists of the *Sendero Luminoso* were to be considered "victims," demanded that Peru resign from the Court.

Although the militants from the *Sendero Luminoso* were brutal in their tactics against a vast range of citizens, the Peruvian Truth Commission found that both the *senderistas* as well as the Peruvian military conducted numerous massacres. It was not, however, until the Inter-American Court ruling, that the notion of "victim" became highly politicized. It was suddenly apparent that the notion of "victim" included combatants, sympathizers, resisters, prisoners awaiting sentencing and inmates already charged as terrorists, thus including those who died on both sides of the civil war.

In reaction to the court's ruling, there were demands to remove the names of specific victims as well as to halt all plans for the memorial park. Some of the press referred to "The Eye" as "The Monument to Terrorism" (Vargas Llosa 2007). Alternatively, there were marches by human rights activists, delegations from the Andes and relatives of victims that adamantly defended the memorial calling for reconciliation. Thus, how to remember those that were brutalized has become a traumatic process as the brutalized were also political beings. There apparently does not exist a post-dirty war reconciliation, as the empathy for the other requires becoming aware of the distinction between one side's perception and the experience of the other. The divisive conversation about who is the victim and who is the perpetrator still rages on.

On October 14, 2007, Alberto Fujimori, who had taken exile first in Japan and then in Chile, was arrested. The Chilean Supreme Court had ruled that Fujimori be extradited to Peru to face criminal human rights and corruption charges. Fujimori's party had represented the elite business community in Peru. On October 15, the day following Fujimori's arrest, approximately twelve men and women attacked "The Eye That Cries," damaging the central stone of *Pachamama* and covering the stone in bright orange paint. The group also beat and tied up a policeman whose duty it was to guard the memorial. While no one claimed responsibility for this violence, Peruvians were aware that bright orange was the color of Fujimori's political party. Moreover, some of Fujimori's supporters, including former presidential candidate, Martha Chávez, applauded the attack, calling the memorial "garbage" on CPN Radio, September 25, 2007. This deliberate denigration of the Indigenous Goddess provoked an angry outcry on the part of human rights groups and Indigenous families who had suffered at the hands both of the military and the Shining Path.

The Peruvian memorial, then, like Peru's divided history, reveals that who has been the victim and who has been the perpetrator is a divisive and violent argument that has been on-going since the colonization of Peru. The architecture of "*Dos Demonios*" appears not to have dissipated in almost 500 years. Consequently, violence has erupted periodically in Peruvian history. In Katherine Hite's interview with Lika Mutal, the sculptor described the destroyed monument as "impossible to restore—[it] represents the wound which in Peru throughout its history was never healed" (Hite 2007, 134).

CONCLUSION

Disguising their intractable hardline stances against Indigenous demands, Guatemala (1988) and Peru (1978) signed and ratified the International Covenant on Economic, Social and Cultural Rights (ICESCR), a United Nations' document created in 1966 and implemented in 1976. This Covenant is part of the declaration on the Gaining of Independence to Colonial Countries and Peoples.

Additionally, both countries participated in the International Labor Organization's Convention 169 on Indigenous and Tribal Peoples in Independent Countries (1989) which grew out of the third wave of democratization in Latin America. Indigenous movements in Ecuador, Bolivia, Guatemala, Mexico, Brazil and Colombia demanded constitutional reforms recognizing the multiethnic and multinational composition of their respective countries. In the ILO's Convention 169, assimilationist policies towards Indigenous peoples were denounced, and Indigenous demands for recognition of a culturally heterogeneous citizenry were addressed. Ratification of Convention 169 provided a mechanism for advocating constitutional reforms that would include Indigenous rights.

Though Peru signed Convention 169 in 1994 and Guatemala signed it in 1996, little accommodation has been made for their Indigenous diverse populations. The inclusion of Indigenous protections in a constitution as hard law has been avoided in Guatemala and largely ignored in Peru. Peru's constitutional trajectory on Indigenous rights has worsened. Peru's previous 1979 Constitution protected Indigenous community lands whereas the 1993 Constitution repealed the "inalienable, indefeasible and inviolable" nature of the Indigenous lands in Peru making these lands "negotiable in accordance with the market economy" (1979 Peruvian Constitution, Article 163).

The phenomenon of *Dos Demonios* implies an intransigent and unrepentant rightist suppression of human rights which births a violent leftist insurgency. This binary divide repeats the violence of the Conquista until one side is completely suppressed, creating the conditions for a violence that is destined to repeat itself throughout history.

The leftist insurgency in Peru, the *Sendero Luminoso*, was far stronger than the Guatemalan leftist insurgency. The blatant abuse of human rights in Guatemala was primarily conducted by the State, with 93 percent of the 200,000 killings listed as civilians killed by the military (Commission for Historical Clarification 2010). In contrast, in Peru, both State security forces and the Shining Path guerrillas carried out massive abuses, and as in Guatemala, most of the terror and atrocities took place in the highlands against the Indigenous peoples. In both cases, then, the Indigenous peoples made up the bulk of victims and Disappeared of the dirty wars involving right-winged military or security forces and left-winged guerrillas. The dirty wars have thus repeated the colonial suppressions of the native peoples in Guatemala and Peru. The recent experience of these dirty wars and the enormity of the trauma have only served to further entrench both countries in an architecture of *Dos Demonios*. There is a refusal by both States to improve the rights or to cede to the needs of their large Indigenous populations.

An important pivotal point is that the land is a primary Indigenous concern. In Peru, the failed land reforms of the SAIS cooperatives were the result of unequal land divisions, breeding resentment among Indigenous groups and, on the other hand, angry *latifundistas*. In Guatemala, US corporate anger and right-winged obsessive fears of communism brought about the failure of land reform by provoking a military coup. Both countries' attempted land reforms failed the Indigenous peoples. At the heart of the rise of the politics of ethnic Indigenous identity in Ecuador and Bolivia is the concern for the control and sustainability of their Indigenous lands. Without such recognition and the accepted space for Indigenous identity and their political action, both Guatemala and Peru continue to harbor the conditions that can provoke the violent confrontations of *Dos Demonios*.

REFERENCES

n.d. Lima, Peru: Instituto de Defensa Legal. Accessed December 27, 2014. http://www.idl.org.pe.

Ball, Patrick, Jana Asher, David Sulmont, and Daniel Manrique. 2003. "How Many Peruvians Have Died? An Estimate of the Total Number of Victims Killed or Disappeared in the Armed Internal Conflict between

1980 and 2000." August 28. Accessed January 3, 2015. https://hrdag.org/wp-content/uploads/2013/02/aaas_peru_5.pdf.

BBC News. 2013. "Guatemala Ex-ruler Rios Montt on Trial for Genocide." March 19. Accessed January 2, 2015. http://www.bbc.com/news/world-latin-america-21851940.

———. 2013. "Guatemala Judge Suspends Trial of Former Military Ruler." April 18. Accessed January 2015, 2015.

———. 2015. "Rios Montt Guatemala Genocide Retrial Suspended." January 5. Accessed January 10, 2015. http://www.bbc.com/news/world-latin-america-30678693.

CIA. 1966a. October 8. "Guatemala--A Current Appraisal." National Security Federal Council Files, Directorate of Intelligence, CIA, Lyndon Baines Johnson Library, Guatemala Box 54.

———. 1966b. "Guatemala after the Military Shake-up." National Security Federal Council Files, Directorate of Intelligence, CIA, Lyndon Baines Johnson Library, Guatemala Box 54, October 8.

———. 1966c. "Prospects for Stability in Guatemala." National Security Federal Council Files, Lyndon Baines Johnson Library, Box 9.

———. 1968. "The Communist Insurgency Movement in Guatemala." National Security Federal Council Files, Directorate of Intelligence, CIA, Lyndon Baines Johnson Library, Box 54, September 20.

Commission for Historical Clarification. 2010. "Guatemala: Memory of Science: Tz'inil Na "Tab"Al." Truth Commission, Guatemala City. Accessed January 2, 2015. http://shr.aaas.org/guatemala/ceh/report/english/toc.html.

Commission, Truth and Reconciliation. 2003. "Final Report for the Truth and Reconciliation Commission Peru." Accessed December 27, 2014. http://www.cverdad.org.pe/ingles/pagina01.php.

Cullather, Nick. 2006. *Secret History: The CIA's Classified Account of Its Operations in Guatemala, 1952-1954.* Stanford: Stanford University Press.

Degregori, Carlos Iván. 1995. "El estudio del otro: cambios en los análisis sobre etnicidad en el Perú." In *Perú 1964-1994: Economía, Sociedad, y Política*, 303-32. Lima: Instituto de Estudios Peruanos.

———. 1996. *Las rondas campesinas y la derrota de Sendero Luminoso.* Lima: IEP.

————. 1997. "After the Fall of Abimael Guzmán: The Limits of Sendero Luminoso." In *The Peruvian Labyrinth: Politics, Society, Economy*, edited by Maxwell A. Cameron and Philip Mauceri, 179–91. University Park: Pennsylvania State University Press.

de-la-Cadena, Marisol. 2000. *Indigenous Mestizos: The Politics of Race and Culture in Cuzco, Peru, 1919-1991.* Durham, NC: Duke University Press.

Earthjustice. 2006. *Bechtel Surrenders in Bolivia Water Revolt Case.* Earthjustice. Accessed April 24, 2015. http://earthjustice.org/news/press /2006/bechtel-surrenders-in-bolivia-water-revolt-case.

Gleijeses, Piero. 1988. *Politics and Culture in Guatemala.* Ann Arbor: University of Michigan Press.

————. 1997. *Shattered Hope: The Guatemalan Revolution and the United States, 1944-1954.* Princeton, NJ: Princeton University Press.

————. 2006. "Afterward: The Culture of Fear." In *Secret History: The CIA's Classified Account of Its Operations in Guatemala, 1952-1954*, by Nick Cullather, XXIII–XXXVI. Stanford, CA: Stanford University Press.

Hale, Charles R. 2002. "Does Multiculturalism Menace? Governance, Cultural Rights, and the Politics of Identity in Guatemala." *Journal of Latin American Studies* 34 (3): 485–524.

Hayner, Priscilla B. 2001. *Unspeakable Truths: Confronting State Terror and Atrocity.* New York: Routledge.

————. 2013. "Reconsidering the Peace-and-Justice Debate: International Justice in Africa and Latin America." In *Sustaining Human Rights in the Twenty-First Century: Strategies from Latin America*, edited by Katherine Hite and Mark Ungar, 143–62. New York: Woodrow Wilson Center Press.

Hite, Katherine. 2007. "The Eye that Cries: The Politics of Representing Victims in Contemporary Peru." *Contracorriente* 5 (1): 108–34.

————. 2013. "Voice and Visibility in Latin American Memory Politics." In *Sustaining Human Rights in the Twenty-First Century: Strategies from Latin America*, edited by Katherine Hite and Mark Ungar, 341–69. New York: Woodrow Wilson Center Press.

Hite, Katherine, and Mark Ungar. 2013. *Sustaining Human Rights in the Twenty-First Century: Strategies from Latin America.* Washington, D.C.: Woodrow Wilson Center Press.

Kinzer, Stephen. 2006. *Overthrow: America's Century of Regime Change from Hawaii to Iraq.* New York: Henry Holt and Company, LLC.

Mauceri, Philip. 1997. "The Transitions to 'Democracy' and the Failures of Institution Building." In *The Peruvian Labyrinth: Politics, Society, Economy*, edited by Maxwell A. Cameron and Philip Mauceri, 13–36. University Park: Pennsylvania State University Press.

McClintock, Cynthia. 1989. "Peru's Sendero Luminoso Rebellion: Origins and Trajectories." In *Power and Protest: Latin American Social Movements*, by Susan Eckstein, 61–101. Berkeley: University of California Press.

Mutal, Lika. 2008. "En Nombre de la Memoria." *Caretas.* Accessed October 19, 2013. http://www.caretas.com.pe/Main.asp?T=3099.

The New York Times. 2007. "Ruling on Shining Path Rebels Angers Peru." *The New York Times*, January 11. Accessed January 5, 2015. http://www.nytimes.com/2007/01/11/world/americas/11peru.html.

Postero, Nancy, and Leon Zamosc. 2004. "Indigenous Movements and the Indian Question in Latin America." In *The Struggle for Indian Rights in Latin America*, edited by Nancy Postero and Leon Zamosc, 1–31. London: Sussex Academic Press.

Psacharopoulos, George, and Harry Patrinos. 1994. *Indigenous People and Poverty in Latin America.* Washington, D.C.: World Bank.

Reid, Michael. 2009. *Forgotten Continent: The Battle for Latin America's Soul.* London: Yale University Press.

Roberts, Kenneth, and Mark Peceny. 1997. "Human Rights and the United States Policy toward Peru." In *The Peruvian Labyrinth: Politics, Society, Economy*, edited by Maxwell A. Cameron and Philip Mauceri, 192–222. University Park: Pennsylvania State University Press.

Sawyer, Suzana. 2004. *Crude Chronicles: Indigenous Politics, Multinational Oil, and Neoliberalism in Ecuador.* London: Duke University Press.

Schlesinger, Stephen, and Stephen Kinzer. 2005. *Bitter Fruit: The Story of the American Coup in Guatemala.* Cambridge, MA: Harvard University David Rockefeller Center for Latin American Studies.

Sieder, Rachel. 2001. "War, Peace, and Memory Politics in Central America." In *The Politics of Memory: Transitional Justice in Democratizing Societies*, edited by Alexandra Barahona de Brito, Carmen Gonzalez-Enriquez and Paloma Aguilar, 161–86. Oxford: Oxford University Press.

———. 2002. *Multiculturalism in Latin America: Indigenous Rights, Diversity and Democracy.* New York: Palgrave.

"The Recovery of Historical Memory." 2010. *Comisión de Esclarecimiento Histórico.* Guatemala. Accessed May 2, 2015. http://www.derechoshumanos.net/lesahumanidad/informes/guatemala /informeCEH.htm.

Thompson, José. 2013. "Particpation, Democracy and Human Rights." In *Sustaining Human Rights int the Twenty-First Century: Strategies from Latin America*, edited by Katherine Hite and Mark Ungar, 73–100. Washington, D. C.: Woodrow Wilson Press Center.

Vargas-Llosa, Mario. 2007. "El ojo que llora." *El País Internacional* 14 (1). Accessed January 10, 2015. www.elpais.com/articulo/opinion/pjo/llora /elpepuint/20070114elpepiopi_5/Tes.

Yashar, Deborah J. 2005. *Contesting Citizenship in Latin America: The Rise of Indigenous Movements and the Postliberal Challenge.* New York: Cambridge University Press.

CHAPTER 7

Destructive Narratives: The Latin American Indigenous Struggle against Western Narratives and Western Citizenship

Since the 1990s, Latin American Indigenous groups have mobilized to create a vibrant politics of ethnic identity, to oppose globalization and to demand that their settler-states recognize their autonomy and their rights. For Latin American Indigenous groups, the political, economic and environmental effects of globalization have mirrored the upheaval of the Conquista. Neoliberal interests in oil, mines and water privatization have threatened Indigenous lands and the sustainability of their land-based cultures. These threats have provoked massive protests and accelerated significant political organization of Latin American Indigenous confederations. The traumatic effects of globalization—toxic pollution of native lands, the neoliberal redefinition of Indigenous lands as market-available to resource development, and the commodification of the commons have ignited the demand for a different definition of Indigenous citizenship. Analyses based on the Indigenous historical experience with settler-nations have led to new initiatives to define what Indigenous citizenship in settler-nations means. In redefining the notion of citizenship, they are seeking a fundamentally better balance between the state and its Indigenous societies.

A LATIN AMERICAN "WESTERN" DILEMMA: THE DEFINING OF WHO IS INDIGENOUS

Today, there are estimated to be more than 40 million Latin Americans who openly define themselves as Indigenous peoples (Reid, 2009, 223). This figure does not include the numerous Indigenous groups who refuse to participate in census-gathering. Approximately 90 percent of the Latin American Indigenous societies live in just five Latin American nations: Bolivia, Ecuador, Peru, Guatemala, and Mexico.

Historically, census gathering engendered great distrust among Indigenous groups in Latin America as they feared being targeted for increased taxes, a reduction of social benefits or the loss of their land. Today, most census analyses warn that the Indigenous population numbers should be interpreted as a significant undercount. Eva Morales, the first Indigenous president of Bolivia, refers to this fear or resistance to be counted as a "colonized mentality" (Mallén 2013). Being seen as Indigenous has long been a socially reductive label of colonization. Estimates by Indigenous institutes and confederations suggest that the Indigenous populations are much higher than officially recorded. Despite the significant inaccuracies and the colonized perspectives, 48 percent of Bolivians openly declared themselves Indigenous in the 2012 census. Forty-five percent of Peruvians recently claimed Indigenous heritage. Approximately 60 percent of Guatemalans and 25 percent of Ecuadorians consider themselves Indigenous. Mexico, whose Indigenous population rivals the high number of the Peruvian Indigenous peoples, only identifies Indigenous identity by languages spoken. The National Indigenous Institute (INI) in Mexico estimates that 10.7 percent of Mexicans are Indigenous.

In the western capitalist perspective, these Indigenous groups make up some of the most economically disadvantaged people in their respective regions, with less education, poorer health, and worse living conditions than those who are not Indigenous (Psacharopoulous and Patrinos 1994). From the Indigenous perspective, their relationship with settler-nations has remained colonial to its roots. The relationship has always been characterized by a form of domination and dispossession by the settler-state. It is a relationship of power—economic, racial and state power—drawn by a web of Western, hierarchical and social relations that continues to dispossess Indigenous peoples of their lands and their self-determining authority. Consequently, admission of Indigenous identity to western ideas of statistics and census-gathering only identifies them as targets.

THE UNDERLYING PRESUPPOSITIONS OF A
WESTERN VERSUS INDIGENOUS DEFINITION OF CITIZENSHIP

The definition of citizenship has been a western script that constitutes membership in a polity, but insinuates a rigid, dialectical competition between inclusion and exclusion. Originally Greek in articulation, the polity in question is no longer a city-state but a nation-state. In the nation-state there are those who are considered eligible for citizenship, and there are others who are denied the elevated status of citizenship.

The Aristotelian ideals of citizenship that were imported to Latin America following the Conquista were *jus sanguinis and jus solis*. In the former framework of thinking, citizenship was historically restricted to white, property-owning males who were literate. Consequently illiteracy, race, and gender exclusions meant that the Indigenous were not citizens but subjects. *Jus sanguinis* defended a political manifestation of one ethno-national identity, that is, the exclusion of Indigenous peoples. *Jus solis* granted citizenship along territorial lines for those who were born in a given territory. There was no recognition that a political community was one of blood, kinship and descent. *Jus solis* only sanctified the individual (liberalism) and his or her political ties to a nation-state. Thus, *Jus sanguinis* excluded the Indigenous on the basis of ethnicity and lack of western education while *jus solis* refused to recognize the cultural importance of the Indigenous community as a political player with rights and responsibilities.

Iris Marion Young extrapolates on the entitlement of a citizen and the reductive nature of the non-citizen, emphasizing that historically "the exclusion of groups defined as different was explicitly acknowledged" (Young 1989). The liberal idea that citizenship is the same for all translated in practice to the requirement that all citizens be the same (Young 1989). The excluded "other" functioned as the point of comparison and as a permanent scapegoat (Alejandro 1998). Thus the very dual nature of the definition of citizenship created the excluded or the non-citizen. This western definition of citizenship, then, either assimilates and equalizes or alienates and ostracizes (Fleischmann, Van Styvendale, and McCarroll 2011). The dual war-like perspective is part of the heritage of Western civilization from the Greeks and Romans; it explains some of the predominant narratives that Latin American Indigenous groups have had to face—those of forced exclusion because of race or forced assimilation to erase difference.

Thus, Indigenous groups have been locked in protracted struggles to define which of the most basic of human rights should be accorded them by countries that demand their assimilation yet insist upon their exclusion or separation. This contrary predicament reveals a dual *modus operandi* to erase the Indigenous cultures by difference or distance. Historical Indigenous resistance to both forms of erasure have challenged many of the discourses of power that serve to entrench vested racial, economic and juridical interests.

Not only does the terminology of citizenship evoke a Western contentious hierarchy of inclusion versus exclusion, but the terminologies "sovereignty" and "nation" also reflect a Euro-American bias toward hierarchy and centralized power. The very architecture of western competitive thought rejects, trivializes, or ignores the nucleus of the Indigenous world view.

In the Indigenous perspective, citizenship is an understanding of a common social interdependence with the community, the tribal web of kinship rights and responsibilities that link the people, the land and the cosmos together (Fleischmann, Van Styvendale, and McCarroll 2011). This web is an ongoing and dynamic system of mutually affecting relationships (Weaver 2006). Its structure privileges the group as the primary political actor, the central unit of political life.

The Western conception of citizenship is based upon an *a priori* that is aggressively individualistic. In contrast, the Indigenous notion of citizenship respects the communal and honors the idea of the commons which belongs to all. The Indigenous relationships between human beings and the natural world are built on principles of reciprocity, non-exploitation and respectful coexistence. These ideas deeply permeate and sustain Indigenous modes of thought. They could also form the ethical practices and preconditions for a more just and sustainable world order.

The complete incompatibility of the two definitions of citizenship has caused Indigenous groups to point out the limitations of Western nation-state citizenship. Indigenous NGOs have emphasized the rising concern in the global south for universal human rights. Just as globalized citizenship has transcended the nation-state, Indigenous constructs of citizenship and the nation exceed the comparatively insular and restrictive western ideas of both terms (Fleischmann, Van Styvendale, and McCarroll 2011). In this respect, globalization has forged a reaction to create a transformed notion of citizenship that also conforms to international concepts of human rights.

FOUR NARRATIVES OF DOMINATION AND
TWO RECENT NARRATIVES OF RESISTANCE

From an historical Indigenous perspective, the settler-colonial relationship is characterized by multiple forms of domination. There have been many Western narratives that have been used extensively against Latin American Indigenism. In the twentieth and twenty-first centuries, the major narratives include the Narrative of Forced Exclusion, the Narrative of Assimilation, the Narrative of Communism, and the Narrative of Neoliberal Market-Based Dispossession. The recent resurgence of Indigenous political action along with the support of the southern global civil society of NGOs and human rights, have responded to these narratives of domination with the demands of Recognition. Although some of the settler-nations are practicing a more conciliatory set of discourses that emphasize this native recognition, the Narrative of Recognition appears to have been emptied of accommodation on the part of most settler-states. Dialogue becomes a disguise which cloaks the state's lack of accommodation. Born out of the frustration of more deception, the Narrative of Indigenous Anticolonial

Nationalism postulates the impossibility of ever changing the colonial attitude of the settler-states, and as a consequence, Indigenous interests must practice an active and continued critical opposition to Latin American settler-nations. They must be the critical thorn in the flesh as a preventive prescription against the colonial and reductive attitudes toward their peoples.

In the succeeding sections of this article, contextual and historical examples will be presented to illustrate the powerful effect of the different narratives.

THE NARRATIVE OF VIOLENT EXCLUSION OF THE INDIGENOUS PEOPLES: GUATEMALA

Today there is much better documentation on the genocidal practices of forced exclusion of the Guatemalan Indigenous peoples. Despite this knowledge, there is a continuing practice of colonial domination in Guatemala. The colonial attitude of the oligarchy has long been the generator of structured and continued dispossession of the Guatemalan Indigenous *pueblos*.

Where such authoritarian control by the elites and their military is evident, justice and accountability for human rights violations are normally sham exercises, retreading the old colonial path of *Dos Demonios*. The on-going deliberate rightist suppression of human rights provokes leftist insurgencies, a duality that appears destined to repeat the violent confrontations. The lasting effect of these repetitive confrontations points to the great difficulty of shedding a colonial past with its strong racist implications.

Historically home to part of the great Mayan civilization, Indigenous peoples make up greater than 60 percent of the Guatemalan population. However, these Indigenous groups are confronted with settler-state environments that are hostile and have frequently overridden Indigenous demands by violence or threats of violence.

Since the Conquista, Guatemala has endured an unbalanced system of land ownership that has been at the root of the problem of poverty for Indigenous natives. However, with the advent of the breakdown of some of the hacienda systems next door in Mexico (1948), the hope of land ownership for Indigenous pueblos caught fire, rapidly developing into a progressive movement in Guatemala. Guatemala underwent a "democratic spring" from 1944–1954 (Kinzer 2006). In 1952, President Jacobo Arbenz Guzmán's Agrarian Reform Law was the crowning achievement of Guatemala's momentary democratic revolution. The purpose of the land reform was to convert Guatemala from a dependent nation status with a semicolonial economy into an economically independent nation. It would allow the participation of Indigenous peoples in the move away from a colonial feudalism into a modern multinational state.

From January 1953 to June 1954, 500,000 *campesinos*—one-sixth of Guatemala's population—received the land they desperately needed to survive. "For the first time in the history of Guatemala, the Indigenous were offered land rather than being robbed of it (Gleijeses 2006). However, in June 1954, a US corporation, United Fruit, instigated a military coup to stop the land reform, depose President Arbenz and reinstate the colonial control by the Guatemalan elites and the Guatemalan military. This was the first instance of a US corporation waging a propaganda campaign as well as a military coup to undermine a president of a foreign country so to protect its land and its profits. It was the early dawn of neoliberal dispossession.

The coup provided the death knell to any hope of change for the Indigenous plight in Guatemala. The *encomienda*-like conditions of the Indigenous laborer would not be allowed to change. Like the Guatemalan elites and military, the absolute deafness of the wealthy US stockholders of United Fruit to the Indigenous worker's deplorable conditions guaranteed the dispossession.

Since Arbenz's overthrow and the abrupt removal of the new Indigenous occupants from the land they had just received, the Guatemalan elites and military have ruled Guatemala. To discourage any possible repetition of a democratic spring, the Guatemalan military undertook what the CIA called "it extralegal terror campaign"—a wave of "kidnappings, torture and summary executions", which today is recognized as a thirty-six-year war primarily against the Indigenous peoples (Gleijeses 2006). Amnesty International documented a similar pattern of violence: "Tortures and murders are part of a deliberate and long-standing program of the Guatemalan Government" (Amnesty International 1981).

In 1998, the Comisión de Esclarecimiento Histórico (CEH), the Guatemalan Truth Commission for Historical Clarification, submitted the first report on the violent events in Guatemala from 1960 to 1996. Made up of anthropologists, historians, social workers and diplomats, the Truth Commission's report was far more than the Guatemalan military had bargained for; it was a report that portrayed the traumatic history of inequality, racism and cultural prejudice. The CEH members had accumulated over 8,000 testimonies from their interviews on human rights and Indigenous groups. Using a truth-telling model of the careful documentation of victims' stories, the project was known as "The Recovery of Historical Memory." The Guatemalan military's reaction was instantaneous. Two days after the report was released, in April of 1998, the project's director, Bishop

Juan Gerardi, was assassinated. The assassination only underscored the continued levels of violence and atrocities practiced by both the Guatemalan military and elites against their Indigenous peoples. The CEH also found that greater than 93 percent of the 200,000 killings from 1960 to 1996 were civilians who were murdered by the military (Sieder 2001; The Recovery of Historical Memory 2010). The Guatemalan military and elites systematically practiced abuse and massacres of the Indigenous peoples who made up most of the Disappeared.

The Narrative of Forced Exclusion has been practiced to the extreme in Guatemala. In order to protect the economic interests of the privileged elite minority, the military carried out a genocide against the Indigenous Mayans. General Efraín Rios Montt, who conducted both scorched earth policies and genocides against Indigenous groups, recently had his court case indefinitely suspended (*BBC News: Latin America & Caribbean* 2015). The clout and power of the Guatemalan military has been able to cancel accountability for crimes against humanity. Violent exclusion of Guatemala's Indigenous peoples has had no real deterrent.

THE NARRATIVE OF COMMUNISM USED AGAINST INDIGENOUS PEOPLES: GUATEMALA

The anticommunist narrative of the west has been primarily a corporate narrative that fears a government's seizure of its natural resources, and thus, corporate exclusion from making profits off of those resources. That those natural resources belong to the people of another sovereign nation appears to be irrelevant to corporate minds. Nationalization of natural resources, restriction of access to primary resources, higher regulation and the threat of taxation have galvanized multinational corporations and their dollars to buy political muscle to avoid such outcomes. In the US, this political muscle has stretched as far as the implementation of military coups in order to guarantee a US corporation's profits. Communism has been the narrative; big money has been the motive. The obsessive fear of nationalization of a country's resources also has taught corporate minds a strategy to invert their position of vulnerability to a position of strength. Instead of a progressive government restricting corporate access, corporations now restrict sovereign governments by privatization and trade deals, a neoliberal tactic. Corporate manipulation and control of politics appears to be formidable.

From the 1950s to the 1990s, the accusation of communism became a corporate weapon of political warfare. The warring duality was communism versus capitalism. Only one of these warring ideologies of the twentieth century could win, a mindset that also explains many of the wars of the twentieth century and the pre-programmed mentality of most US citizens. Communism became a metaphoric architecture that was broadcast as evil with no critical distinctions established among progressive nationalism, socialism, or true communism.

For the Indigenous peoples of Guatemala, the Narrative of Communism not only paralleled the aftermath of the Narrative of Racial Exclusion but greatly magnified it. The accusation of communism gave the Guatemalan elites and military the license to massacre Indigenous people. The fact that most of the Indigenous Guatemalans were not and did not understand communism appeared to be irrelevant. The Guatemalan Truth Commission backed this data. They found that greater than 93 percent of the 200,000 killings from 1960 to 1996 were native civilians who were murdered by the military. Only the remaining 7 percent were killed by leftist guerrillas with an ideological position (Sieder 2001; The Recovery of Historical Memory 2010).

Louis Halle, a US State Department official scoffed at the label of communism as applied to native Guatemalans. He asserted that Guatemala was in desperate need of social reform, and its government was "nationalist and anti-Yanqui" but not pro-communist (Kinzer 2006). The charge of communism came from the corporate board of the Boston-based United Fruit Company. United Fruit perceived the Agrarian Reform Law as a direct challenge because the company controlled more than one-fifth of Guatemala's arable land, but cultivated less than 15 percent of it. When President Arbenz also subjected the company to new regulations and taxation, the company howled in protest, charging that the Guatemalan government was communist (Kinzer 2006).

However, no real evidence ever backed corporate America's paranoia of Soviet involvement in Guatemala nor was there any substantial evidence that Arbenz was leading Guatemala toward communism. Communists never held more than four out of sixty-one seats in the National Assembly and no communist ever sat in Arbenz's cabinet. After the US-backed military coup and the ouster of Arbenz, the Guatemalan military and elites sought US arms and financial support to continue the Narrative of Communism as a war to suppress the Indigenous peoples. The Narrative of Communism cloaked their Narrative of Racial Exclusion as well as their determination to retain their lands and profits.

It should be noted that the definition and practice of communism is historically European, not Indigenous. Indigenous leaders have long rejected Marx's declaration that Indian societies have no history at all. Michael Hardt and Antonio Negri remind us that non-Western societies at the lower end of the economic scale were considered peoples without a history by western nations.

Moreover, Marx believed that these Indigenous societies should ultimately be subjected to "development for the human good." In Marx's purview, capitalism was a historically inevitable process that would eventually have a beneficial effect on those violently drawn into the capitalist storm. They would serve as poor laborers, the proletariat. But in Guatemala, under a feudal hacienda system, there has only been an abuse and degradation of the Indigenous proletariat. The claim that cultural destruction is an unfortunate prelude to a better life is an exceedingly hollow assertion, especially for those targeted.

It is a fallacy of Western thinking that equates Indigenism with communism. Most Indigenous groups have completely rejected Marx's theories as an outside set of ideas that would only serve to help the colonizer. Marxist organizations have undermined Indigenous communal values and have not tolerated Indigenous forms of organization; such was the case of the Shining Path in Peru. Marxist theories are an example of how western ideas have only served to undermine and further dispossess Indigenous peoples.

THE NARRATIVE OF ASSIMILATION OF THE INDIGENOUS PEOPLES: THE LIBERAL NATION BUILDING PROJECT OF PERU

Prior to 1975, Latin American federal policies concerning the Indigenous peoples were frequently assimilationist, that is, Indigenous identity was discouraged and reframed as an economically lower class citizenry to be incorporated into the mainstream culture. Ethnicity could be seen as a form of racism; it was to be replaced by a vision of class. The objective of settler nations was to create an erasure of cultural and racial difference by conformity and hybridization into western patterns. The savages had to be either civilized and assimilated or encouraged to disappear (Unzueta 2000).

In Peru, General Juan Velasco Alvarado (1968–1975) initiated the 1970 Statute on Peasant Communities in which the Indigenous were redefined as "peasants." The intent was to undermine their ethnic identification and restructure the Indigenous ideas of land and working relationships. Under these pressures of assimilation and the growing pejorative association with the word "Indian," many Indigenous groups no longer admitted their Indigenous heritage openly, especially for reasons of census. Yet because the Indian population was so large, assimilation was not a short-term possibility. The repeated saying "One will no longer be discriminated against when one stops being an Indian" expressed the Indigenous reactions of derision and scorn. Consequently, these efforts of cultural assimilation to reframe Indigenous identities were not met with success, and the

Indigenous continued to suffer an intrinsic ingredient of humiliation in the social treatment as a subaltern class.

From the government's perspective, the liberal republican attempt to assimilate the Indigenous was presumed to be for the good of the nation of Peru because "Indigenism was considered to be the cause of backwardness" (Rivera Cusicanqui 1984). However, the project of assimilation was not successful because concealed behind the universal republican ideals, the culturally defined characteristics that elites held as preconditions for citizenship were not met by Indigenous social behavior. The elites' assumptions about Indigenous barbarous and communal natures justified their exclusion.

As a result, the Narrative of Assimilation was not only met with a strong resistance from the Indigenous peoples but also a quiet rejection from the Peruvian elites. The narrative and the practice did not sync as the practice of exclusion continued. Although the political reforms promised universal inclusion, the cultural clash of race continued to produce profoundly exclusionary results. The cultural *mestizaje* that had become the basis of the Revolutionary national identity in Mexico did not apply to Peru, Ecuador, Guatemala and Bolivia. The racial boundaries of the old caste system between the "whites" and the "Indigenous" remained.

THE NARRATIVE OF NEOLIBERAL MARKET-BASED DISPOSSESSION: MEXICO AND THE ZAPATISTAS IN THE FIRE OF ADVERSITY

It was the Indigenous Zapatistas of Chiapas, Mexico, that rebelled openly against Neoliberalism on January 1, 1994, the day that the North American Free Trade Agreement (NAFTA) went into effect. For the Zapatistas, it was a war against the globalization of the market, against the destruction of nature, the confiscation of resources, the consequent termination of the Indigenous Peoples and their communal lands. NAFTA and trade agreements like it would increase the unequal distribution of wealth and would incur a decline in standards of living for all but the rich elites (Kopkind 2002, 19). The Chiapas revolt stirred up crucial questions and sympathy from human rights activists worldwide.

The forces of globalization soon required the Mexican government to scrap its constitutional protection of communal lands on which the Indian economy and culture depended. This was a bitter refrain that has been echoed in the histories of Peru, Ecuador and Bolivia. At the heart of ethnic Indigenous identity is the deep concern for the control and sustainability of their lands; theirs is a land-based economy. Yet with the money proffered by corporate interests to governments for access to lands and natural resources, the once inviolable nature of Indigenous lands became negotiable in accordance with the market economy and wealthy corporate interests.

The fight for their lands in Chiapas repeated the history of Emil Zapata's struggle for Indigenous lands in the Mexican Revolution. Yet, for the Zapatistas of the 1990s, the effects of globalization had greatly accelerated the corporate resource war. From the *chiapanecos'* perspective, neoliberalism was an increasingly aggressive form of recolonization by the Western financial web and the Washington Consensus. It was a powerful rigging of the game of life against the poor and especially against the Indigenous.

In 1994, the state of Chiapas was still under the iron-fisted control of the business-oriented Partido Revolucionario Institucional (PRI). The PRI controlled Mexico from 1929 to 2000 and was the force that repeatedly subjected Chiapas to military suppression: the bombing of Indigenous communities (1994), displacing 20,000 *campesinos* and turning the Zapatistas' strong hold into an army base (1995), conducting the Acteal Massacre of a church community (1997), expulsing human rights observers from Chiapas (1998), and invading four Indigenous communities with over 1,000 troops and police (1998).

In 1995, Chase Manhattan Bank issued a report demanding that the Mexican Government "eliminate the Zapatistas." (Hansen 2002). Outside corporate interests wished to influence a crushing repression of the Zapatistas in order to have rapid access to their land and resources. The 1994 strong uprising in Chiapas against neoliberalism was repeated in Ecuador (1994) when an agrarian law was passed to appease the World Bank while disenfranchising the Indigenous poor. In response, corporate interests feared a pattern that needed to be suppressed.

By 1998, the Bishop of Chiapas, Samuel Ruíz García, tired of trying to mediate the sham procedures for seeking peace accords, accused the Mexican government of having already chosen the path of war and repression. Bishop Ruíz García, the champion of the Maya, had been the target of numerous death threats and his motorcade had been sprayed with gunfire (1997).

By 1999, three million Mexicans voted for a program of land reform, Indigenous autonomy and the respect of Indigenous cultural rights (the San Andrés Accords). A rising sympathy from the Mexican citizenry for the *chiapanecos* affected the national elections in 2000. The PRI lost the Mexican presidency for the first time in seventy-one years.

The Partido de Acción Nacional (PAN) took over with the new President, Vincente Fox, promising to "resolve the problems in Chiapas in 15 minutes" (Hansen 2002). The Zapatistas requested that three demands be honored before the resumption of peace talks: 1) to withdraw troops from seven of the 250 military encampments in Chiapas, 2) to release Zapatista political prisoners, and 3) to implement the San Andrés Accords. Fox honored the first demand, however, he urged Congress to significantly modify the San Andrés peace accords (known as the *Cocopa* proposal).

In February of 2001, the Zapatistas with their commanders and *Subcomandante* Marcos, undertook a two-week caravan, known as the *Zapatour*, from Chiapas to Mexico City in order to lobby for the *Cocopa* law. The *Zapatour* echoed Gandhi's well-documented march to the sea and Martin Luther King's celebrated march through Selma, Alabama. Along the way, hundreds of thousands of Mexicans hailed the caravan. Many citizens joined the march to Mexico City to support the Indigenous land reform, Indigenous autonomy, and cultural rights.

Despite the outpouring of popular support for the Zapatistas, the Mexican legislature heavily modified the *Cocopa* law. A few months later, President Fox signed the Plan Puebla Panama agreement which outlined a strong neoliberal vision of economic development for Southern Mexico *ergo* Chiapas. For the Zapatistas, the betrayal repeated the PRI's emphasis on business and corporate development. President Vincente Fox was championing neoliberal development and corporate moneyed interests.

Thus, the fate of the Indigenous *chiapanecos* was cast as a loser, a declining influence. Though the Zapatistas gained tremendous moral authority from their rebellion, they withdrew from political influence in elections and refused participation in political coalitions. Globalization erases Indigenous sustainability more effectively than republican governments. The Neoliberal web of financial interests can buy the necessary influence to facilitate corporate access to resources on Indigenous lands. The economic clout of the world's large multinational corporations and banks eclipses the sovereignty of settler-nations. Settler-nations are merely pawns to the big banks and trade deals in which corporations can sue governments if their profits are threatened. Thus, the Narrative of Neoliberal Market-Based Dispossession is perceived as a death-knell for Indigenous societies—the loss of their land, the loss of a sustainable way of life and a consequent degradation of their societies. For this reason, the Indigenous peoples compare the advent of neoliberalism to the Conquista.

The Morphing of the Indigenous Narrative of Recognition: An Asymmetrical Lie

The demand for Indigenous recognition has emerged as a dominant expression of Indigenous self-determination in the past thirty years. In Latin America,

Indigenous regimes have been created which demand recognition of their land rights, their cultural distinctiveness and their political autonomy. Most of the recognition models push for the delegation of land, political control, capital to be transferred from the state to Indigenous development projects and self-government. Nation-states have had to reassess their relationship with Indigenous groups adapting a more conciliatory set of discourses that emphasize native recognition and accommodation. The past three decades have produced a proliferation of state institutional mechanisms that promote "forgiveness" and "reconciliation." This represents a formal transition from the violent history of openly authoritarian regimes (still present in Guatemala and Peru) to more democratic forms of rule (in Ecuador and Bolivia) such as state apologies, commissions of inquiry, truth and reparations (Coulthard 2014).

However, such apologies come with an unrealistic price. The state wishes to situate the abuses of colonization firmly in the past, as if the aftermath of colonization were no longer an issue. Indigenous peoples who have undergone centuries of colonization cannot suddenly grant the settler-state a clean slate for a ceremony of a few words. On-going mediation efforts with the settler-state continue to fall on deaf ears despite the Narrative of Recognition. For the settler-state and its development initiatives, there appears to be a hope that the Indigenous voice will become weary, and the business of dispossession can then continue as usual. It is as if the relationship of Hegel's master-slave has allowed recognition of the slave, but not of the master's actions (Markell 2003).

Consequently it does not appear that the politics of recognition have transformed the colonial relationship between Indigenous regimes and the settler-states that contain them. State violence may no longer constitute the regulatory norm that governs colonial dispossession; rather, the current *modus operandi* of recognition and accommodation appears in fact to be a deception.

In Peru (1994) and in Guatemala (1996), international pressure to dial down the racial violence against their Indigenous populations led to the ratification of the ILO Convention 169 on Indigenous and Tribal Peoples in Independent Countries. Convention 169 delineates the rights of Indigenous peoples and the responsibilities of the settler-states toward them. It requires the states to recognize ethnic heterogeneity where they had previously advanced homogeneity. These reforms constituted an important symbolic victory for the recognition of Indigenous peoples. However, it appears that both Peru and Guatemala cooperated for public appearances, rubber-stamping recognition, but with little intention of accommodation for their Indigenous populations. In 2007, the monument to the victims of Peru's Dirty War, the sculpture of *Pachamama* (the

Andean Indigenous goddess) was vandalized and destroyed by sympathizers of Fujimori's conservative party as a refusal of accommodation. In Guatemala, the authoritarian rule of the elites and the military has continued to deny Indigenous access to land and sustainability. For the Peruvian and Guatemalan Indigenous peoples, the Narrative of Recognition has only contained empty words. If there is any accommodation, it ends up being determined by and in the interests of the hegemonic partner thus reproducing nonmutual and unfree relations, an asymmetrical lie (Coulthard 2014).

Frantz Fanon, a black physician, and author of *The Wretched of the Earth* and *Black Skins, White Masks*, challenges all colonized peoples to transcend the fantasy that the settler-state apparatus which has always practiced domination and dispossession might somehow be capable of allowing liberation of the colonized (Coulthard 2014). Fanon states that settler–state power requires the production of colonized subjects. This production commits the colonized to the types of practices that are required for their continued domination. Fanon also recognizes the deception of the state apparatus in situations where colonial domination does not exercise state violence. Rather, the state attempts to entice Indigenous peoples to identify with the profoundly asymmetrical and nonreciprocal forms of recognition imposed on them by the settler state (Coulthard 2014). This asymmetrical and nonreciprocal form of recognition is imposed not as a cultural liberator but a cultural straitjacket (Phillips 2007).

If the Indigenous response expresses anger or resentment at the lack of accommodation, it is conveniently considered no longer the state's problem as those who refuse to reconcile are represented in policy literature as unable or unwilling to move on because of resentment (Coulthard 2014). Thus, the relationship of the Indigenous to the state remains colonial despite the procedure of formal recognition precisely because of its asymmetrical and nonreciprocal nature that perpetuates colonial domination. Many Indigenous peoples have clearly understood the fallacy, that is, the empty process practiced by the Narrative of Recognition. For them, recognition by the settler-state is an asymmetrical lie that merely allows the continued domination to become invisible, cloaked by a political process that appears conciliatory but is not.

THE NARRATIVE OF INDIGENOUS ANTICOLONIAL NATIONALISM: SAFEGUARDING THE COMMONS IN BOLIVIA AGAINST THE SETTLER-NATION, CORPORATIONS, AND THE WORLD BANK

The Narrative of "Indigenous Anticolonial Nationalism" (Fleischmann, Van Styvendale, and McCarroll 2011) replicates Fanon's Discourse of Resentment and takes as its principle objective, the deliberate unsettling of the colonial master narrative of Western civilization. Great effort is made to counter the Western Mirror of Reality with an Indigenous Mirror of Reality to critique the corruption and destruction brought about by greed. Since 2008, there has been a larger world-wide audience receptive to this critical perspective as corporate greed, white collar crime, and the tacit cooperation of the big banks brought about a world-wide recession that crippled the poor and the middle classes in many nations. Relationships of sustainability, bedrock concepts in Indigenous cultures, appear to have entered the discourses of many universities, with the apparent notable exception of the practice of money and banking. The concept of maintaining a highly critical assessment of the colonial-corporate master narrative appears to be a necessary and prudent endeavor that is garnering international support.

The attitude and involvement of the Indigenous peoples in Bolivia in response to the corporate takeover of their water rights reflects the Narrative of Indigenous Anticolonial Nationalism. When the World Bank imposed the privatization of Cochabamba's water supply, Cochabamba's municipal water service (Servicio Municipal del Agua Potable y Alcantarillado or SEMAPA) was forced to accept a concession to International Water, a subsidiary of the Bechtel Corporation headquartered in California (Barlow and Clarke 2003). Cochabamba, Bolivia's third largest city, is situated in an arid region which is a center for many Indigenous communities. Within a short period of time, water bills jumped 60–90 percent and in some cases, doubled. These increases forced some of the poorest families in South America to choose between food and water. The initial mass mobilization (La Coordinadora de Defensa del Agua y de la Vida) in protest of Bechtel and the jump in water prices managed to shut down Cochabamba for four days.

In the following several weeks, millions of Indigenous Bolivians marched on the city, stopping all transportation and holding a general strike. The protesters demanded protection of universal water rights, the termination of the water contract with Bechtel, and the participation of the Bolivian population in setting up a public water service. For the Indigenous communities, water was a part of the "commons," a centerpiece of Indigenous belief. Water was life, and a foreign corporation was denying them the right to life. The Indigenous Mirror of Reality was demanded. Protests against the commodification of water and the inability to pay such high prices for water continued for months. These protests gathered steam when Indigenous Bolivians who could not afford the water increases were jailed for attempting to collect rainwater.

The Bolivian government was constrained by the obstacles in the GATS treaty that permit corporate interests to sue governments and that prohibit the interference of any cultural objections to the treaty. Bechtel threatened suit for breach of contract. Consequently, the Bolivian government attempted to shut down the water protests through the use of martial law. The Indigenous Bolivians refused to back down. Violence flared and the situation in Cochabamba became a flagrant water war. As Vandana Shiva points out, denying the poor access to water by privatizing water distribution is, for them, a form of terrorism (Shiva 2002).

Eighteen months after Bechtel was forced to leave Bolivia, the multinational corporation and its coinvestor, Abengoa of Spain, filed a $50 million legal suit against Bolivia. Bechtel sought $25 million in damages and $25 million in lost profits. The case was filed before the International Centre for Settlement of Investment Disputes (ICSID), the World Bank trade court, located in New York. The ICSID process bars the public and the media from being present at its proceedings or even allowing disclosures of who is testifying. The secrecy and the exclusivity of such proceedings favor multinational corporations and their investors.

For four years following the filing of this suit, NGOs and citizen groups on five continents waged a global campaign against Bechtel, demanding that the corporation drop the case. Groups from forty-three nations endorsed a legal petition to the World Bank insisting that the court case be opened to public participation (Bechtel Surrenders in Bolivia Water Revolt Case 2006). Bechtel was strongly criticized on the world stage and the international support for the Bolivian Indigenous groups earned Bechtel a very negative notoriety in the international media. Bechtel subsequently dropped the case for a token payment of approximately thirty cents (Bechtel Surrenders in Bolivia Water Revolt Case 2006).

As a consequence, the power of an informed public stepped into the position vacated by the settler-state, a state that was controlled by corporate trade deals. On this issue, the Indigenous Bolivians inverted the power relationship of Indigenous citizens to the settler-state. The only answer to corporate control of states was to establish the priority of the citizenry's power over the power of the state. Shortly thereafter, Bolivia elected its first Indigenous president to protect the Indigenous Mirror of Reality that its citizens had fought so hard to erect. Reflections of that critical proactive Indigenism continue in Bolivia today.

A SECOND EXAMPLE OF INDIGENOUS ANTICOLONIAL NATIONALISM: SAFEGUARDING THE COMMONS IN ECUADOR

Historically, Ecuador's political history controlling the Indigenous populations has been geographically regulated. There exist two very distinct regional Indigenous communities, one in the highlands of the Andes, and one in the Amazon. The Ecuadorian settler-state has actively sought to incorporate and control Indigenous peoples in the Andes since its inception; however, the state largely neglected the Amazonian Indigenous communities until the second half of the twentieth century. The history of the development of Indigenous confederations reflects the separateness of their geographical condition, and their traditional mistrust of each other.

By the 1990s, the state, lured by neoliberal interests and potential money, had backed away from land reforms and social provisions that had been promised to the Indigenous Andeans. In addition, state-supported oil exploration and toxic dumping of 30 billion gallons of toxic waste in the Amazon had ignited a significant reaction among Indigenous Amazonians (Schemo 1998).

Demanding participation, Indigenous networks mobilized. Powerful groups such as CONFENAIE and ECUARUNARI emerged as the regional Indigenous organizations of the Amazon and the Andes respectively. Compounded by the economic crises of the 1980s and the 1990s, protective land reform was rescinded and oil money fueled a neoliberal state policy of growth in oil exploration. Indigenous demands for land security and an accountability for environmental pollution increased. From this hotbed of Indigenous discontent, the strongest, oldest and most recognized national Indigenous confederation, CONAIE, was born, bringing together the two regional confederations from the Andes and the Amazon that were so distinct. CONAIE represents the first national mobilization of the Indigenous peoples of Ecuador.

In 1990, CONAIE gained national and international notoriety with an uprising that blocked roads, cut off commercial transport and occupied churches for ten days. The uprising catalyzed a process of consciousness raising, capturing the attention of governing circles and mobilizing outside Indigenous groups to participate. The demand to make Indigenous lands secure and to participate in governance was central. The concept of the national mosaic of Ecuador's citizens, the pluri-national state, was raised, challenging the Western idea of a state built on unity.

When the settler state tried to privatize property with the 1994 Agrarian Development Law, CONAIE instigated a second uprising, *Movilización por la Vida*, because the law opened the doors for the disappearance of communal lands.

The nation-wide protests forced the settler-state to include Indigenous leaders to reform the Agrarian Development Law. CONAIE emerged as a significant political actor promoting a more democratic, inclusive and pluri-ethnic politics. As a result of their strong involvement, communal lands could not be sold or privatized without an Indigenous vote of two-thirds of the residents approving the sale (Andolina 1999).

When confronted with new neoliberal political regimes that threatened Indigenous interests, CONAIE helped to bring down two national governments— President Bucaram in 1997 and President Mahuad in 2000. In a country in which civil society has been notoriously weak (Pachano 1996), the recently strong activity of Ecuador's national Indigenous confederation stands out in contrast. The Narrative of the Anti-Citizen stance has aligned the inner resentment of centuries, the pride of Indigenous values and the critical analysis of Western master narratives, giving strength to Indigenous Ecuadorean's political activity.

THE ICONOGRAPHY OF THE INDIGENOUS ANTI-CITIZEN

In the labyrinthine world of on-going colonial and neo-colonial structures, the oft-quoted words of Michel Foucault in *Nietzsche, Genealogy, History* confirm an awareness that many Latin American Indigenous groups have come to acknowledge when dealing with the settler-state.

> Humanity does not gradually progress from combat to combat until it arrives at universal reciprocity, where the rule of law finally replaces warfare. Humanity installs each of its violences in a system of rules and thus proceeds from domination to domination.

If the never-ending reality of Indigenous peoples is to struggle against forms of domination and neocolonialism, Latin American Indigenous groups, particularly in Ecuador and Bolivia, have turned away from the colonial state and found in their own de-colonial praxis the source of their liberation (Coulthard 2014). The exercise of recognition by the settler-nation is not sufficient as it appears to exclude accommodation. Recognition by the settler-state will only continue to cloak forms of domination.

But self-recognition empowers. A resurgent politics of self-recognition based on self-actualization and direct action has engendered a renewal of Indigenous values. On the bedrock of those values, cultivating a persistent critical attitude that perpetually seeks to unsettle colonial-corporate master narratives of a capitalist west could be considered a necessary academic exercise of checks and balances. That the settler-state perceives Indigenous resentment as an unwillingness to get over the past is a short-sighted perspective that avoids the spotlight of critical analysis and accommodation. For the Indigenous Bolivians, the settler-state had to get over it. Because of the strong momentum of self-empowerment, they proceeded to elect an Indigenous president, Eva Morales, for the settler-state. By combining Indigenous interests into a strong national movement, Indigenous Ecuadorians have entered into the fray of Ecuadorian politics, blocking neoliberal interests and ousting several presidents who would not accommodate Indigenous interests. The neoliberal order of power, corporations-governments-citizens, is being reversed: citizens who control government to block neoliberal corporations. An Indigenous over-riding influence over the politics of the settler-state is the only successful tactic to limit outside corporate interests and to reject the web of neo-colonial financial strings by banks and their treaties. Naomi Klein documents this new politics aided and abetted by Indigenous involvement:

> "In 2005, Latin America made up 80 percent of the International Monetary Fund's total lending portfolio; by 2007, the continent represented just one percent—a sea change in only two years" ... In April 2007, Ecuador's president, Ralph Correa, revealed that he had suspended all loans from the IMF and declared the institution's representative in Ecuador *persona non grata*—an extraordinary step. Two years earlier, Correa explained, the World Bank had used a $100 million dollar loan to defeat economic legislation that would have redistributed oil revenues to the country's [Indigenous] poor. "Ecuador is a sovereign country, and we will not stand for extortion from this international bureaucracy," he said. At the same time, Evo Morales announced that Bolivia would quit the World Bank's arbitration court, the body that allows multinational corporations to sue national governments for measures that cost them profits." (Klein 2007)

Today's Latin American Indigenous Anti-Citizen functions to protect his or her cultural core both against the settler-state and against neoliberal corporations and banks. He or she is not afraid to fight for justice by exposing violations of human rights and the greed of Western institutions that dispossesses Indigenous peoples of their lands, their resources and their rights. What Fanon defined as *ressentiment*, is an adamant refusal to forget the past, a permanent posture of self-defense, and focused critical analysis on the part of today's Latin American Indigenous Anti-Citizen.

TOWARD A NEW DEFINITION OF CITIZENSHIP: AN OVERVIEW

Latin American nations have not had an historical tradition of accepting their Indigenous populations as citizens. "Rhetoric aside, the history of ethnic relations in Latin America has been one of violence, subordination, marginalization and assimilation" (Yashar 2005).

For centuries the notion of citizenship was defined along Aristotelian lines; Latin American citizenship was frequently restricted by property, literacy, and gender. The Narrative of Exclusion was essentially defended by medieval philosophical doctrine. Subsequently, the liberal nation-building projects of the twentieth century incorporated measures designed to turn their Indigenous populations into national peasants. Categorizing the Indigenous as "backwards," the assimilation policies of the states encouraged miscegenation to "whiten" the Indigenous populations while discouraging the public display of Indigenous dress and identity.

In the second half of the twentieth century, the violence against Indigenous identity was exponentially accelerated by the Narrative of "Communism" and the Neoliberal resource war. The Narrative of Communism was a convenient tactic of US neoliberal corporations, co-opted by elites in settler-states against Indigenous identity when in fact, most Latin American Indigenous groups were not "communists." However, the arrival of neoliberal regimes, the privatization of the commons, the destruction of Indigenous lands by oil and mining corporations and the web of neoliberal financial controls repeated the intense dispossession of the Conquista. Neoliberalism spelled the death of Indigenous sustainability by the loss of their lands, by toxic pollution, and by disease.

Out of this fire of adversity, Indigenous regimes coalesced to form confederations that demanded Indigenous recognition. Both international efforts (the ILO Convention on Indigenous rights) and settler-nations' modification by conciliatory dialogue utilizing the Narrative of Recognition did not result in Indigenous accommodation in most cases. Rather the political process engendered the appearance of cooperation by conciliatory dialogue but accommodation to Indigenous demands was rarely put into practice.

Contrarily, in a twist of meaning, the Narrative of Self-Recognition has invoked a pride of Indigenous identity which when combined with the Narrative of the Indigenous Anti-citizen has produced the greatest positive political results for Latin American Indigenous groups. Ever vigilant, always critical of the colonial-corporate master narratives, the resentment and refusal to forget the past fuels the on-going energy of Indigenous confederations in the political arena of their settler-nations. The recent successful overturns of the political culture of two settler-states, Ecuador and Bolivia, are the results of this energy.

Latin American Indigenous confederations have come to demand inclusion and equal treatment, challenging the homogenizing impulses of the settler-state, its hierarchies of power and its liberal precepts. Rather, they are demanding a heterogeneous notion of who is a citizen and how he or she is defined. They have changed the venues where authority is vested. No longer do they endure one overarching Western political culture. Indigenous movements in Ecuador, Bolivia, Mexico, and Guatemala have demanded constitutional reforms to recognize the multiethnic and pluri-national composition of their countries, and refer to this plurality constantly.

Yet so much remains to be done. Even CONAIE, Ecuador's largest and most prominent Indigenous movement, states boldly: "In Ecuador the fundamental principles of democracy—equality, liberty, fraternity, and social peace—have not been achieved" (Yashar 2005). In the competing visions of how to accommodate a multiethnic citizenry, the active critical stance of the Indigenous Anti-citizen toward his or her settler-state will be, in all likelihood, a permanent one.

REFERENCES

Albro, Robert. 2005. "Indigenous in the Plural in Bolivian Oppositional Politics." *Bulletin of Latin American Research* 24 (4): 433–53.

Alejandro, Roberto. 1998. "Impossible Citizenship." In *Citizenship After Liberalism*, edited by Karen Slawner and Mark E. Denham, 9–32. New York: Peter Lang.

Altamirano-Jiménez, Isabel. 2013. *Indigenous Encounters with Neoliberalism: Place, Women and the Environment in Canada and Mexico.* Vancouver: University of British Columbia Press.

Amnesty International. 1981. *Guatemala: A Government Program of Political Murder.* London.

Andolina, Robert James. 1999. *Colonial Legacies and Plurinational Imaginaries: Indigenous Movement Politics in Ecuador and Bolivia.* Minneapolis: University of Minnesota Press.

Barlow, Maude, and Tony Clarke. 2003. *Blue Gold: The Battle Against Corporate Theft of the World's Water.* London: Earthscan.

BBC News: Latin America & Caribbean. 2015. "Rios Montt Guatemala Genocide Retrial Suspended." January 5.

http://publicinternationallawandpolicygroup.org/wp-content
/uploads/2015/01/WCPW_011215_masternew.html.

Beiner, Ronald, ed. 1995. *Theorizing Citizenship*. Albany: State University of New York.

Bennett, David. 1998. *Multicultural States: Rethinking Difference and Identity*. London: Routledge.

Boyle, Alan E., and Michael R. Anderson. 1998. *Human Rights Approahes to Environmental Protection*. Oxford: Clarenden Press.

Brysk, Alison. 2000. *From Tribal Village to Global Village: Indian Rights and International Relations in Latin America*. Stanford, CA: Stanford University Press.

Coulthard, Glen Sean. 2014. *Red Skin White Masks: Rejecting the Colonial Politics of Recognition*. Minneapolis: University of Minnesota Press.

Cullather, Nick. 2006. *Secret History: The CIA's Classified Account of Its Operations in Guatemala, 1952-1954*. Stanford, CA: Stanford University Press.

Davis, Shelton. 2002. "Indigenous People, Poverty, and Participatory Development: The Experiences of the World Bank in Latin America." In *Multiculturalism in Latin America: Indigenous Rights, Diversity, and Democracy*, edited by Rachel Seider, 227–50. London: Palgrave.

Earthjustice. 2006. *Bechtel Surrenders in Bolivia Water Revolt Case*. Earthjustice. Accessed April 24, 2015. http://earthjustice.org/news/press/2006/bechtel-surrenders-in-bolivia-water-revolt-case.

Fleischmann, Aloys N. M., Nancy Van Styvendale, and Cody McCarroll. 2011. "Narratives of Citizenship." In *Narratives of Citizenship*, edited by Aloys N. M. Fleischmann, Nancy Van Styvendale and Cody McCarroll, XI–XLV. Edmonton: University of Alberta Press.

García, María Elena. 2005. *Making Indigenous Citizens: Identity, Development, and Multicultural Activism in Peru*. Stanford, CA: Stanford University Press.

Gleijeses, Piero. 1988. *Politics and Culture in Guatemala*. Ann Arbor: University of Michigan.

———. 1997. *Shattered Hope: The Guatemalan Revolution and the United States, 1944-1954*. Princeton, NJ: Princeton University Press.

———. 2006. "Afterward: The Culture of Fear." In *Secret History: The CIA's Classified Account of Its Operations in Guatemala, 1952-1954*, by Nick Cullather, XXIII–XXXVI. Stanford, CA: Stanford University Press.

Hale, Charles R. 2002. "Does Multiculturalism Menace? Governance, Cultural Rights, and the Politics of Identity in Guatemala." *Journal of Latin American Studies* 34 (3): 485–524.

Hansen, Tom. 2002. "Zapatistas: A Brief Historical Timeline." In *The Zapatista Reader*, edited by Tom Hayden, 8–15. New York: Avalon Publishing Group Inc.

Hardt, Michael, and Antonio Negri. 2009. *Commonwealth.* Cambridge: Harvard University Press.

Hayden, Tom, ed. 2002. *The Zapatista Reader.* New York: Nation Books/Avalon Publishing Group, Inc.

Hite, Katherine and Mark Ungar. eds. 2013. *Sustaining Human Rights in the Twenty-First Century: Strategies from Latin America.* New York: Woodrow Wilson Center Press.

Kinzer, Stephen. 2006. *Overthrow: America's Century of Regime Change from Hawaii to Iraq.* New York: Henry Holt and Company, LLC.

Kirsch, Stuart. 2014. *Mining Capitalism: The Relationship Between Corporations and Their Critics.* Oakland: University of California Press.

Klein, Naomi. 2002. "The Unknown Icon." In *The Zapatista Reader*, 91. New York: Avalon Publishing Company.

———. 2007. *The Shock Doctrine: The Rise of Disaster Capitalism.* New York: Picador.

Kohl, Ben. n.d. "Restructuring Citizenship in Bolvia: El Plan de Todos." *International Journal of Urban and Regional Research* 27 (2): 337–51.

Kopkind, Andrew. 2002. "Opening Shots." In *The Zapatista Reader*, edited by Tom Hayden, 19–21. New York: Avalon Publishing Group Inc.

Kovach, Margaret. 2010. *Indigenous Methodologies.* Toronto: University of Toronto Press.

Laurie, Nina, Robert Andolina, and Sarah Radcliffe. 2002. "The Excluded "Indigenous? The Implications for Multi-Ethnic Policies for Water Reform in Bolivia." In *Multiculturalism in Latin America: Indigenous Rights, Diversity, and Democracy*, edited by Rachel Seider, 252–75. New York: Palgrave McMillan.

Mallén, Patricia Rey. 2013. "Bolivian Census Highlights How Changes In Bolivian Demographics Might Affect President Evol Morales' Power Base." *International Business Times*, August 7. Accessed 2015. http://www.ibtimes.com/bolivian-census-highlights-how-changes -bolivian-demographics-might-affect-president-evo-morales.

Markell, Patchen. 2003. *Bound by Recognition*. Princeton, NJ: Princeton University Press.

Mehta, Uday. 1997. "Liberal Strategies of Exclusion." In *Tensions of Empire: Colonial Cultures in a Bourgeois World*, edited by Frederick Cooper and Ann Laura Stoler, 59–85. Berkeley: University of California Press.

Moreno, Fernando Romero. 1996. "Desarrollo sostenible y participación popular ciudadana." In *El pulso de la democracia: participación ciudadana y la descentralización de Bolivia*. La Paz: MDH/SNPP/Nueva Sociedad.

Pachano, Simón. 1996. *Democracía sin sociedad*. Quito: ILDIS.

Philips, Anne. 2007. *Multiculturalism without Culture*. Princeton, NJ: Princeton University Press.

Postero, Nancy, and Leon Zamosc. 2004. "Indigenous Movements and the Indian Question in Latin America." In *The Struggle for Indian Rights in Latin America*, edited by Nancy Postero and Leon Zamosc, 1–31. London: Sussex Academic Press.

Psacharopoulos, George, and Harry Patrinos. 1994. *Indigenous People and Poverty in Latin America*. Washington, D.C.: World Bank. http://documents.worldbank.org/curated/en/541051468757195444/pdf /multi-page.pdf.

Reid, Michael. 2009. *Forgotten Continent: The Battle for Latin America's Soul*. London: Yale University Press.

Rivera Cusicanqui, Silvia. 1984. *Oprimidos pero no vencidos: Luchas del campesinado aymara y ahechwa de Bolivia, 1900-1980*. La Paz: HISBOL-CSUTCB.

Samosc, Leon. 2004. "The Indian Movement in Ecuador: From Politics of Influence to Politics of Power." In *The Struggle for Indian Rights in Latin America*, edited by Nancy Postero and Leon Zamosc, 131–57. London: Sussex Academic Press.

Sawyer, Suzana. 2004. *Crude Chronicles: Indigenous Politics, Multinational Oil, and Neoliberalism in Ecuador*. London: Duke University Press.

Schemo, Daine Jean. 1998. "Ecuadoreans Want Texaco to Clear Toxic Residue." *The New York Times*, February 1. http://www.nytimes.com/1998/02/01 /world/ecuadoreans-want-texaco-to-clear-toxic-residue.html.

Schlesinger, Stephen, and Stephen Kinzer. 2005. *Bitter Fruit: The Story of the American Coup in Guatemala.* Cambridge, MA: Harvard University David Rockefeller Center for Latin American Studies.

Segarra, Monique. 2013. "Challenging Neoliberalism and Development: Human Rights and the Environment in Latin America." In *Sustaining Human Rights in the Twenty-First Century: Strategies from Latin America*, edited by Katherine Hite and Mark Ungar, 303–40. Washington, D.C.: Woodrow Wilson Center Press.

Shiva, Vadana. 2002. *Water Wars: Privatization, Pollution and Profit.* Cambridge, MA: South End Press.

———. 2004. "Water Democracy." In *¡Cochabamba! Water War in Bolivia*, edited by Oscar Olivera and Tom Lewis. Boston: South End Press.

Sieder, Rachel. 2001. "War, Peace, and Memory Politics in Central America." In *The Politics of Memory: Transitional Justice in Democratizing Societies*, edited by Alexandra Barahona de Brito, Carmen Gonzalez-Enriquez and Paloma Aguilar. Oxford: Oxford University Press.

———. 2002. *Multiculturalism in Latin America: Indigenous Rights, Diversity and Democracy.* New York: Palgrave.

Szeminski, Jan. 1983. *La utopía tupamarista.* Lima: Pontificia Universidad Católica del Perú, Fondo Editorial.

Taylor, Charles. 1992. *Multiculturalism and "the Politics of Recognition."* Princeton, NJ: Princeton University Press.

"The Recovery of Historical Memory." 2010. *Comisión de Esclarecimiento Histórico.* Guatemala. Accessed May 2, 2015. http://www.derechoshumanos.net/lesahumanidad/informes/guatemala /informeCEH.htm.

Thompson, José. 2013. "Particpation, Democracy and Human Rights." In *Sustaining Human Rights in the Twenty-First Century: Strategies from Latin America*, edited by Katherine Hite and Mark Ungar, 73–100. Washington, D.C.: Woodrow Wilson Press Center.

Unzueta, Fernando. 2000. "Periódicos y formación nacional: Bolivia ensus primeros años." *Latin America Research Review* 35 (2): 35–72.

Weaver, Jace. 2006. "Splitting the Earth: First Utterances and Pluralist Separatism." In *American Indian Literary Nationalism*, edited by Jace Weaver, Craig S. Womack and Robert Warrior, 1–89. Albuquerque: University of New Mexico Press.

Yashar, Deborah J. 2005. *Contesting Citizenship in Latin America: The Rise of Indigenous Movements and the Postliberal Challenge*. New York: Cambridge University Press.

Young, Iris Marion. 1989. "Polity and Group Difference: A Critique of the Ideal of Universal Citizenship." In *Feminism and Political Theory*, edited by Cass R. Sunstein, 117–41. Chicago: University of Chicago Press, 1990.

CHAPTER 8

The Corporate Script: The "Free Trade Agreements and Commissions that Led to the "Rigged" Economic and Political Game in Latin America—Neocolonial Control, Eroding Sovereignty, and Corrosive Democracy

Since 1945, the ruling elite classes of Western corporates and their bankers have set in motion five successive ideological blueprints and commissions to control and safeguard their interests in trade with Latin America: Bretton Woods (1944), the GATT (1948), the Trilateral Commission (1973), the largest modification of the GATT, known as the Uruguay Round (1983), and NAFTA (1994). Each trade agreement and its modifications would tighten a strong-hold on Latin American resources, sovereignty and progressive movements well into the twenty-first century. What Senator Elizabeth Warren of Massachusetts has referred to as a "rigged game" for multinational corporations, large banks, and the corporate wealthy has long been perceived as such by Latin Americans. Latin America was one of the first experimental laboratories for corporate planning to control world trade. The North American multinational corporations wanted access to lucrative natural resources in Latin America on their terms.

The extent to which these blueprints and the ideology behind them have affected Latin America is glaring: military coups, torture of progressives labeled "subversives," the large number of the disappeared, the plight of miners and unions, CIA interference, increased social inequality, the steep income rise of the Latin American elites, the rise in immigration of poor farmers and asylum seekers to the US, the selling off (privatization) of many Latin American industries to foreign investors, and the commodification of the public commons (such as water). The Latin American experience of this "disaster capitalism" (Klein 2007) explains Latin America's 2005 rejection of the Free Trade Agreement of the Americas (FTAA), its abrupt retreat from the International Monetary Fund (IMF) in 2007 and the withdrawal of some Latin American nations from the entangling web of free trade regulations with the North.

This investigation has three objectives. The first objective is to review the architecture that constructs the monolithic vision of free trade that has affected Latin America. The second goal is to capture in a few poignant historical examples the magnitude of the effect of disciplinary neoliberalism and free trade in Latin America. The third objective is to emphasize the fallacies behind the common assumptions that have justified this vision of free trade. It is not in this investigation's purview to offer solutions or alternatives to the current architecture of free trade as that would exceed the parameters of this text.

THE CLASH OF THEORETICAL SKELETONS

The cumulative effects of the internationalization process might be said to constitute a major structural change in the global political economy since the 1930s (Gill 4). These structural changes have been deliberately constructed by the creation of free trade agreements and related commissions, many of which have been dominated by North American material interests and frameworks of thought and ideology. Contributing institutions—the Council on Foreign Relations, the Trilateral Commission, the Ford Foundation, the Brookings Institution, parts of the International Monetary Fund, the World Bank, and the World Trade Organization to mention only a few—have fostered conservative think tanks where a monolithic "world view" predominates and intellectual interlocking memberships and relationships prevail (Gill 1990, 9). This hegemonic perspective which has been under the tutelage of the American foreign policy establishment continues to reflect realist, neorealist and liberal theories of international trade that primarily stress market efficiency (read: profits) over goals of equality, and secondarily, political order over human rights.

Theoretically, the assumptions behind the theories of neoliberalism and free trade have clashed with Latin American perspectives. Many of these assumptions were blatantly contradicted by the Latin American experience with North American corporate "free trade," as this investigation will demonstrate. The North American hegemony's material capabilities, their institutions, and ideas have been contested by Latin American perspectives which reject the neocolonial dependency to which they have often been relegated. In contradiction, many Latin American theorists emphasize the conflicts of international inequality and injustice. In their experience from 1954 to 2007, such problems of inequality and injustice became acutely disruptive socially under North American neoliberalism and free trade. Latin thinkers appear to parallel a Neo-Gramscian theoretical perspective and have been behind the efforts to delink from the North American capitalist network.

Gramsci's ideas of hegemony reflect the Latin American historical experience. His conception of "historic blocs"—such as the institutions, free trade blueprints, commissions and think tanks that constitute a monolithic vision of global trade—act as one "organic intellectual" group that forges the ideology of neoliberalism and the primacy of corporate power. Neo-Gramscian theory perceives the sovereignty of states as subjugated to a financial system and a system of production. For Latin Americans, the GATT, the IMF, the World Bank and NAFTA have formed such a historic bloc that has exercised global hegemony while imposing a single regulatory regime, the World Trade Organization. Latin American resistance to this historic bloc has provoked counter-hegemonies whose priorities emphasize class struggle and reject free trade's "harmonization." Harmonization invalidates all claims to protect health, safety, consumer rights and environmental protections that would slow down or impede trade. Moreover, harmonization is perceived as a threat by Latin American Indigenous communities that leads to the loss of their protected lands and subsequently, to an eventual cultural oblivion.

THE ANTI-DEMOCRATIC NATURE OF "FREE TRADE" AGREEMENTS

Free trade agreements with the US have acquired notorious reputations today. They reflect the tradition of elite ideology and corporate planning that crafts the rules of trade, banking and business to their advantage, circumventing democratic laws that restrict trade and eliminating public interests that cut into their profit margins. To ensure the success of such trade agreements, these contracts are written in secrecy behind closed doors by elite business interests and corporate lobbyists with no accountability to the public, allowing no public access to the blueprints of the trade agreements until the agreement is a *fait accompli.* Consumer interests, environmentalists, health representatives, small businesses, labor interests, Indigenous Peoples and general citizens are excluded from the process. All protective countermoves on the part of the public that might oppose the control of money and power by multinational corporations have been nullified and outlawed as "non-tariff trade barriers" in these trade agreements.

By signing these complex legal agreements, nations have surrendered their sovereignty to a globalization of corporate power. By not signing the trade agreements, however, their governments had reduced alternatives for trade until the 1990s. They either molded themselves to a Western model of control by corporate and banking interests, or they faced isolation. Most countries found it difficult resisting the pressure to sign on given that their export income would be diminished.

Counter Trade Agreements to Oppose the North American Monolithic Bloc

Since the 1990s, some Latin American nations chose to retreat from trade with the North rather than be reduced and controlled by the institutions that ensure foreign corporate interests. The GATT required that smaller countries increasingly relinquish all remnants of sovereignty, and the rules favored the wealthier nations of the Northern Hemisphere. Both these conditions worked to the detriment of Latin America, particularly the smaller countries of the South. Corporate attempts to depress Latin American wages, bankrupt family farms, erode cultural heritages, dismantle health, safety, and environmental protections provoked a preference for smaller nations' systems of local production. Rather than participate in a "race to the bottom" (Nader 1993, 8) perceived as the end game of entering the Northern corporate trade-maze by Latin American small businesses and laborers, some Latin American countries preferred to safeguard their democratic autonomy.

Since 1992, approximately twenty Latin American intraregional free trade agreements have sprung up creating a web of Latin American trade with rules tailored to Latin American local and sectoral pressures such as the Common Market of the South (Mercosur). Founded in 2004, ALBA, the *Alianza Bolivariana para los Pueblos de Nuestra América*, promotes socialist forms of trade. The Andean Community of Nations (CAN), revitalized by this intraregional desire for trade, entered talks with Mercosur, thereby creating a larger trade organization, UNASUR, in 2008. This regional trend deliberately opposed the free trade agreements with the complex financial systems of the North, preferring to encourage intraregional trade or trade with Asia which required less disadvantageous trade regulations.

It is impossible to extrapolate on all the ramifications of these blueprints for "free trade" with Latin America in this short paper; such a task could fill books. The trade agreements will be briefly presented as they affected the public in Latin American, along with the timing of each blueprint on the Latin American context. Only a few of the many effects on Latin America can be delineated in this short investigation. These results will be used to illustrate the invalidity of the initial assumptions or justifications that have spawned the ideology behind free trade.

The Bretton Woods Agreement 1944–1971

In 1944 while World War II was still in process, delegates from forty-four Allied countries met for an economic conference in Bretton Woods, New Hampshire.

The attendance by so many nations implied an awareness that the failure to manage monetary exchange rates for trade during the interwar years had exacerbated trade disagreements and political tensions, leading to World War II. Also, the 1931 banking crisis partially due to unrecoverable loans from World War I led to the Treaty of Versailles' imposition of the debt upon Germany. This punitive stranglehold on Germany also fanned tensions that spawned the conditions for the Second World War. The Bretton Woods conference was not only an attempt to "peacefully regulate" world trade, but it concealed an intended effort on the part of corporate interests to expand their control over world trade. In the words of Jerry Mander, a former senior fellow at the Public Media Center, "the vast expansion of corporate power had actually been predicted and planned for…at the Bretton Woods meetings held after World War II" (Mander 1993, 14). Those involved with the successive meetings believed 1) that world problems could be solved by a push for Western-style economic development, and 2) that the benefits would "trickle down" to the world's poorest populations. 3) Not only did corporate capitalism believe itself to be the solution for world peace, but they would also guarantee open competition. 4) The multinational corporate enterprises perceived themselves to be the most efficient enforcers of this overall economic program. These four assumptions formed the initial foundation of ideas for the coming monolithic vision of free trade.

The Bretton Woods Agreement set up a system of rules, procedures, and institutions such as the International Monetary Fund (IMF) and the International Bank for Reconstruction and Development, which is today part of the World Bank. The International Monetary system was to be regulated by the gold standard and the US dollar to maintain fixed exchange rates. As the United States was the largest holder of gold after World War II, this fact gave the US unprecedented power to cement the terms of Bretton Woods favoring large corporate and banking interests. The Bretton Woods regulations would reduce trade barriers such as tariffs, oppose nationalization of resources so that Northern corporations could retain access to foreign natural resources, and prevent rapid devaluations of currencies for competitive purposes.

LATIN AMERICA'S DEVELOPMENTALISM BEFORE BRETTON WOODS

In Latin America, the abundance of mineral resources had already attracted Northern corporations by the 1930s and '40s. In particular, the Chilean mines were recognized to be highly profitable resources for extraction.

In the early 1940s, Latin American economics reflected the Social Democrats of Europe and the Keynesian economic policies in the United States with an emphasis on developing jobs and businesses and improving the conditions of labor. Latin American economists predicted that their countries could escape poverty if the policy of "Developmentalism" were pursued. Developmentalism was an economic plan that favored a locally oriented strategy of industrialization and protectionism rather than relying on the exports of natural resources. Exports to the North had proven to be less and less lucrative for Latin Americans as Northern corporations had already been siphoning off large portions of the profits. As a consequence, developmentalists argued for the nationalization of oil, minerals and other natural resources so that the profits would benefit government-led developmental projects for their countries rather than enriching foreign corporations. By the 1950s, numerous success stories surrounding the policies of Developmentalism had taken root, particularly in the Southern Cone of Latin America.

From a historical perspective, these years of economic expansion under Developmentalism prompted predictions of prosperity for Latin America that started to resemble the progress of Northern economies. However, the growing prosperity was protected by high tariffs, restricting foreign competition while Latin American industries and businesses grew. New factories flourished; salaries in unions increased. Under Developmentalism, hope and pride in domestic growth had become a reality.

CORPORATE CAPITALISM'S RESPONSE TO LATIN AMERICAN DEVELOPMENTALISM

Access to Latin America's resources was highly restricted as a result of the policies of Developmentalism. Northern exports to Latin America were non-competitive due to the high tariffs assessed to imports, protecting growing Latin American factories and businesses. Meanwhile, the conditions for a counter-revolution in economics were festering in the corporate sector of the United States. The laissez-faire capitalism that the multinational corporations so favored was being suppressed by Developmentalism in Latin America and by Keynesian economics in the United States.

As early as the 1950s, the corporate response in the United States was three-fold. 1) Corporate elites co-opted Milton Friedman's conception of "free trade" as a theoretical and ideological underpinning of their position. 2) They sought out young Latin Americans to enter Friedman's department of economics at the University of Chicago. The Latin Americans were indoctrinated in the corporate ideology of neoliberalism and free trade. When these students returned to Latin America, they became known as the "Chicago Boys," the mouthpiece for neoliberalism and free trade. 3) The third response was the corporate and banking sector's most strategic move, the creation of the General Agreement on Tariffs and Trade (GATT), a precursor to the World Trade Organization (1995).

THE CORE ARTICLES OF THE 1947 GENERAL AGREEMENT ON TARIFFS AND TRADE (GATT)

By October of 1947, twenty-three founding member nations signed on to the GATT during the first round in Havana, Cuba. Successive rounds met to modify the GATT: the Annecy Round in France 1949, the Torquay Round in England in 1951, the Geneva Round in 1955–1959, the Dillon Round in Geneva from 1960–1962, the Kennedy Round from 1962–1967, and finally the most ambitious Uruguay Round in Geneva from 1986–1995 which created the World Trade Organization (WTO). Until the establishment of the WTO in 1995, GATT was the only multilateral instrument governing international trade. However, all rounds that contributed sub-agreements and modifications for trade had to remain compatible with the initial GATT of 1947.

In the early years, the trade rounds of the GATT primarily concentrated on reducing tariffs. The GATT became effective January 1, 1948. Latin American nations were immediately urged to enter the GATT, resulting in Brazil and Cuba joining in 1948, Chile in 1949, Haiti, the Dominican Republic and Nicaragua in 1950, Peru in 1951, and Uruguay in 1953. Of these initial countries, most were under the rule of dictators and leaders of military or elite business interests, naturally favoring the interests of a small percentage of Latin American business elites. Ten Latin American nations did not sign on to the GATT until years later: Argentina (1967), Colombia (1981), México (1986), Venezuela (1990), Bolivia (1990), Costa Rica (1990), El Salvador (1991), Guatemala (1991), Honduras (1994), and Paraguay (1994).

Articles delineated by the GATT significantly affected Latin America:

Article I of the General Agreement on Tariffs and Trade granted the status of "Most Favored Nations" to signers of the GATT. GATT countries, in direct opposition to Developmentalism, could not favor their domestic products over the competitive products of other GATT nations. Exclusions on how a product was harvested or produced were not permitted; considerations such as environmental hazards or exclusions because of child labor were not allowed. GATT signers could not limit the importation of products. Tariffs, quotas, and taxes were forbidden as trade barriers, and would be phased out.

Article III also reiterated the illegality of national legislation, taxes or tariffs to provide differential treatment to imports. Article III explicitly ended the use of trade restrictions to protect domestic industries, a key policy of Developmentalism in Latin America.

Article XI reinforced the above articles by rejecting the application of quotas, licensing systems or bans on imports to protect national industries.

Article XX allowed for general exceptions to the preceding articles in the protection of life, national security and resistance to slave labor. However, increasingly in the effort to be less trade restrictive, conservation of life was not perceived as a goal of free trade.

In summary, the GATT destroyed the policies of Latin American Developmentalism. Furthermore, competition was not encouraged; the large corporations with economies to scale effectively eliminated smaller companies from the competition.

An Example of the Magnitude of the Effects of the GATT on Chile

The original GATT consisted of sixty pages, and superficially, trade disputes appeared to be primarily economical in content. But the collective strengthening of the corporate will under the experience of drafting the GATT reinforced the future outspoken response of North American corporations to Latin American politics and leftist movements. The hardball push of North American corporations for cooperation from the US government against Latin American progressive politics guaranteed US military intervention against the rise of the Latin American left. American corporations feared their access to Latin American natural resources would be effectively cut off by the nationalization of Latin American industries and resources. As a result, the newly established corporate blueprint to "prevent war" (the GATT) became the program that instigated war to protect its corporate vision of trade. The first and most basic assumption behind the free trade monolith—that of trade promoting peace—was blatantly contradicted. Thus, in the Latin American perspective, its assumption to prevent war was a form of deceptive doublespeak. It was AT&T Corporation which operated 70 percent of the telephone service in Chile that scripted the eighteen points of the military coup for Chile under the Nixon administration.

It was corporate America that declared war on Latin American progressives and socialists from 1954 (the Guatemalan coup instigated by corporate members of United Fruit Company) to 1992 (The Panama Invasion to check a rogue strongman, Noriega, and to regain access and control over the Panama Canal). In particular, the success of the Guatemalan Coup for the US corporation, United Fruit, was a historical precedent for the Chilean Coup.

Consequently, a dramatic effect of the original GATT was an iron-fisted strengthening of corporate political involvement in world affairs. For Latin America, the GATT's vision launched more than economic trade reform; it provoked and supported coups and military governments. Where democracy in Latin America had not been a hospitable fit for US-based multinational corporations, military dictatorships would create the conditions that protected their corporate profits (Klein 2007, 169). As Eduardo Galeano, an Uruguayan journalist and writer expressed it, "the theories of Milton Friedman gave him the Nobel Prize; they gave Chile General Pinochet" (Galeano 1978, 38). When the dust from the Chilean coup settled (1973), the Chicago Boys had already finished *The Brick*, a 500-page set of instructions to guide Pinochet's most important economic decisions to impose neoliberalism and free trade. *The Brick* was an obvious mirroring of Milton Friedman's book, *Capitalism and Freedom*. In essence, the induction of Latin American students to the University of Chicago for Milton Friedman's neoliberal indoctrination was perceived by many Latin Americans as pure academic imperialism. Juan Gabriel Valdés, Chile's foreign minister, documents it as "the organized transfer of ideology from the U.S." (Valdés 1995, 6). Chile was the first Chicago School laboratory, a corporate experiment to remake a country along the neoliberal lines of free trade. Chile was targeted because of the election of a socialist president, Allende, whom corporate interests saw as a threat because Chile was the country with the most known mineral wealth in Latin America.

Although the US refers to this change of government in Chile as a *coup d'état*, General Augusto Pinochet referred to the events around September 11, 1973, as "war." To the Chileans, it indeed felt like a war. After 160 years of peaceful democratic rule, Chile underwent an immediate reign of terror. Although the numbers are contested because of the consistent attempts by Pinochet's regime to cover up the terror, respective journalists and authors (Kandell, Bethell, and Cornwell) have estimated that, in total, more than 3,200 people were disappeared or executed, at least 80,000 were imprisoned, and 200,000 fled the country for political reasons (Kandell 2006). Inside the National Stadium, prisoners were hooded, hundreds were executed while others were carted off as subversives to be tortured. General Sergio Arellano Stark and his Caravan of Death, a roving death squad, undertook helicopter missions to the Northern provinces to seek out "subversives," those opposed to the new military government (Klein 2007, 93).

Within a very short period, Pinochet had unseated three military leaders that were part of his initial junta so that he could embrace the Chicago Boy's economic vision of a complete overhaul of the status quo. Pinochet opened the doors to foreign competition. He initially privatized businesses, cut government spending by 10 percent, and removed trade barriers such as protective tariffs and price controls. The shock of the flood of foreign competition led to an inflation rate of 375 percent, almost twice the level of inflation under Allende (Gunder Frank 1976, 62). Because of the cheap imports, thousands of Chileans experienced unemployment as Chilean small businesses could no longer compete and closed. Only foreign corporations and a small group of Chilean business elites known in Chile as the Piranhas benefited from this economic shock therapy. In response to the alarming inflation, in March 1975, Milton Friedman and his colleague from the Chicago School, Arnold Harberger, landed in Chile to counsel Pinochet. Friedman's advice, however, was to embrace the free market, "the shock treatment," and to include the Chicago Boys in Pinochet's administration (Klein 2007, 98). As a result of Friedman's strong directive, public spending in Chile was cut an additional 27 percent and hundreds of state-owned companies were privatized (Klein 2007, 100).

The strongest criticism of Pinochet came from a former Chicago Boy, André Gunder Frank, who had worked under the Allende administration and saw firsthand the connection between the violence instituted by the Pinochet's regime and the brutal economics imposed by the Chicago Boys. By 1982, Chile suffered an economic crash with the exploding debt, hyperinflation, and unemployment at 30 percent (Klein 2007, 104). What economic journals in the US touted as the "Chilean Miracle" was in the eyes of Chileans a war of foreign corporations and wealthy Piranhas versus the Chilean middle and lower classes. Forty-five percent of the Chilean population had fallen below the poverty line; only the wealthiest ten percent of Chileans, the business elites, profited with their incomes increasing by 83 percent (Klein 2007, 105). From this point on, Chile has frequently been referred to as one of the most unequal societies of the world (World Bank 2007). Chile is a prime examples of free trade provoking significant social inequality where only the biggest corporations and the wealthiest businesspeople profit. One of the primary assumptions of neoliberalism's free trade--that the economic benefits from free trade would "trickle down" and benefit the poor and middle class—was first proven wrong in Chile. Today, the trickle-down theory has been debunked by many celebrated economists, including a Nobel Prize winner, Joseph Stiglitz.

THE RISE OF TRILATERALISM AND THE VISION OF CORPORATE WORLD DOMINANCE

The desire for global economic governance by corporate and banking interests was further encouraged by the Trilateral Commission, a "brainchild" of David Rockefeller (Lydon 1977). The Trilateral Commission was widely understood to be an off-shoot of the Council on Foreign Relations which was well known for its influence on the US government. David Rockefeller was both the chairperson of the Council on Foreign Relations and the founding Chairman of the Trilateral Commission.

Many of the primary assumptions about elite world management in the Council on Foreign Relations were carried out as policy by the Trilateralists. The commission was labeled "trilateral" to link elite businesses and political leaders from three sides of the globe—North America, Europe and Japan. According to the Commissioners, these trilateral regions contained the lion's share of world trade and finance, producing approximately two-thirds of the world's output (Sklar 1980, 8). Trilateralists reinforced multinational corporations as the centers of power for the elites of these countries. Global corporations were considered the "best means yet devised for utilizing world-resources according to the criterion of profit: a standard of efficiency (Ball 1967). In contrast, nationalism and sovereign governments were perceived as obstacles to free trade objectives.

The Trilateralists conflated economics with politics; they strongly opposed and equated two distinct types of government in Latin America—communism (an ideology) and socialism (an economic distribution). The real issue was an economic obstacle—the blocking of access to raw materials when the Trilateralists believed the world should be the corporate playground. The potential for nationalization of resources by leftist governments was a threatening impediment to US control of world trade. As a consequence, the tactic of equating socialism with communism became a US obsession for decades reinforced by negative propaganda-like messages in US literature and the media. All government policies from the three sides of the Trilateralists' regions had to ensure that corporate capitalism would not only endure but prosper. Neither communism nor socialism was to be tolerated. This unbridled intolerance had devastating effects on Latin America.

The Trilateral model's overall objectives were the suppression of national laws and the homogenization of cultures within a Western economic paradigm. Like those who had worked on the GATT, the Trilateralists saw themselves as the world's elite players who should restructure the playing field so that the world favored transnational corporate activity. In particular, it was to favor the agendas of the corporations of the North—North America, Europe, and Japan. Trilateralists predicted a moving away of advanced nations from the post-industrial age toward a post-national age controlled by free trade regulations and corporate elites.

GUIDING ASSUMPTIONS AND POLICIES BEHIND TRILATERALISM THAT VIOLATED THE LATIN AMERICAN COLLECTIVE

For US Commissioners, Trilateralism was a form of global collective management under US tutelage (Sklar 1980, 8). Trilateralists intended to shape future conditions by managing interdependence presumably for the common interest, but in actuality, they shaped conditions for the profits of the multinational corporations. All individual economies were to surrender to transnational corporate capitalism. In Latin America, however, this "tutelage" was perceived as a strategy for managing dependence, a form of neocolonialism and a revitalization of imperialism. The system of global corporate control under US tutelage reenacted the privilege of Latin American elites, also a persistent colonial trait, and the ruling business classes of Latin American nation-states were "to ensure and maintain" this favorable investment climate.

The Trilateralists' development and distribution of global resources benefited the rich in the developed and underdeveloped countries at the expense of the middle class and poor in all countries. Capitalist economists continually refer to the "big tradeoff between efficiency and equality" (Okun 1975, 1). More efficiency for corporate profits as cultivated by the Trilateralists meant less equality and poorer pay for the average worker. For much of the Latin American public, private corporate profit as a system from 1954–1992 made a mockery of Latin American democracies, paid workers poorly, appropriated Latin American lands and resources, making repression a necessity. The Trilateralists' assumption of "building an international system that is pluralistic enough to permit cultivation of the values of trilateral countries in all those countries" was, in reality, a euphemism for imperialism (Cooper, Kaiser, and Kosaka 1977, 19).

Although Latin American nations had formal political sovereignty, in reality, debt dependency was one of the neocolonial leashes that ensured Western development projects would return massive profits to foreign corporations and banks. The Trilateral Commission called for an expansion of the IMF's role in managing "interdependence" by creating the "art of debt diplomacy" (Sklar 1980, 28–29). IMF programs consistently required the dismantling of social welfare programs for the poor and the maintenance of low wages to encourage foreign investment. In reference to the violation of human rights, James Petras' ironic article on the new morality of the Trilateralists points out that "morality is the recurring ideological expression of US imperialism in a period of crisis: it is what is offered to the world in place of substantive changes in the world's economic and social order (Petras 1977, 38). For Latin Americans, the economics promoted by the Trilateralists provoked an unceasing exploitation and fanned the conditions for human rights abuses. The so-called "New Morality" of the Trilateralists only increased the violation of human rights and operated in solidarity by and for the oppressor.

Andrew Young, himself a Trilateralist, pointed out that a common goal of trilateral policies toward the Third World was to promote neocolonialism:

> I don't think the U.S. has but one option, and that's neocolonialism. As bad as that has been made to sound, neocolonialism means that multinational corporations will continue to have a major influence in the development and productive capacities of the Third World…I just think capital and technology happen to be in the hands of the people who are called neocolonialists. (Sklar 1980, 564)

Philip Wheaton, the codirector of EPICA, Ecumenical Program for Inter-American Communication and Action, states this idea even more succinctly: "In the Third World, the West hopes to discard its colonial robes while maintaining its neocolonial throne" (Shank, Wheaton, and Lockwood 1977).

The powerful influence of the Trilateralists stabilized the GATT, based no longer on gold but on the US dollar. Trilateralists also increased corporate pressure on the US government to oppose any form of US and Latin American leftist populism. Trilateralists came from the financial world's top corporate players, bankers, and politicians that would favor transnational corporate activity. Their influence galvanized strong political support in the US government for the Chilean coup as well as its aftermath. The militarization of Latin America was firmly backed by the Trilateralists who perceived socialism as a form of "communism" and consequently, as an extreme threat to free trade, market economics, and especially their profit structure.

In May 1975, the rising conservatism of the Trilateral Commission and its anti-democratic sentiments came to the foreground with a controversial document, the "Report of the Trilateral Task Force on Governability of Democracies." In a well-known article, "Capitalism Shows Its Face: Giving Up on Democracy," Alan Wolfe remarks on two striking features of the Trilateralists' report: "the dominant tone of pessimism" arising among Trilateralists due to fear of class conflict and "the unmediated authoritarianism" of their newer approach to liberal democracy (Wolfe 1980, 297).

The intense controversy that arose from this report provoked a retreat by Trilateralists behind the walls of secrecy for the succeeding years. As Alan Wolfe pointed out, publicly expressing anti-democratic sentiments is an American taboo. Furthermore, as a tactic, it is much harder to stop an elite agenda when the general public is unaware of their existence, their publications, and their intentions. Nevertheless, the hidden influence of the Trilateralists led to major modifications of the GATT—the Uruguay Round—followed by another Trilateral agreement, the North American Free Trade Agreement (NAFTA).

THE URUGUAY ROUND OF THE GATT (1986–1993): SECURING THE MONOLITH

The Uruguay Round of modifications was concluded in 1993, and its modifications were established within the following five years. Where the original GATT was less than sixty pages in length, the Uruguay Round expanded the GATT to approximately 500 pages. In these modifications, the Uruguay Round significantly increased control of global trade regulations by creating the Multilateral Trade Organization (MTO) later known as the World Trade Organization (WTO), established in 1995. It was this global commerce agency that would wield powerful legal control to enforce compliance with the free trade regulations where the previous GATT did not have sufficient power to enforce such compliance. Dispute resolutions among trade officials and investors continued to be closed to the public. The ruling by the panel of commerce officials in the International Centre for Settlement of Investment Disputes (ICSID) would be automatically adopted unless there was an immediate appeal by all opposing parties or nations involved to stop the ruling.

Essentially, global corporate control was now not only legislative (the GATT), but it had just become an institutional judicial power (the WTO) over sovereign nations in ethical, social and economic issues. The WTO proceedings and the ICSID courts excluded public access and public testimony. They defied all democratic principles, and when applied to Latin Americans, this control evoked strong memories of colonialism. In the words of Ralph Nader, "the Uruguay Round expansion of GATT and NAFTA would establish a world economic government dominated by giant corporations, but they [did] not propose a democratic rule of law to hold this economic government accountable" (Nader 1993, 3).

As a consequence, the Uruguay Round promoted what has famously become recognized as a downwards "harmonization" of environmental and consumer standards. Environmental and health standards were not considered legitimate objectives to bar trade. The Uruguay Round expanded the concept of "nontariff trade barriers" to include all measures that would restrict trade or increase costs. Consequently, under the modifications of the Uruguay Round, environmental, health, and safety measures could be classified as obstacles that prevented access to any domestic market. Thus, restrictions on hormones in meat, pesticides sprayed on foods, and usage of asbestos would be struck down in trade agreement dispute resolutions as "nontariff trade barriers." After the expansion enacted by the Uruguay Round, the GATT could nullify national laws, and assess fines against countries that resisted the trade regulations.

The Uruguay Round aligned the GATT with the standards of the Codex Alimentarius Commission as an example of international standards. Strongly influenced by large agribusinesses, the Codex is part of the UN Food and Agriculture Organization. The lowered standards are dictated by corporates and their courts. Other world views, cultural, ethical, medical or religious, have been denied validity. "Harmonization" essentially forced countries to have to accept the lowest common denominator as a standard.

The trade agreements created to profit corporate interests began to arouse strong resistance among Indigenous groups in Latin America. A growing perception of neocolonialism in Latin America was increased by the new inclusion of agricultural products, probably one of the most controversial product groups under the Uruguay Round of the GATT. Once again, Latin American nations became producers of monoculture crops, the production of one large crop for the markets of the North, a repetition of colonial patterns. Thousands of small farmers were pushed out of their livelihoods, and mutually beneficial connections between agribusinesses and government officials were cultivated, repeating the social structure of the elites under colonial rule.

Eight Latin American nations that signed onto the GATT in the time frame before the Uruguay Round was enforced, came to understand the meaning of the new modifications in the turbulent years of the 1990s: México (1986) , Venezuela (1990), Bolivia (1990), Costa Rica (1990), El Salvador (1991), Guatemala (1991), Honduras (1994), and Paraguay (1994). In addition to the new regulations of the Uruguay Round, Mexican farmers and Indigenous groups were threatened by a new trilateral trade agreement, the NAFTA, which was enacted on January 1, 1994.

THE NORTH AMERICAN FREE TRADE AGREEMENT (NAFTA) AND THE MEXICAN REACTION

The NAFTA reflected the Trilateralists' influence, creating a trilateral rules-based trade bloc of Canada, Mexico and the US. However, the preparations for the signing of the NAFTA were highly controversial in all three countries. In Mexico, the intent of the Mexican government to sign the NAFTA sparked a revolution which the Mexican government downplayed to hide the dissension.

In the early 1990s, the Mexican government under President Carlos Salinas de Gortari canceled Article 27 of its Constitution in preparation for the NAFTA. A landmark piece of legislation reflecting Emilio Zapata's fight to acquire land for the Indigenous in the Mexican Revolution of 1910–1919, Article 27 protected Indigenous communal landholdings against sale and privatization. Under the NAFTA regulations, Article 27 was an obsolete barrier to trade and investment (Hayden 2002, 82). For the Indigenous, unable to compete with the money of large corporations, it was the nightmare of the Conquista all over again. They felt deeply threatened with the incursion of corporate speculation upon their remaining lands. For them, it spelled a loss of their lands and their way of life. Tied to the Earth culturally, the loss of control over their land was perceived as a "death sentence" by the Indigenous groups of Chiapas. This threat to their identity galvanized *chiapanecos* to prepare for war. The battle was more than another resistance against repressive landowners and paramilitaries. President Bush's proclamation of the "New World Order" would propel a forced cultural assimilation, an eventual obliteration of the Indigenous cultures and practices. Only physical separation by owning their lands had ever guaranteed the Indigenous Mayans occasional periods of respite. With no physical separation, the overriding dominate culture would denigrate and erase the Indigenous way of life, eventually destroying their cultural identities.

By the time President George Bush signed the preliminary text of the North American Free Trade Agreement (NAFTA) in 1992, Mexican Indigenous groups had clearly learned about the consequences of the Uruguay Round of the GATT and the NAFTA. In an outright campaign against the signing of the NAFTA by

President Salinas de Gortari of Mexico, they rejected neoliberalism and free trade. Chanting that "NAFTA is Death," the Chiapas Rebellion that started on the first day of NAFTA's enforcement was the first denunciation of Bush's "New World Order" (Hayden 2002, 2). Their Indigenous identity became a motivational weapon to uproot the rule of free trade which they perceived as relegating them to a cultural death of oblivion.

In contrast, the corporate mentality was "oblivious" to the "oblivion the Zapatistas were fighting." "One mindset floated in the bubble of [market] modernity while the other tried to shake off a 500-year nightmare" (Hayden 2002, 77). The free trade corporate mentality had already "eclipsed the democratic process, human rights, and environmental concerns" by buying out legislative support with a flood of dark money and claims about the "inevitability of globalization" (Hayden 2002, 78–79).

The Chiapas revolt raised critical questions by human rights activists globally. The basic demand of the Zapatistas was a "world in which many worlds fit," and not an Anglo-Saxon "mono-world with no space for them" (Hayden 2002, 2). *Comandante* Marcos, the leader of the Zapatistas, restated the Indigenous objections: "The new distribution of the world excludes minorities.... The majority who make up the world basements are disposable" (Klein 2002). Historically today, there is a recognition that the Conquista, which is so monumental in the Latin American Indigenous consciousness, was indeed a genocide. But to recognize the Conquista as a genocide is to undermine Western legitimacy. Western and North American minds have long had the ability to annihilate Indigenous peoples who have stood in their way, and subsequently have denied the massacres they propagated. The same behavior defined the free trade corporate mentality. The elite claim is that cultural destruction is an unfortunate preliminary condition to a better, more democratic world. Chase Manhattan Bank issued a report calling for the Mexican government to "eliminate the Zapatistas" (February 13, 1994). Apparently, David Rockefeller, the Bank President, and a Trilateralist, appeared to negate the need for "a more democratic world," reflecting the Trilateralist' agenda of antidemocratic sentiment as seen in their aforementioned 1975 report.

From a Latin American perspective, free trade has discouraged democracy. Rather, it has encouraged right-winged military dictatorships and control by the elites. For Latin Americans, the rise of the *chiapanecos* was a "war against the globalization of the market, against the destruction of nature, the confiscation of resources, against the termination of Indigenous peoples and their lands, against the growing maldistribution of wealth and the consequent decline in standards of living for all but the rich" (Kopkind 2002, 19.). In Chiapas, the ideological underpinnings and political effects of the new globalization merely repeated the cycle of violence suffered by the Indigenous in the Conquista.

The enforcement of the NAFTA allowed the Mexican military, many of whom were trained at the ill-famed School of the Americas, to persecute the Indigenous Zapatistas. Within twenty-four hours of the implementation of the NAFTA, the army bombed Indigenous communities and killed approximately 145 Indigenous people. The military displaced 20,000 Indigenous *campesinos* from their town in Aguascalientes to construct an army base. This harassment led to the Acteal massacre of December 22, 1997, where forty-five Indigenous victims who were praying in a church were executed (Hayden 2002, 91). Forty-three were shot in the back. Two were killed by blows to the head. The Mexican army was carrying out the dictates of Chase Manhattan Bank: "to eliminate the Zapatistas." To avoid bad press, the Mexican administration denied the existence of "paramilitaries" in Chiapas. The Mexican military was not "officially at war," however they bombed Indigenous civilians, cleared their villages and executed Indigenous peasants by death-squad tactics. Following the Acteal Massacre, human rights observers and activists were expelled from Chiapas.

By 2000, the internal upheaval had caused the Mexican elections to overturn seventy-one years of the PRI's (Partido Revolucionario Institucional) governmental rule. Nevertheless, despite an unprecedented two-week march to Mexico City and a demonstration by 250,000 citizens for the Zapatistas in 2001, President Vicente Fox of the Partido Acción Nacional (PAN) signed yet another trade agreement, the Plan Puebla Panama agreement. This free trade agreement outlined a neoliberal vision of free trade and development for Mexico and Central America. As Rigoberta Menchú, an Indigenous Nobel Prize winner, has famously pointed out, for the Latin American Indigenous, nothing has changed since the Conquista. Free trade is just another name for the appropriation of Indigenous lands and the acceleration of Indigenous cultural destruction.

DOMINATION BY A SYSTEM OF RULES AND REGULATIONS: THE CORPORATE MONOLITH OF TRADE

The system of rules that has imposed forms of violence in Latin America has grown exponentially since 1947 into a monolithic structure of trade contracts, trade commissions, the World Trade Organization and ICSID, the disciplinary court. Sovereign countries are subjugated to the rules and regulations established by a capitalist economic system and controlled by an elite corporate minority. This domination has no democratic recourse, promotes exploitation of resources by outside corporations and reduces the value of human life and labor. Any in-depth study of Latin American social, economic and political history from 1954–2016 will portray the intensity of that exploitation by neoliberal corporate elites and their practices of free trade.

This exploitation has not abated. In 2016, a US mining corporation, Tobie Mining and Energy, launched a $16.5 billion lawsuit against Colombia for its refusal to allow the company to establish a gold mine in its Amazon forest. Given the infamous precedent of Chevron-Texaco that dumped toxic waste from oil extraction in the Ecuadorian Amazon rainforest (1967–1990), polluting an area the size of Rhode Island, Colombia preferred to establish a national park. In 2011, Chevron-Texaco was fined $18.2 billion for its extensive pollution that uprooted Ecuadorian Indigenous lives; however, Chevron-Texaco blatantly refused to pay anything for the damages of dirty extraction, the significant rise of cancer for inhabitants of the region and their loss of their sustainable lands. Gold extraction is also a dirty process that contaminates the land. Colombia, a sovereign country, is not given the right to reject a US mining company from polluting their forest, from extracting the lion's share of the profits, nor from having any likely responsibility to restore possible damages. The Uruguay expansion of the GATT demanded no restrictions on investing in any part of the world. Corporate domination of Latin American resources and lands has had and continues to have devastating effects on Latin Americans—their land, their resources, and their lives.

For Latin Americans, the September 11, 2001, attack on the twin World Trade Center towers in New York City was a highly symbolic retribution for the first 9/11. On September 11, 1973, the United States, pushed by US corporate interests involved in Chile, was successful in its efforts to overthrow the democratic government of Salvador Allende and to install General Augusto Pinochet and a neoliberal program. Noam Chomsky, in his book, "Who Rules the World?" (2016) makes two observations. The first observation considers the economic destruction, the torture, and kidnappings to demonstrate just how much more devastating the first 9/11 was (Chomsky 2016, 19). Then Chomsky reminds his reader of the conclusions of Nixon's National Security Council—that if the United States could not control Latin America, it could not expect "to achieve a successful order elsewhere in the world" (Chomsky 2016, 19–20). Chomsky is referring to The Grand Area doctrine that was developed in the US during World War II. The doctrine stated that the United States was to dominate the Western hemisphere, the Far East, and the former British Empire with its Middle East energy resources (Chomsky 2016, 45). The structure to control the Grand Area included the blueprints of trade agreements, trade commissions, the World Trade Organization, and the US military that would enforce this dominance outside of the United States.

Today, however, those whom Adam Smith called the "Masters of Mankind" are not nations but rather multinational conglomerates, large financial institutions, and their elites. The real infrastructure of the architectural maze of power has been built by the "Masters of Mankind," trade agreement by trade agreement, creating the institutions that will secure their control. Chomsky reminds us that even Adam Smith, a founding theorist of capitalism, pointed out the "vile maxim" to which the "Masters of Mankind" are dedicated: "All for ourselves and nothing for other people"—a doctrine known otherwise as bitter and incessant class war (Chomsky 2016, 239). Certainly, the Chilean public who lived through the bitter years of 1973–1996 would agree that the neoliberal policies imposed on them incited not only an ugly class war but increased social inequality. The neoliberal agenda of these "Masters of Mankind" has succeeded in arousing strong resistance, particularly in Latin America, which was the first test laboratory for the neoliberal push for global control, and therefore, well acquainted with the significant violence and destabilization that accompanies it.

THE CONTRADICTORY ASSUMPTIONS BEHIND NEOLIBERAL FREE TRADE

The original assumption, the most frequent defense of neoliberal free trade, was that opening markets to free trade would ensure global peace. For Latin Americans, this has been a blatantly false myth. The rise of US military interventionism and direct CIA interference to protect US corporations in Latin America provoked considerable structural adjustment to Latin American societies by the shock therapy of coups, internment camps, torture of "subversives", and US backed military dictatorships. War and violence were inflicted to ensure that the neoliberal vision of free trade was imposed. Both the military coups in Guatemala and Chile were scripted by North American corporations, and the ensuing chaos brought about by these coups encouraged three decades of genocide in Guatemala and two decades of economic upheaval for Chileans.

A second assumption leading off of the first claimed the rise of free trade would guarantee an open democratic competition. It did not take long to understand that such open competition only profited the large corporations which could outlast and cripple the mainstream of small businesses.

The third assumption—that benefits would "trickle down" to the world's poorest populations--would become a major mantra of corporate capitalism for years. Today, we know that rather than improve labor, labor conditions, and wages, free trade has marginalized labor's voice and kept wages flat. Poverty as a global phenomenon has increased significantly. Neoliberal societies are being severely criticized for their marked social inequality. The deflationary thrust brought about by free trade caused unemployment, reduced public spending, and engendered frequent economic crashes that brought about an impoverishment of masses of people. These results portray the opposite of the projected assumption of the "trickle-down" theory or "the rising tide that is supposed to lift all boats."

In the fourth assumption, multinational corporate enterprises perceived themselves to be the most efficient enforcers of corporate capitalism. In Latin America, the trade-off for such "efficiency" has been marked loss of human life, massive human rights violations, social upheaval, and increased poverty for the masses. But such "efficiency" has safeguarded investor-rights, corporate profits, and predatory capitalism, especially for Anglo-American corporations. It is therefore not surprising that corporate "efficiency" and its mislabeled "free trade" agreements have provoked an angry rejection against Bush's monocultural world and the homogenization of all cultures within a Western economic paradigm. From the perspective of the Latin American experience with the monolithic hegemony of corporate capitalism and free trade, the "efficiency" of corporate capitalism is not only in question but it is also an unfairly "rigged" neocolonial game favoring corporate elites that has been highly destructive of Latin American societies.

REFERENCES

Altamirano-Jiménez, Isabel. 2013. *Indigenous Encounters with Neoliberalism: Place, Women and the Environment in Canada and Mexico*. Vancouver: UBC Press.

Ball, G. 1967. "Cosmocorp: The Importance of Being Stateless." *Columbia Journal of World Business* 2 (6): 26–28.

Barlow, Maude, and Tony Clarke. 2003. *Blue Gold: The Battle against Corporate Theft of the World's Water*. London: Earthscan.

Chomsky, Noam. 2016. *Who Rules the World?* New York: Metropolitan Books.

Cooper, R., K. Kaiser, and M. Kosaka. 1977. *Towards a Renovated International System*. Triangle Paper 14, The Trilateral Commission, 19.

Coulthard, Glen Sean. 2014. *Red Skin White Masks: Rejecting the Colonial Politics of Recognition*. Minneapolis: University of Minnesota Press.

Cullather, Nick. 2006. *Secret History: The CIA's Classified Account of Its Operations in Guatemala, 1952-1954.* Stanford, CA: Stanford University Press.

Davis, Shelton. 2002. "Indigenous People, Poverty, and Participatory Development: The Experiences of the World Bank in Latin America." In *Multiculturalism in Latin America: Indigenous Rights, Diversity, and Democracy*, edited by Rachel Seider. 227–50. London: Palgrave.

de-la-Cadena, Marisol. 2000. *Indigenous Mestizos: The Politics of Race and Culture in Cuzco, Peru, 1919-1991.* Durham, NC: Duke University Press.

Galeano, Eduardo. 1978. *Days and Nights of Love and War.* Cuba: Casa de las Américas.

Gill, Stephen. 1990. *American Hegemony and the Trilateral Commission.* Cambridge: Cambridge University Press.

———. 2008. *Power and Resistance in the New World Order.* 2nd Edition. New York: Palgrave Macmillan.

Gleijeses, Piero. 1997. *Shattered Hope: The Guatemalan Revolution and the United States, 1944-1954.* Princeton, NJ: Princeton University Press.

Gunder Frank, André. 1976. "Economic Genocide in Chile: Open Letter to Milton Friedman and Arnold Harberger." *Economic and Political Weekly* 11 (24): 880–88.

Hansen, Tom. 2002. "Zapatistas: A Brief Historical Timeline." In *The Zapatista Reader*, edited by Tom Hayden, 8–15. New York: Avalon Publishing Group Inc.

Hayden, Tom, ed. 2002. *The Zapatista Reader.* New York: Nation Books/Avalon Publishing Group, Inc.

Hayner, Priscilla. 2001. *Unspeakable Truths: Confronting State Terror and Atrocity.* New York: Routledge.

Kandell, Jonathan. 1976. "Chile, Lab Test for a Theorist." *The New York Times*, March 21. http://www.nytimes.com/1976/03/21/archives/chile-lab-test -for-a-theorist.html?_r=0.

———. 2006. "Augusto Pinochet, 91, Dictator Who Ruled by Terror in Chile, Dies." *The New York Times*, December 11. http://www.nytimes.com/2006/12/11/world/americas/11pinochet.html.

Kinzer, Stephen. 2006. *Overthrow: America's Century of Regime Change from Hawaii to Iraq.* New York: Henry Holt and Company, LLC.

Kirsch, Stuart. 2014. *Mining Capitalism: The Relationship Between Corporations and Their Critics*. Oakland: University of California Press.

Klein, Naomi. 2002. "The Unknown Icon." In *The Zapatista Reader*, edited by Tom Hayden, 91. New York: Avalon Publishing Company.

———. 2007. *The Shock Doctrine: The Rise of Disaster Capitalism*. New York: Picador.

Kopkind, Andrew. 2002. "Opening Shots." In *The Zapatista Reader*, edited by Tom Hayden, 19–21. New York: Avalon Publishing Group Inc.

Letelier, Orlando. 1976. "The 'Chicago Boys' in Chile: Economic Freedom's Awful Toll." *The Nation*, August 28. https://www.thenation.com/article/the-chicago-boys-in-chile-economic-freedoms-awful-toll.

Lydon, Christopher. 1977. "The Trilateral Commission was David Rockefeller's Brainchild." *The Atlantic*, July. https://books.google.com/books?id=Jvbl5o9_rm8C&pg=PA93&lpg=PA93&dq=Lydon,+Christopher.++%E2%80%9CThe+Trilateral+Commission+was+David+Rockefeller%E2%80%99s+Brainchild.%E2%80%9D&source=bl&ots=dbSyWWTJFs&sig=5VGO0MGQ-eWAvHUnE9jFqD0TKA8&hl=en&sa=X&ved=0ahUKEwiAoYDv2dHSAhXogVQKHXRHAu8Q6AEINzAF#v=onepage&q=Lydon%2C%20Christopher.%20%20%E2%80%9CThe%20Trilateral%20Commission%20was%20David%20Rockefeller%E2%80%99s%20Brainchild.%E2%80%9D&f=false.

Mallén, Patricia Rey. 2013. "Bolivian Census Highlights How Changes in Bolivian Demographics Might Affect President Evol Morales' Power Base." *International Business Times*, August 7. Accessed 2015. http://www.ibtimes.com/bolivian-census-highlights-how-changes-bolivian-demographics-might-affect-president-evo-morales.

Mander, Jerry. 1993. "Megatechnology, Trade and the New World Order." In *The Case against Free Trade*, edited by Ralph Nader, 13–22. San Francisco, CA: Earth Island Press.

Mehta, Uday. 1997. "Liberal Strategies of Exclusion." In *Tensions of Empire: Colonial Cultures in a Bourgeois World*, edited by Frederick Cooper and Ann Laura Stoler, 59–85. Berkeley: University of California Press.

Nader, Ralph, ed. 1993. *The Case against Free Trade: GATT, NAFTA, and the Globalization of Corporate Power*. San Francisco, CA: Earth Island Press.

Okun, A. M. 1975. *Equality and Efficiency: The Big Tradeoff.* Washington, D.C:
   The Brookings Institution.

Petras, J. 1977. "President Carter and the 'New Morality.'" *Monthly Review* 28
   (June): 14–17.

Philips, Anne. 2007. *Multiculturalism without Culture.* Princeton, NJ: Princeton
   University Press.

Postero, Nancy, and Leon Zamosc. 2004. "Indigenous Movements and the Indian
   Question in Latin America." In *The Struggle for Indian Rights in Latin
   America,* edited by Nancy Postero and Leon Zamosc, 1–31. London:
   Sussex Academic Press.

Power, J. 1979. "The Thoughts of Andy Young." *The Observer.*

Psacharopoulos, George, and Harry Patrinos. 1994. *Indigenous People and
   Poverty in Latin America.* Washington, D.C.: World Bank.
   http://documents.worldbank.org/curated/en/541051468757195444/pdf
   /multi-page.pdf.

Reid, Michael. 2009. *Forgotten Continent: The Battle for Latin America's Soul.*
   London: Yale University Press.

Rose, Andrew K. 2004. "Do We Really Know That the WTO Increases Trade?"
   American Economic Review I (94): 98–114.

Samosc, Leon. 2004. "The Indian Movement in Ecuador: From Politics of
   Influence to Politics of Power." In *The Struggle for Indian Rights in
   Latin America,* edited by Nancy Postero and Leon Zamosc, 1–31.
   London: Sussex Academic Press.

Sawyer, Suzana. 2004. *Crude Chronicles: Indigenous Politics, Multinational Oil,
   and Neoliberalism in Ecuador.* London: Duke University Press.

Schemo, Daine Jean. 1998. "Ecuadoreans Want Texaco to Clear Toxic Residue."
   The New York Times, February 1. http://www.nytimes.com/1998/02/01
   /world/ecuadoreans-want-texaco-to-clear-toxic-residue.html.

Schlesinger, Stephen, and Stephen Kinzer. 2005. *Bitter Fruit: The Story of the
   American Coup in Guatemala.* Cambridge: Harvard University David
   Rockefeller Center for Latin American Studies.

Segarra, Monique. 2013. "Challenging Neoliberalism and Development: Human
   Rights and the Environment in Latin America." In *Sustaining Human
   Rights in the Twenty-First Century: Strategies from Latin America,*
   edited by Katherine Hite and Mark Ungar, 303–40. Washington, D.C.:
   Woodrow Wilson Center Press.

Shank, Wheaton, and Lockwood. 1977. "Jimmy Carter's Foreign Policy, Human Rights and the Trilateral Commission." ACTS. Washington, D.C., September.

Shiva, Vadana. 2002. *Water Wars: Privatization, Pollution and Profit.* Cambridge: South End Press.

Shiva, Vandana. 2004. "Water Democracy." In *¡Cochabamba! Water War in Bolivia,* edited by Oscar Olivera and Tom Lewis, ix–xi. Boston: South End Press.

Shoup, Laurence H., and William Minter. 1980. "Shaping a New World Order: The Council on Foreign Relations'Blueprint for World Hegemony, 1939-1945." In *Trilateralism: The Trilateral Commission and Elite Planning for World Management,* edited by Holly Sklar, 135–56. Cambridge, MA: South End Press.

Sieder, Rachel. 2002. *Multiculturalism in Latin America: Indigenous Rights, Diversity and Democracy.* New York: Palgrave.

Sklar, Holly, ed. 1980. *Trilateralism: The Trilateral Commission and Elite Planning for World Management.* Cambridge, MA: South End Press.

Stiglitz, Joseph E. 2012. *The Price of Inequality.* New York: W.W. Norton & Company.

Taylor, Charles. 1992. *Multiculturalism and "the Politics of Recognition."* Princeton: Princeton University Press.

The World Bank. 2007. *The World Bank Report 2007: "Development and the Next Generation."* Washington, D.C. http://documents.worldbank.org/curated/en/556251468128407787/pdf/359990WDR0complete.pdf.

Thompson, José. 2013. "Participation, Democracy and Human Rights." In *Sustaining Human Rights int the Twenty-First Century: Strategies from Latin America,* by Katherine Hite and Mark Ungar, edited by Katherine Hite and Mark Ungar, 73–100. Washington, D.C.: Woodrow Wilson Press Center.

Valdés, Juan Gabriel. 1995. *Pinochet's Economists: The Chicago School in Chile.* Cambridge: Cambridge University Press.

Wolfe, Alan. 1980. "Capitalism Shows Its Face: Giving Up on Democracy." In *Trilateralism: The Trilateral Commission and Elite Planning for World Management,* edited by Holly Skylar, 295–307. Cambridge, MA: South End Press.

Yashar, Deborah J. 2005. *Contesting Citizenship in Latin America: The Rise of Indigenous Movements and the Postliberal Challenge*. New York: Cambridge University Press.

CHAPTER 9

The Parallel: The Crumbling of Imperial Peace—
The Violence of External Acquisition Is Turning Internal

The US has often been described as empire. It is imperial as it has exported a domestic political and financial system to the world. Concrete imperialism has evolved to abstract financial controls by the rules of Neoliberalism and the Washington Consensus. In Latin America, these financial controls have devalued the sense of national sovereignty and increased the great inequality of income between the few elites and the poorer majority. Today, in the US, there is a growing awareness that our system of capitalism has taken the wrong track because the poor and the middle class majority have been targeted. The rapidly rising inequality of income has become an alarming statistic that points to a monopolizing private ownership of the earth and its resources by the very wealthy few. The network of large banks and mega-corporations in the US have become the power players that control the US Congress by lobbying dollars, corporate contributions, and an advertised narrative that disguises the root of their efforts for profits. The dispossession of the resources, programs and incomes of the many will continue to enrich the few. Imperial peace was always false; the internal violence against the American worker is coming to mirror what already happened in Latin America (1954–1990).

A GLOBAL PERSPECTIVE

The US has often been described as an empire, particularly by those who live outside the US borders and have undergone the financial constraints imposed by the Washington Consensus. The US has been imperial as it has aggressively exported its domestic political and financial agenda to the world (1953–2016), that is, a combination of free-market competition and very limited government intervention. The search for commodities by European and US businesses propelled the concrete imperialism of the nineteenth and the first half of the twentieth centuries in Latin America; that imperialism was a physical exploitation of cheap labor, a tangible, visible dispossession of land and resources for corporate profit.

In the latter part of the twentieth century, the imperial control had become abstract. The control became constrained by debt, explained by balance sheets, bankers' language and economic theory to which the average global citizen had little access, less understanding, and no voice. Only the results of this control were visible. Wielded by the rules of Neoliberalism and the Washington Consensus—that is, the International Monetary Fund, the World Bank, the World Trade Center, and the US Treasury all located between 15th and 19th Street in New York City—this control stressed a neoliberal narrative. The narrative claimed neoliberal policies would stimulate economic growth. These policies were imposed on the American nations of the Southern Hemisphere for the second half of the twentieth century. However, for many countries in Latin America, the enforced neoliberal program demonstrated the exact opposite of the neoliberal narrative: 1) a reduced economic growth rate, 2) a perceived colonial return to supplying cheap resources for large corporate profits, 3) a deepening social inequality, and 4) currency instability and disastrous events such as a plan to privatize water in Bolivia or the Chevron-Texaco pollution of Indigenous lands.

Since the turn of the century in Latin America, the neoliberal policies of the Washington Consensus have been perceived not only as an ideological market fundamentalism but also as a form of neocolonialism meant to subordinate Latin American national sovereignty to the Washington Consensus. Simultaneously, these policies have enriched the US and multinational bankers and corporations that no longer have to be physically present. In the imaginations of many, the US has become another decaying Rome with economic might that has reduced all competition by military intervention, stringent economic policies or large corporate production that destroys competing internal Latin markets.

As a result of this image of empire, a spate of dystopian movies such as *Hunger Games* have captured these perceptions very well, drawing a clear parallel to the perceived hierarchy of the world. The movie, *Hunger Games*, expresses a public resonance globally. It contains numerous obvious overtones about the origins of western culture that reflect both the competitive games of Greece and the violence of the Roman Empire. In *Hunger Games*, the frivolity, inhumanity, and disinterest of the singularly privileged first world contrast sharply with the suffering in the twelve other districts of the world. The twelve "colonies" must cooperate in a war-like global competition for survival and give their lives as tribute to the amusement of the first world. In our parallel universe, the US is like the first world that imposes a global war-like competition for resources. From the point of view of those outside the US who are caught in the neoliberal financial web of the Washington Consensus, the US reflects the inhumanity, the disinterest and the frivolity of the first world in *Hunger Games*. The movie mirrors the perspective of the global outsider who is forced to compete for survival in a cruel colonizing game that favors the wealthy of the first world and kills smaller competition. In *Hunger Games*, only winners of competitions survive, and not only history but the present and the future are scripted by the conqueror, that is, the first world.

The implied parallel suggests that US neoliberal interests write the script and the colonizing rules of the competitive resource game-wars. The movie, *Hunger Games*, expresses a global perspective of empire shared by many outside the US. But it is more a twentieth-century perspective, and in Latin America, this perspective is based on their experience of imperialism in the second half of the twentieth century. The nation-state of the US was considered to be the face of Empire.

Empire in the twenty-first century has become a more problematic paradigm. According to Michael Hardt and Antonio Negri, the declining sovereignty of nation-states and their decreasing ability to regulate economic and cultural exchanges is one of the primary symptoms of the Empire of the twenty-first century (Hardt and Negri 2001, xii–xiv). The face of the Empire has become virtual; the US nation-state was a mask. The Empire machine is evolving into a decentered apparatus of rule in which a new imperial form of sovereignty has emerged. No nation-state now forms the face of this imperialist project. The machine of capitalism is primarily run by wealthy US and multinational corporate and banking interests. Their wealth buys power and economic and political control. Today it appears that this new paradigm of Empire works to the detriment of most labor and the majority of workers, even in the US. In contrast to the rest of the world that experienced nineteenth- and twentieth-century imperialism, it is the twenty-first-century paradigm of Empire that has awakened public awareness of imperial control in the US. Many US citizens finally recognize that this corporately controlled machine of capitalism that runs on neoliberal policies wields enormous powers of oppression and destruction for a great majority of people.

FROM THE US INTERNAL PERSPECTIVE: DENIAL OF EMPIRE

Until the twenty-first century, the perceptions within the US were for many years very different. There had long been an avoidance or denial of the state of empire that we had projected on the world. Americans' persistent denial of their nation's imperial past had many reasons—our historical tendency to seclusion, our narcissism, our blind complicity, our myth of exceptionalism as portrayed in our comics and the abysmal performance record of our students in history.

The New York Times (2011, June 1) reported the results of a nationwide test (the Nation's Report Card) in which US students were "less proficient in their nation's history than in any other subject." Thus, Americans' denial of empire does not take into account that the US was historically grounded on an imperial understanding, that is, expansion of European populations and territory at the expense of a corresponding reduction and dispossession of Indigenous populations and territories. William Appleman Williams, one of the earliest students in the US to define the existence of an American Empire, describes this imperialism: "The routine lust for land, markets or security became justifications for noble rhetoric about prosperity, liberty and security" (Williams 1980, 61). Public blindness was fed by a disjuncture of two distinct visions of the United States—the academic study of the national culture in our textbooks versus what Oliver Stone and Peter Kuznick term the "darker side," the history of US imperialism (Stone and Kuznick 2012, x). This darker side has been mostly excluded from US textbooks.

Complicating this one-sided version of US history is the tendency of Empire to efface history. In 1845, John L. O'Sullivan, founder and editor of *The United States Magazine and Democratic Review* coined the phrase "manifest destiny" to explain the future project of unlimited onward expansion of the United States. In the same editorial, he also eloquently described the ahistorical thinking so characteristic of Americans. America constitutes the "beginning of a new history...which separates us from the past and connects us with the future only." America is the "Great Nation of Futurity" (O'Sullivan 1845, 426–30). Michael Hardt and Antonio Negri, in their book *Empire*, confirm this elimination of the past: "Empire exhausts historical time, suspends history...Empire presents its order as permanent, eternal and necessary" (Hardt and Negri 2001, 11). As a consequence, the American tendency to omit a historical perspective reveals an American fault as well as a noncritical complicity with Empire's objectives.

William Appleman Williams made another famous yet revealing statement pointing out that the perception of empire was not internal or native to the American public. Rather, a perception grew and crystalized which was defined by an opposing Other:

One of the central themes of American historiography is that there is no American Empire. Most historians will admit if pressed, that the United States once had an Empire. They then promptly insist that it was given away. But they also speak persistently of America as a World Power. (Williams 1955, 379)

Amy Kaplan, in her book, *Left Alone with America: The Absence of Empire in the Study of American Culture* (2005), further expands this idea that America's self-identity developed in contrast to the Nazis and the twentieth century Soviets. She points out that the imperial politics denied at home were very visibly projected onto a demonic other; empire is something we do not do, rather, it is something we fight against. We could see the Other; we could not see ourselves. This persistent blindness about US corporate interests abroad has left many American citizens unprepared for the crash of 2008, the post-2008 realities, and the siege of corporate right-winged dollars on US politics.

The binary division of good versus evil rose out of the American struggle of the rugged settler taming nature, out of the perspectives of World War II and out of several generations of Americans that grew up on comics. Batman versus the Joker, Superman versus Lex Luther, the Avengers' struggle with Evil, and Luke Skywalker versus Darth Vader formed some of these binaries. These comics re-created an American mythology of the hero fighting evil, a self-perceived identity that spilled out into Hollywood's early TV series and movies such as *Gary Cooper in High Noon*. This myth of American exceptionalism was a strong recurring narrative encouraged by Hollywood that filled our gaping historical void. By Reagan's nadir in the decade of the 1980s, the US identified with the bright empire of *Star Wars*, another dualistic celebration of good versus evil, not because it was an empire, but because of the exceptional struggle of good versus evil. However, this binary internal American perspective was then forced to mature.

In the final decade of the twentieth century, a shift happened. There was no more demonic Other—the Berlin wall had come down and the Union of the Soviet Socialist Republic had disbanded. Gorbachev was being lauded worldwide for ending the Cold War. In true *fin du siècle* pessimism, the myth of American exceptionalism started to erode, losing its legitimacy in the public milieu. Both the diversion of the heroic struggle against evil and the anticommunist narrative of corporate neoliberalism began to unravel in the public mind despite a resurgence of the neoliberals and their corporate agenda.

Though Americans have long denied the imperial pretensions of the United States, Oliver Stone and Peter Kuznick document a change in that denial in the first few years of the twenty-first century:

> It is only recently that neoconservatives have broken with this pattern [of denial], proudly proclaiming not only that America is an empire but that it is the most powerful and most righteous empire the world has ever seen. To most Americans this is still blasphemy. To the neocons it reflects muscularity.... The *New York Times* Sunday magazine cover for January 5, 2003, read, "American Empire: Get Used to It." (Stone and Kuznick 2012, xiv–xv)

In the twenty-first century, when the American public came to recognize that the real demon was not external but internal, American politics polarized in two groups with each side demonizing the Other, by now a bad American habit. This state of affairs aptly demonstrated a clairvoyant quote from yet another famous American cartoon, Pogo: "We have met the enemy, and the enemy is us." This 1972 quote was resurrected in 1989 by the *Los Angeles Times* and the Kelly family's dedication of a plaque with this quote in 1998. The quote encapsulated the American public's awareness. The first decade of the twenty-first century shredded the consoling myth of American benevolence and exceptionalism. The duality turned internal; civility evaporated, and a biting meanness entered the vocabulary of politicians and political ads. "We [Americans] have only just begun our confrontation with our imperial history, our imperial ethic, and our imperial psychology" (Williams 1980, 6).

Today in the US, Conservatives vilify Liberals and the Liberals point to the conservative corporate wealth that is corrupting both Senators and Congressmen. The US legislative body has been locked in a polarizing war of self-identity since 2009. This "war" to interpret America has become an all-out power struggle for the majority of seats in the US legislative bodies with enormous amounts of money being spent to secure each side's identity and agenda. The fallout from this polarization is an embittered American public who expects no help from its dysfunctional government body and who now recognizes that the disenfranchised of the world includes a large American working class. Thus, in predictable American fashion, the middle and working classes finally came to recognize the demon that had remained hidden from them for so many years—the great corporate and banking wealth that strives to reduce all public benefits and runs away with public dollar bail-outs. The protest, Occupy Wall Street, was born. Why did public recognition of corporate neoliberal interests take so long in the

United States? Because for the majority of American people, they did not recognize an empire and the empire's agenda did not have a name.

NO RECOGNITION OF EMPIRE, NO NAME FOR THE EMPIRE'S SCRIPT

That US citizens have been slow to recognize the decline of the public good at the expense of corporate profits is partially due to the slow death of the American Dream. For many US citizens, the housing crisis from 2008–2012 killed the American Dream. But Americans were also slow to recognize the decline of the public good partially due to the lack of a precise name to pinpoint and explain this decline.

Neoliberalism is a name well recognized in the rest of the world as an economic force that favors corporate and banking interests. Countries with the experience of imperialism clearly understand how neoliberal policies have subordinated their interests to the Empire. But "neoliberalism" is a term that is seldom used in the US. Although there has been a rising realization in the US of class struggle—the 1 percent versus the 99 percent—this class struggle has not been given a clear name either. This lack of an explicit name helps to explain decades of the average US citizen's inability to clearly perceive working class stagnation. Moreover, Karl Marx's identification of class struggle has not been a part of the average American citizen's education. Rather, Karl Marx's name has long been linked to a failed model of government.

Why is the term Neoliberalism seldom used or understood in the US? The base of the word liberal confuses conservatives and liberals (now also called progressives) alike. Liberal in politics supports the 99 percent, the poor and the middle class. However, liberal in economics supports the exact opposite, that is, the extremely wealthy investors, the 1 percent and their corporate interests. So Neoliberalism is an economic term that upholds the business and economic policies favored by the corporates and the elites to expand their businesses and increase their profits.

Neoliberalism has been named the dominant political, economic paradigm of our time globally, yet in the US, the term Neoliberalism is largely unknown and unused by the public at large (McChesney 1998, 7). It has been the narrative of the twentieth century Empire—the Empire that average American citizens didn't acknowledge. But the lack of a precise name and a clear definition has worked in favor of US corporate interests in their home base. Neoliberals preferred the image of the historically valid Republican Party or the Tea Party, referring to the historic uprising against taxation. Neoliberal political control has worked best in labyrinthine chaos where it has not been clearly recognized or defined by the public. It has worked best when the population is diverted from the information necessary for meaningful decision making. It functions best where television channels of information and news rooms are frequently funded or controlled by Big Business.

Furthermore, neoliberal policies in the US have been white-washed with desired associations. Words are pivotal marketing devices and have become the tactical *modus operandi* of the Empire. So "free" market policies encourage private enterprise and consumer choice. "Free" market policies undermine the incompetent, bureaucratic and parasitic government. "Free" market policies increase and elevate liberty. The terminology "liberty" is also a neoliberal mantra that has pushed the corporate agenda—deregulation, privatization and financial liberalization—to increase its profits. "A generation of corporate-financed public relations efforts has given these terms and ideas a near sacred aura" (McChesney 1998, 7) that 2008 could not completely undo, especially in the socially conservative southern and mid-western parts of the United States. The original values of the US founding fathers have been appropriated to equal neoliberal orthodoxy. The father of Neoliberalism, Milton Friedman, stretched this appropriation even further when he called profit making the essence of democracy, and any attempt to control the market for the public good as anti-democratic (*Capitalism and Freedom*).

As Williams pointed out, the founding fathers were imperialistic by constitutional design; nevertheless, they were equally concerned with preventing an oligarchy by the wealthy. Consequently, the equation of the values of the founding fathers to neoliberalism presents a troubling contradiction. The early presidents—George Washington, Thomas Jefferson, James Madison, and John Quincy Adams—all warned against the threat of political and economic control by the wealthy which could undo a democracy and the liberty of the average citizen.

Historically, the Neoliberal movement was initiated by Milton Friedman of the University of Chicago's School of Business in the 1950s. His fervor galvanized a think-tank of conservative economic thought which Daniel Bell, a Harvard sociologist, described as an "idealized system" (Bell 1981, 57–58). The market left to its own devices, would create just the right number of products at precisely the right prices, produced by workers at just the right wages to buy those products (Klein 2007, 61). The immediate downfall to this theory was that there did not exist a country that met the criteria for perfect laissez-faire capitalism to validate the idealized system. According to the neoliberal ideas of the Chicago School, the Keynesian economics enacted by President Roosevelt as a result of the Great Depression of 1929 had left corporations in the US crippled. The mission of the neoliberals was to return to unfettered pure capitalism. Their theories could not be immediately applied to the US (1954–1979) due to the American public support of Keynesian economics in the 1950s and '60s. However, neoliberal policies were vigorously applied to US corporate interests in Latin America for several decades (1953–1979) prior to President Reagan's election in 1980, particularly in the Southern Cone of Latin America—Chile, Uruguay, Argentina, and Brazil.

THE EMPIRE'S SCRIPT

Dani Rodrik, the author of *The Globalization Paradox* describes the change in internal US politics with the arrival of President Reagan who unswervingly supported neoliberal economics:

> The state was no longer seen as an aide to economic growth; it was considered the principal obstacle blocking it. By 1989, an early version of the revisionist package was codified "The Washington Consensus." Coined in 1989 by the economist, John Williamson, the term originally referred to a list of ten distinct reforms, with a heavy emphasis on deregulation, trade and financial liberalization, privatization, avoidance of currency overvaluation and fiscal discipline. But over time, the Washington Consensus was transformed into a more doctrinaire approach, a mantra for the über-liberalizers. By the mid 1990's, the moniker of Neoliberalism had evolved into an agenda that could be summarized in three words: stabilize, liberalize and privatize. (Rodrik 2011, 163–64)

Under the Washington Consensus, the simple and deceptive narrative about the power of globalization to lift developing nations out of poverty ("the rising tide") misled many nations, particularly in Latin America. In the famous Sachs-Warner analysis (1995) by two university economists, they reported countries that opened themselves up to international trade and investment would experience a rising tide of trade to pull them up from poverty. This famous report fueled an "obsessive drive for globalization," the neoliberal quest for hyper-globalization (Rodrik 2011, 166). However, for many Latin American countries, the promised Rising Tide never happened, just as the Trickle Down theory in the US has been proven false by rampantly rising social inequality.

THE EMPIRE'S SCRIPT IMPOSED ON LATIN AMERICA

Historically, the dominant Latin American economic model that spawned prosperity during the years of 1930–1970 was called Developmentalism. To protect their internal industries and businesses, it maintained highly restrictive trade regimes which posed a threat to US corporate expansion. Latin countries such as Brazil and Mexico relied more heavily on their own domestic markets to fuel growth. Under their own protectionist model, Latin nations experienced faster rates of economic growth than in any other time of their economic history. Latin America grew at a rate exceeding 2.5 percent per capita, a pace that far exceeds what Latin America has achieved under the umbrella of the neoliberal policies of the Washington Consensus and the neoliberal drive for globalization.

The Neoliberal project for Latin America during the '60s, '70s, and '80s became a three-pronged thrust that demonstrated Imperial violence: 1) The implementation of a "political solution"—a series of parallel right-winged military coups were installed in Latin America (Operation Success, Operation Condor, and Operation Fubelt). 2) The implementation of an "economic solution"—the transplantation of US Neoliberalism in Latin soil under the tutelage and visits of Milton Friedman and his Chicago Boys. 3) The political genocide—the use of torture and internment for all political dissenters against these conservative military governments was deliberately undertaken. The CIA's manual on torture, the Kubark (1963), was used to instruct almost all the Latin American military "puppet dictators" at the School of the Americas in Panama.

For several decades, policy makers in Latin America were Latins educated at the University of Chicago under Friedman's neoliberal ideology at the US tax payers' expense. These "Chicago Boys" implemented neoliberal policies with fervor. The fervor, of course, was first propelled by the violent imposition of military governments, supported by US tax dollars, to quell socialists' movements and protect US corporate investments. This fervor and the money to spread it came from a US right-winged, ideological nucleus of wealthy men and corporations representing IT&T, the Anaconda and Kennecott mining corporations, Ford Foundation, Heritage Foundation, Chevrolet, Pfizer Chemical, Chase Manhattan, City Bank, IBM, and others (Klein 2007, 78–79, 136, 198). They insisted that the US government financially support their demands with public dollars. The primary objective of their neoliberal ideology was to protect and grow their corporate profits in Latin America.

Chile represented the chance to experimentally impose Neoliberalism on a country. In the US business magazine, *Barron's*, the headlines "Chile, Lab Test for a Theorist," summarized the neoliberal intent (Bleiberg 1987). However, after the military coup, the imposition of neoliberal policies provoked disastrous results, causing a 375 percent inflation rate in the initial years, high rates of unemployment (20 to 30 percent) that lasted for years, marked social inequality and the destruction of Chile's internal markets (Klein 2007, 101). Chileans were thrown out of work because corporate "free trade" was flooding the country with cheap imports. By 1982, after eight years of the neoliberal experiment, Chile's market crashed and unemployment hit 30 percent (Grandin 2006, 171). Even twenty-five years later, Chile still retained vestiges of the imperial violence imposed in 1973. By 2007, Chile remained one of the most unequal societies in the world (CIA 2007).

Chile, as a "laboratory" for free market ideology, demonstrated a very disturbing pattern of imperial violence, a pattern that would later be repeated in the US in 2008. The middle and working classes were impoverished and a small elite, known as the Piranhas, leapt from wealthy to super-rich status in short order. Naturally, when Chile's market crashed in 1982, these elites who had bought up the country's wealth on too much borrowed money were bailed out by public funds. Thus, even great economic crashes, brought about by both elites and corporate overextension, appear to have created times of great prosperity for the corporate elite both in Chile and the United States.

In US journalism, the so-called "Chilean Miracle" touted by Milton Friedman (1974) was a deliberate description of this windfall for corporate profits; it ignored the reality on the ground of the vast majority of Chileans. The misery of the majority is apparently of little concern to the script of the Empire.

By the 1990s, the failure of the neoliberal analysis of a rising tide and trickle down wealth was the final blow to neoliberal credibility in Latin America. Even with a strong ideological fervor in the US during the 1990s, the fallacy of the Empire's script was not at all new to Latin Americans. They had experienced this neoliberal dogma to the extreme and did not wish to participate further in the shackles of "free trade" that repeated imperial assumptions. Their rejection of the neoliberal Empire was quick. The IMF was paid off and abandoned. ALBA (that symbolically means "dawn"), the Bolivian Alternative for the Americans, is one of the many Latin American answers to reject the Free Trade Area of the Americas (FTAA). Latin American countries announced they would no longer send students to the School of the Americas. Between 2005 and 2007, the revolt against the neoliberal Empire was most advanced in Latin America as they had endured the intensity of the Empire's violence longer than most. For them, neoliberal globalization was dead; it was no longer the only economic option.

THE POLITICAL TRILEMMA BROUGHT ABOUT BY THE EMPIRE'S SCRIPT

Thus, in Latin America, the effects of empire left a debilitating record of violence—thousands of Disappeared, destruction of the democratic process and weakening of national sovereignty. Dani Rodrik in *The Globalization Paradox* points out exactly this scenario, labeling it a political trilemma:

> We cannot have [neoliberal] hyper-globalization, democracy and national self-determination all at once. We can have at most two out of three. If we want hyper-globalization and democracy, we need to give up on the nation state. If we must keep the nation state and want hyper-globalization too, then we must forget about democracy. (Rodrik 2011, 200)

In the '70s and '80s, under the US-supported military governments in Latin America, the imposition of neoliberal trade globalization and the political internment of all voices that disagreed with this arrangement meant many Latin Americans had no democracy and no voice. In Argentina alone, 30,000 disappeared for their opposition to the forced military coup and the imposed economic program. From the 1980s through the first decade of the twentieth century, the demands of hyperglobalization, neoliberal privatization, and debt control by the Washington Consensus left Latin Americans with two results: 1) Countries that demonstrated democracy, but they had a significantly weakened nation state controlled by the IMF. 2) The complete suppression of democracy by puppet dictatorships such as Chile (1973–1990). By 2000, in Latin American eyes, the real power of their national sovereignty had been lost to the Washington Consensus; the demands of the IMF and WTO had effectively neutered national sovereignty. Because of privatization, many Latins felt that their country and its resources no longer belonged to them. Their democracies had also been violently suppressed. As Bolivia's Vice President, Álvaro García Linero told the *Christian Science Monitor* in March 2007, "We are searching for a road to post-neoliberalism, for ways to disassemble the process of financial colonization and public resource privatization of the 1980's and 1990's" (Bremmer 2010, 172).

For Latin Americans today, the neoliberal narrative for US and multinational corporate profits is thinly tolerated. The Empire and its script are to be resisted. National sovereignty and democracy must be maintained; neoliberal globalization is dangerous. Brazil paid off its debts to the Washington Consensus in order to regain the control of its own sovereignty. It has even modified its take on capitalism to include some traits of state-capitalism (China as a model) over free-market capitalism. (It appears, however, that today Brazil cannot come back from its own corruptive influences.) Those who have had to dance to the demands of the Washington Consensus such as Bolivia reflect a strong disenchantment with the political and financial constraints of empire that have brought such havoc to their economies and to their lives.

The Bolivian Water Wars of 2000 exemplify this distaste for US corporate profits at the expense of Bolivian lives. Because of the IMF debt, the sovereignty of Bolivia had been eaten away by the demands of the Washington Consensus to privatize everything. The demand to privatize water allowed Bechtel, the fifth largest corporate structure in the US, to monopolize the drinking water of Cochabamba, Bolivia and to double the cost of water. This monopoly outraged the large Indigenous populations who not only could not afford the steep increases in water, but who perceived this monopoly as a violation of the commons—that which is common to all men and should not be owned for the profits of elites.

Indigenous Bolivians believe that water is the blood of *Pachamama* and utilizing her sacred gift to impoverish her own people while making a foreign corporation rich is an outrage. The arrest of those Bolivians who collected rainwater because they could not afford the high price increases on water proved the last straw. Bechtel's monopoly on water for profit provoked a great uprising of the people of Bolivia against the US-based corporation of Bechtel. Martial law had to be enforced, restoring order, and Bechtel was kicked out of Bolivia. The Empire's script had lost its credibility and appeal.

THE EMPIRE'S VALUES AND ITS EVOLUTION

Imperial values stand in opposition to the values of the collective commons. The idea of the collective commons is deeply rooted in many of the world's cultures, particularly in many Indigenous cultures. In the eyes of collective cultures, nature's basic resources are for all, not to be owned or monopolized by the wealthy few. In the Indigenous perspective, the imperial values of wealth, privilege, and dispossession for the profits and private ownership of all resources promote violence. In Latin American eyes, imperial values point to the subordination of the state, the suppression of democracy, glaring social inequality and human misery—such as the starvation and thirst of the poor.

Today, in the US, the collective commons are mainly represented by programs. Since Obama's presidential election in 2008, these programs—Social Security, Medicare, Medicaid, Obamacare, labor unions, and public education—

have all been under relentless attack by right-winged neoliberal conservatives. Neoliberal voices have voted to dismantle Obama-Care countless times demonstrating the vehemence and the continuity of the attack. That US citizens are subject to a weakening of democratic rights by court cases (Citizens United 2010 and McCutcheon 2014), by suppression of voter rights, and by suppression of unions is not a surprise to Latin Americans. In the Latin American experience, democracies were crushed, people were shot, tortured, and disappeared to impose imperial values. As Eduardo Galeano expressed it: "people were in prison so that prices could be free" (Weschler 1990, 147). Nor is it a surprise to Latin Americans that there is a weakening of the government of the United States as wealthy corporations, and their lobbyists buy congressional support for their agendas. The court cases, Citizen's United and McCutcheon, have made this corruption legal. The Latin American experience of the values of empire point to puppet dictators installed by the Empire's economic support (US corporations, the CIA, and US presidents) for the purpose of creating favorable political environments for their profits. As Noam Chomsky succinctly pointed out, the Empire's script places "profits over people" (Chomsky 1999). William Appleman Williams also synthesizes what Empire is about: "Locke said it as well as anyone and more honestly than most: Empire as a way of life involves taking wealth and freedom away from others to provide for your own welfare, pleasure and power" (Williams 1980, 30).

History documents that imperial peace is false. "When an individual converts to the values of the imperial, he or she reorients his or her feeling of worthiness to a mode of individual gain, regardless of the well-being of others" (Hopkins 2013, 15). The successful capitalist believes that he is entitled to a disproportionate share of goods even though his activity dispossesses the goods of others. He or she acquires a sense of false imperial peace. Economic wealth, according to Hopkins, becomes valued as one of the highest virtues and the hunger for this ownership, akin to the addiction of gambling, controls the person's perception of the worth of his life or death.

On a grand scale, this accelerated acquisition, which is practiced by many and that is unregulated, leads to destabilizing swings in the market and violent dispossession of others, as demonstrated by the market and housing crash in 2008 in the US and Chile's 1982 crash. These downward crises also appear to greatly benefit elites and corporate profits at the expense of the general population.

The US general population, today, has experienced this violence of dispossession—the loss of homes, high unemployment, reductions in work income, the destruction of benefits and retirement incomes, economic strangulation of educational institutions, the loss of programs and resources for the poor—at the hands of the wealthy banking and corporate interests. The predatory capitalism that the US corporations imposed on Chile in the '70s has turned inward against its own citizens. The efforts of dispossession are intense and unrelenting.

The Neoliberal policies of the past thirty-six years, starting with President Reagan have brought about what Joseph Stiglitz, a Nobel Prize-winning economist, terms a great social inequality and a divided society. While incomes for the working class and the middle class have remained stagnant for forty years, incomes for the top 1 percent have dramatically increased by 80 percent between 1980 and 2005 under neoliberal policies. According to Stiglitz, by 2007, the top one-tenth of 1 percent had incomes that were 220 times larger than the average of the bottom 90 percent (Stiglitz 2012, 2). The wealthiest 1 percent owned more than one-third of the nation's wealth before the crash, and it is now estimated that this 1 percent owns 40 percent of the nation's wealth. This acquisition of wealth by the 1 percent significantly accelerated after the global depression of 2008 while the middle and working classes weakened, repeating the pattern of neoliberalism applied to Chile. In 2010, the top one percent of Americans gained 93 percent of the additional income created in that year (Stiglitz 2012, 3).

"Even before the burst in inequality that marked the first decade of this century, the U.S. already had more inequality and less income mobility than practically every country in Europe, as well as Australia and Canada"(Stiglitz 2012, 5). In the United States today, income distribution is now more unequal than in Uruguay, Nicaragua, and Venezuela. Social mobility has frozen; it is harder to rise from poverty in the neoliberal Empire than in almost any comparable developed country. "We [in the US] are now approaching the level of inequality that marks dysfunctional societies" (Stiglitz 2012, 22). A striking illustration of this is the Walmart Corporation owned by the Walton family's six heirs that commands a wealth of $69.7 billion, equivalent to the wealth of the entire bottom 30 percent of the United States (Stiglitz 2012, 8). Mark Twain's (1901) claim that there must be two Americas, one that sets the captives free and one that takes away the captive's freedom has now become an internal American dilemma.

Because imperial ventures have been rejected abroad in the last decade, corporate interests have now turned inward and are reducing the American worker, his national identity and his democratic voice. The Empire's violence of acquisition has turned internal. Dani Rodrik's political and economic trilemma appears to apply to the United States as well. Some believe the nation-state of the

US has weakened. Others believe the real threat is a loss of democracy; the US has become an oligarchy. Corporate dollars will not allow the suppression of globalization, the third concept of the trilemma. The American public has not only denied the existence of Empire; it has not understood what the Empire's script will do to its own middle and working class people. All commons for the public good will be suppressed if the neoliberal empire can impose its program. The paradox of the American worker is that he and she are within Empire, yet they will be reduced by Empire.

Finally, the reality of Empire today is in a different place. Twenty-first century Empire does not need to be geographically situated; it is decentered. It avoids taxation. So why is there such a concerted effort to control the US government? The newly found resources of gas within the territory of the US have replaced the loss of access to resources in the Southern Hemisphere. The oil and gas industries are driving this effort. The resources for corporate profits are now located within the US; thus, the laws and policies of the US must protect corporate resources and their profits. In the neoliberal purview, corporations should not be subject to the democratic review processes that protect "the commons" or the public. However, if they are seriously challenged, these corporate interests have already moved to off-shore accounts (many times, a mailbox or a bank account) that are even more abstract and difficult to trace. They can evade accountability.

Thus, being imperial has evolved. The nineteenth century's model of tangible dispossession of another's land and resources became the twentieth century's model of festering military coups followed by an intangible web of financial controls by the Washington Consensus. The third level of Empire, the twenty-first century model of imperialism, has become a study in the virtual art of deception to escape taxes and accountability. Large corporations consider themselves above the law; they are governments unto themselves operated by an elite few who hide behind labyrinthine layers of dummy corporations. Elysium's violence of acquisition is now becoming an untraceable, decentered, de-territorializing and destructive global apparatus as described by Michael Hardt and Antonio Negri. These corporations are not answerable to either nation-states, democracies, or judicial judgments. Chevron-Texaco's abject refusal to comply with penalties (Keefe 2012) assessed for dumping toxic waste into Amazonian tributaries is an example of such contempt for judicial decisions.

Today, it is recognized that the tenants of neoliberalism create deeply stratified income inequality. The view that free trade and small government are the best way to promote economic growth and development is recognized as a game rigged for the wealthy. The Great Divergence during the nineteenth century—the division of the US between a rich industrial core of the elite and a poor commodity-producing periphery of the many—has reoccurred, becoming a division of the corporate-financial sector, the 1 percent versus the 99 percent. Far from eliminating master narratives as postmodernism would have had us believe, this imperial machine produces and reproduces ideological narratives in order to validate and celebrate its own power (Hardt and Negri 2001, 34). It legitimizes its own authority. To this end communications industries have become critically important because power narratives wield control in the same manner that propaganda brainwashes the multitude. These power narratives are bent on controlling elections. Empire sets in motion a dynamic of "right" that suspends time, cancels history and discourages critical thought.

Imperial peace is an oxymoron that juxtaposes opposing meanings. It is false. There are two Americas visible today within the boundaries of the US, and theoretically, as with all binaries at war, one side usually subjugates, reduces or destroys the other. Acquisition by the few requires dispossession of the many; imperialism has always promoted dualities and violence.

Imperial violence has been a phenomenon often repeated in history, and the destruction it brings usually is remembered for a long time. However, where there exists a public deficiency in critical understanding of history as in the United States today, there is little memory. Public memory was Latin America's greatest tool of resistance to Empire.

The pattern of violence against the public good has become a documented repetitive phenomenon, first in Latin America under US neoliberal corporations and now in the United States, under the neoliberal or globalization policies of the corporate financial Empire. The internal "imperial" aggression to control the US government has become a defining economic and political struggle of our time. It will define the power of the twenty-first century Empire and its imperialism. The original "imperial incubator" (Williams 1980, 7) has deserted the American worker. If not regulated, the corporate neoliberal Empire will consume its own citizens' future.

REFERENCES

Abbas, Asma. 2010. *Liberalism and Human Suffering: Materialist Reflections on Politics, Ethics, and Aesthetics.* New York: Palgrave MacMillan.

Bell, Daniel. 1981. "Models and Reality in Economic Discourse." In *The Crisis in Economic Theory*, edited by D. Bell and I. Kristol, 46–80. New York: Basic Books.

Bleiberg, R. M. 1987. "Why Attack Chile?" *Barron's*, June 22.

Bremmer, Ian. 2010. *The End of the Free Market: Who Wins the War between States and Corporations?* New York: Portfolio Penguin.

Burt, Jo-Marie. 2013. "The New Accountability Agenda in Latin America: The Promise and Perils of Human Rights Prosecutions." In *Sustaining Human Rights in the Twenty-First Century: Strategies from Latin America*, edited by Katherine Hite and Mark Ungar, 101–41. Washington, D.C: Woodrow Wilson Center Press.

Central Intelligence Agency (CIA). 2007. "Field Listing—Distribution of Family Income—Gini Index." World Factbook. www.cia.gov.

Chomsky, Noam. 1999. *Profit over People: Neoliberalism and Global Order.* New York: Seven Stories Press.

Clements, Jeffrey D. 2012. *Corporations Are Not People: Why They Have More Rights Than You Do and What You Can Do about It.* San Francisco: Berrett-Koehler Publishers.

Dillon, S. 2011. "U.S. Students Remain Poor at History, Tests Show." *The New York Times*, June 15. http://www.nytimes.com/2011/06/15/education/15history.html.

Duggan, L. 2003. *The Twilight of Equality? Neoliberalism, Cultural Politics and the Attack on Democracy.* Boston: Beacon Press.

Dworkin, Peter. 1981 "Chile's Brave New World of Reaganomics." *Fortune*, November 2.

Ferguson, Niall. 2004. *Colossus: The Price of America's Empire.* New York: Penguin.

Freedland, J. 2002. "Is America the New Rome?" *The Guardian*, September 18.

Friedman, Milton. 1982. *Capitalism and Freedom.* Chicago: University of Chicago Press.

———. 1974. "Economic Miracles." *Newsweek*, January 21.

Grandin, Greg. 2006. *Empire's Work: Latin America and the Roots of U.S. Imperialism.* New York: Metropolitan Books.

Gunder Frank, André. 1976. "Economic Genocide in Chile: Open Letter to Milton Friedman and Arnold Harberger." *Economic and Political Weekly* 11 (24): 880–88.

Hardt, Michael, and Antonio Negri. 2001. *Empire.* Cambridge, MA: Harvard University Press.

Hopkins, D. N. 2013. "Resisting Imperial Peace: Theological Reflections." In *The Reemergence of Liberation Theologies: Models for the Twenty-First Century*, edited by Thia Cooper, 13–18. New York: Palgrave-MacMillan.

Kaplan, A. 2005. *Left Alone with America: The Absence of Empire in the Study of American Culture.* Cambridge, MA: First Harvard University Press.

Keefe, P. R. 2012. "Reversal of Fortune." *The New Yorker*, January 4.

Kinzer, Stephen. 2006. *Overthrow: America's Century of Regime Change from Hawaii to Iraq.* New York: Times Books.

Klein, Naomi. 2007. *The Shock Doctrine: The Rise of Disaster Capitalism.* New York: Picador.

Kornbluh, Peter. 2003. *The Pinochet Files: A Declassified Dossier on Atrocity and Accountability.* New York: The New Press.

Lira, Elizabeth. 2013. "Chile: Coming to Terms with a Traumatic Past." In *Sustaining Human Rights in the Twenty-First Century: Strategies from Latin America*, edited by Katherine Hite and Mark Ungar, 219–42. Washington, D.C.: Woodrow Wilson Center Press.

McChesney, Robert. 1998. "Introduction." In *Profit over People: Neoliberalism and Global Order*, by Noam Chomsky, 7–16. New York: Seven Stories Press.

O'Sullivan, J. 1845. "Annexation." *The United States Magazine and Democratic Review*, July.

Reid, Michael. 2007. *Forgotten Continent: The Battle for Latin America's Soul.* New Haven, CT: Yale University Press.

Rodrik, D. 2011. *The Globalization Paradox: Democracy and the Future of the World Economy.* New York: W.W. Norton's Company.

Said, Edward. 1993. *Culture and Imperialism.* New York: Alfred A. Knopf, Inc.

Segarra, Monique. 2013. "Challenging Neoliberalism and Development: Human Rights and the Environment in Latin America." In *Sustaining Human*

Rights in the Twenty-First Century: Strategies from Latin America, edited by Katherine Hite and Mark Ungar, 303–40. Washington, D.C.: Woodrow Wilson Center Press.

Schoultz, Lars. 1998. *Beneath the United States: A History of U.S. Policy toward Latin America*. Cambridge, MA: Harvard University Press.

Stiglitz, Joseph. 2012. *The Price of Inequality: How Today's Divided Society Endangers Our Future*. New York: W. W. Norton.

Stone, Oliver, and Peter Kuznick. 2012. *The Untold History of the United States*. New York: Gallery Books.

Twain, Mark. 1901. "To the Person Sitting in Darkness." *North American Review*, edited by George Harvey.

Valdés, Juan Gabriel. 1995. *Pinochet's Economists: The Chicago School in Chile*. Cambridge: Cambridge University Press.

Weiner, Tim. 2008. *Legacy of Ashes: The History of the CIA*. New York: Anchor Books.

Weschler, L. 1990. *A Miracle, a Universe: Settling Accounts with Torturers*. New York: Pantheon Books.

Weyland, Kurt, Raúl Madrid, and Wendy Hunter, eds. 2010. *Leftist Governments in Latin America*. Cambridge, MA: Cambridge University Press.

Williams, William Appleman. 1980. *Empire as a Way of Life: An Essay on the Causes and Character of America's Present Predicament along with a Few Thoughts about an Alternative*. New York: Oxford University Press.

———. 1955. "The Frontier Thesis and American Foreign Policy." *The Pacific Historical Review* 24 (November): 379–95.

CHAPTER 10

"Democratic Distemper": The Deceptive Architecture of Corporate Capitalism, Its Cracks and Its War on Leftist Populism

THE CRACKS OF POPULISM

The first crack in the Monolithic labyrinth of corporate capitalization or globalization was Latin America's rejection of the Free Trade Agreement of the Americas (FTAA) in 2005. The corporatist response to that refusal was incredulity and anger. In reaction to that rejection, Latin America was to be ignored, like Cuba, and the Latin American rejection was downplayed in the US media. One of corporate capitalism's weapons is a media white-out. The crack was quickly covered up, and the subsequent media silence was intended to imply that Latin America was not a significant player in the game of free trade.

The Latin Americans, however, were proven correct in their assessment of the destructive nature of corporate capitalism and its banking practices within three short years. The market crash of 2008 followed by the housing crisis broadcasted that message globally. Latin American populism had emerged ahead of other nations globally. Their experience with the fires of adversity caused by corporate neoliberalism came before globalization had coalesced into the perceived "inevitable" future (with the collapse of the Berlin Wall, the dissolution of the Soviet Union and the end of the Cold War). Latin America had borne the brunt of neoliberal violence several decades ahead of other nations. They were made the testing laboratory of Milton Freedman's ideology, and that ideology spawned military coups, internment camps, torture, years of fear and the slaughter of thousands of citizens perceived as "unacceptable" for corporate profits. The Latin American rejection of the FTAA in 2005 was well founded. US corporate accountability as assessed by courts could apparently be ignored by corporate interests. So the Latin American judgment of North American corporate accountability came in the form of a rejection of the Free Trade Agreement of the Americas. It was also a rejection of the US's perceived hegemony over the Americas, the Monroe Doctrine and the Grand Area Doctrine.

Despite the events of 2008, President Obama attempted to reach out to Latin American nations, listening to their requirements, one of which was the recognition of Cuba as part of the Latin American family of nations. That recognition was granted by his executive powers in 2015–2016, but once again, that recognition was completely ignored by a US Republican pro-business legislature because Cuba had shut out and long refused to play the "rigged game" of US corporate capitalism that had impoverished the many for the profits of the few.

Thus, a primary reason for the dearth of Latin American coverage and acknowledgement in our corporately sponsored media was payback for that first crack in the meticulously constructed Monolith of corporate capitalism (the free trade agreements, the WTO, the IMF, the World Bank, the strategies of the trade commissions, and the conservative think tanks).

On June 24, 2016, the second populist crack in the Monolithic labyrinth of corporate capitalism occurred, and it was seismic. Brexit, Great Britain's referendum to Stay or Leave the European Common Market, was a shock to corporate objectives. The vote to Leave the EU overcame the massive media blitz by US corporations to defend the Stay campaign.

Brexit, like the Latin American rejection, violated the world elite players' vision of their corporate strategy, a vision that suppressed culture, nationalism, and sovereign governments. National laws were to be supplanted or nullified by the requirements of the trade agreements, and the diverse populations of the world were to be "homogenized" within a Western paradigm of trade and consumption. The twenty-first century was supposed to be the fulfilment of their "post-national" age controlled by free trade regulations and corporate elites. Elite corporatists perceived nationalism and sovereignty as huge obstacles to free trade objectives.

The influence of discontented citizenry in a large common market is negligible; the influence of discontented citizenry on a national scale could be more acute. "Democratic distemper" was to be discouraged in a large global system in which the people's voices could not be heard. However, the elite claim that the loss of cultural and national identity are the unfortunate preliminary conditions to a more "democratic" world, rang hollow. Brexit, then, was a betrayal by the nation with the closest ties to the US corporate interests. Nationalism and the "democratic distemper" of the British citizens had raised their ugly heads and shaken the corporate Monolith. The vote was populist on the political right; the English were objecting to the loss of their national sovereignty and their voice. They were displaying the discontent of the working and middle classes against the economic model that favors the elites. "The Brexit vote is a popular reassertion of national sovereignty in the face of supranational economic policies that have beggared the British middle and working classes" (Carden 2016).

Trade is not a distasteful word. Nations favor trade; but in the case of Latin America, they rejected the neoliberal free trade model that privileges the wealthier nations and the corporate elites. Free trade agreements influenced by the US corporate model have eroded the meaning of national identity and national sovereignty. For Latin Americans, the corporatist model of free trade was a return to the shackles of Neocolonialism, the loss of identity. It is interesting that British citizens in describing their reasons to exit the EU have also expressed their objection to losing their identity and feeling colonized. The overarching model of corporate control was finally politically recognized and rejected by Brexit.

THE DECEPTIVE DUAL STRUCTURE OF OPERATION CONDOR: THE MODEL OF THE TRANSPARENT STATE AND THE COVERT SHADOW STATE

Operation Condor remained a clandestine system, shrouded in secrecy for several decades, a well-kept secret of the Cold War (McSherry 2005, xix). Critical documents, the Archives of Terror in Paraguay, were discovered in police files in 1992. Subsequently, the investigation of Operation Condor by the Spanish judge, Baltazar Garzón, produced new evidence which led to the extradition request and arrest of General Pinochet in 1998. These revelations were then expanded by President Bill Clinton's release of one third of the US classified files on Condor. The CIA and the Pentagon refused to release the rest of the files. Nevertheless, since then, a veritable flood of information on Condor has emerged (McSherry 2005, xix).

The operations of Condor were carried out on three levels. On the first level, mutual cooperation among military intelligence services of the US, Argentina, Chile, Uruguay, Paraguay, Bolivia, Brazil, Ecuador, and Peru was set up to identify "subversives." *Condortel*, the network's secure communications system, coordinated member nations and the parent station in a US facility located in the Panama Canal Zone. Exchange of intelligence information was highly effective despite the fact that some of these nations had formerly been adversaries. Consequently, in the 1980s, Operation Condor was expanded to include parts of Central America.

On a second level, a form of offensive unconventional warfare was covertly enacted for the purpose of concealing the perpetrators that inflicted "political genocide" (Rozanski 1998). The military actions of disappearing citizens were cloaked as paramilitary, or handled outside of the state structure in a covert shadow state to afford the state legal cover and the ability to deny disappearing citizens.

The third level of Condor was Phase III in which special operations in teams of assassins traveled globally to eliminate influential "subversive enemies." These enemies consisted of political leaders that had the potential to mobilize public opinion and opposition to the imposed military governments in Latin America. Orlando Letelier, a foreign minister in the Allende government and his US colleague were assassinated in Washington, D.C. by one of the death squads of Phase III in 1976. In some Phase III assassinations, neofascist organizations in Italy (Ordine Nuovo and Avanguardia Nazional) and right-winged Cuban exiles (CORU) in the United States were contracted to carry out the crimes (McSherry 2005, 5). Operation Condor was not a rogue or ad hoc operation, but a well-organized, sophisticated, and well-equipped network with systematized planning, training, communications centers and a chain of command in each country (McSherry 2005, 6).

With the strong anticommunist indoctrination of the CIA, elites from these Latin American states were galvanized into state terrorism as a means of controlling their societies and maintaining their elite power. The elites and their militaries sought to extinguish the hopes for social justice and better democracy held by millions of Latin American progressives, socialists, union leaders, social democrats, Christian Democrats, nationalists, dissident generals, former presidents, and congressional leaders. Targeting all these actors as "communists" was a convenient justification to eliminate them. The repression by Operation Condor was to guarantee the privilege of business elites in Latin America and the North American corporates' access to Latin American resources.

The use of the shadow state—black operations, paramilitary teams, secret prisons, fleets of unmarked cars, unregistered aircraft, mass graves and secure communications centers—was funded by "black budgets" from the CIA, the Nixon-Kissinger executive office and big corporate interests. This shadow state shielded Latin American nation states from accountability, permitting nations the appearance of legitimacy, the ability to avoid international law and human rights' entanglements. The perpetrators were hidden to escape accountability.

García Márquez's metaphorical mind recognized this structure as a labyrinth, because a classical labyrinth is dual. Its upper structure represents the state and transparency while its lower structure hides the dark site of sacrifice and death. Perceived Minotaurs—political prisoners—are incarcerated there. This dual image captured the function and *modus operandi* of Operation Condor. He clearly understood the architecture of deception, the function of the shadow state and the terror it elicited.

Operation Condor demonstrated both counterinsurgency theory and parallel state structures. A classified US Army Special Forces (December 1960) explicitly stated in the section labeled "Terror Operations" that the use of counterinsurgent terror was a legitimate tactic (McClintock 1991, 121–54). The United States whose mantra has been the War on Terror, has long taught counterinsurgent terror as a legitimate tactic. In a March 1961 article of the *Military Review*, this counterinsurgent terror is further described: "Political warfare, in short, is warfare [that] embraces diverse forms of coercion and violence including strikes and riots, economic sanctions, subsidies for guerrilla or proxy warfare and, when necessary, kidnapping or assassination of enemy elites (McClintock 1991, 131). In essence, the US parent control of Operation Condor embraced and encouraged counterinsurgent terror and consequently, the reign of state sponsored terror in Latin America. Condor eliminated political adversaries and extinguished their ideas outside of the rule of law.

THE STRUCTURE OF THE TRANSPARENT STATE (THE US GOVERNMENT) AND THE SHADOW STATE (THE MONOLITH OF CORPORATE CAPITALISM) AND ITS WARFARE AGAINST LEFTIST POPULISM

Supported by a plethora of corporate lawyers, corporate interests today motivate and corrupt the puppet players—local agents, congressmen, senators, lobbyists, governors, cabinet and executive officers, and foreign elites—with money and equipment. The voices of the people are lost. The puppet players get their hands dirty, not the puppet-masters; the puppet-masters remain hidden to the public. The *modus operandi* is an extension of black operations like Condor, and the public continues to be the destabilizing influence, the potential enemy, as it was in Latin America. For that reason, their voices should be suppressed or eliminated.

The "democratic distemper" and the problems of class warfare by an aroused public have long been a concern of corporate capitalists. In May 1975, the rising conservatism of the elite corporates in the Trilateral Commission and their anti-democratic sentiments came to the foreground with their "Report of the Trilateral Task Force on Governability of Democracies." In response, the well-known article, "Capitalism Shows its Face: Giving Up on Democracy," by Alan Wolfe, remarks on two striking features of the Trilateralists' report: "the dominant tone of pessimism" arising among Trilateralists due to fear of class conflict and "the unmediated authoritarianism" of the Trilateral approach to liberal democracy (Wolfe 1980, 297).

The Trilateralists' report defined the causes that triggered their rising fear of class consciousness in the US. The report listed the causes: 1) the disintegration of traditional agencies, 2) a lack of deferential attitudes as people no longer accepted the guidance of authorities, 3) a radically changed structure of values, and 4) the threat of rising expectations of the college-educated class. The suppression of labor, by ideas, debt, and flat-lined salaries, became a Trilateralists' objective. The analysis stated "democratic societies cannot work when the citizenry is not passive," a pronouncement that echoes the dystopia, *Nineteen Eighty-Four*. The report emphasized the decline of faith in government and authority that demonstrates a "democratic distemper" (Wolfe 1980, 298).

In response to these troubling social changes perceived by corporatists, the Trilateralists' report called for 1) better control of economic planning, 2) a stronger US president, 3) "balance in the sources of campaign finance," 4) restrictions on the freedom of the press, 5) the cutting back on education to lower job expectations and instill passivity, and 6) the restructuring of higher education to discourage the development of critical thought.

In this 1975 report, an excess of democracy was not to be tolerated; democratic procedures had to be limited and reduced. Passivity on the part of citizenry was to be encouraged. For the following four decades (1976–2016) in the US, this report clearly predicted the outcome to reign in and reduce democracy for the benefit of the elite corporatist class.

The Trilateralists' report explicitly identifies the disadvantages that US citizens have come to experience in those forty years: 1) economic inequality as a result of "better economic planning," 2) President Bush's tax cuts for the wealthy and the lax banking practices leading to the 2008 crash, 3) the landmark court case of Citizens United and the resulting reign of corporate dark money over American elections and politics, 4) the monopolizing control of the media by very conservative media tycoons such as Rupert Murdoch and Steve Forbes, 5) the engineered cuts on education both federally and by state governments, and 6) the discrediting of the critically thinking citizen as an educational outcome. If world management under the tutelage of the US corporations is the goal of corporate and elite planning, control over the US society is imperative. The US government is their transparent state. But the real management and impunity comes from the shadow state—the Monolith of the corporate and banking elites. The elite attention and control imposed on Latin Americans by US corporations in the twentieth century has now turned inward to target US citizens in the twenty-first century.

The intense controversy that arose from the Trilateralists' report provoked their retreat behind the walls of secrecy for the succeeding years. As Alan Wolfe pointed out, publicly expressing antidemocratic sentiments is an American taboo. As a tactic, however, it is much more difficult to stop an elite agenda when the general public becomes unaware of their existence, their publications and their antidemocratic agenda. There is the face of the US government, and there is the control of the US government by the shadow state of the elites. This dual structure of the puppet-masters is convenient. Only the paid puppet players, the politicians who are seen, can take the fall.

THE CORPORATIST AGENDA: GLOBALIZATION, THE ERASURE OF NATIONAL SOVEREIGNTY, AND THE CORROSION OF DEMOCRACY

Corporate capitalism acquired its three populist cracks from strong displays of nationalism. Latin Americans resented the loss of their sovereignty and the crumbling of their national identity. The British majority who voted to Leave in Brexit, carried the same resentments. LA-Exit and Brexit have just been followed by the US-Exit in the 2016 US presidential election, a third populist crack showcasing "democratic distemper." Globalization and free trade appear to have created an unsustainable social and economic inequality.

Dani Rodrik reminds her readers in *The Globalization Paradox* that "we cannot simultaneously pursue democracy, national determination [identity], and economic globalization." She calls it the "fundamental political trilemma of the world economy" (Rodrik 2011, xvii). In conclusion, she points out the "great diversity that marks our current world renders hyper globalization incompatible with democracy (Rodrik 2011, xix). This trilemma appears to be backed up— historically by the Latin American experience with imposed military governments. The current buying out of the legislative branch of the US government by corporate lobbyists has also reduced democracy. The elites' anti-democratic agenda as presented in the 1975 Trilateralists' report has become a growing concern of the voting public in the United States.

Today most US citizens recognize that they no longer have a republic/democracy with democratic principles but an oligarchy or a plutocracy, a government bought out and run by the very wealthy. Labor's salaries have been flat-lined for years. It is this realization that has triggered the angry populist surge in the 2016 US presidential election. Labor's voice has been left powerless, a condition which will likely continue to feed a class war on the scale of the very divisive class war that Chileans experienced. Corporate capitalism appears to have caused the erasure of citizens' rights, their national identity, and for the many, their earning power. The danger of the US-Exit is that the corporate influence in the US President's cabinet and their corporate and banking elites will alter Mr. Trump's campaign promises; they may derail the hopes of the US working class. In effect, Mr. Trump's cabinet implies a deliberate corporate coup d'état, the inversion of the American workers' hopes.

Consequently, it is not only the loss of the democratic tradition in the US as Dani Rodrik predicted, but we are following the pattern that Latin America experienced—the loss of our national sovereignty. When corporations can frack in our national parks, and legally there is not a thing that citizens can do because of the legalese found in trade agreements or in newly established laws, we will recognize that we, too, have lost not only our democratic voice in government, but the sovereignty of our people. Our politicians have sold us out. We, too, will be disposable like the Chilean people were during the years of the US-backed military coup in Chile. The alarming parallels between US corporate control in Latin America and what is happening in the US today are based upon the agenda of corporate capitalism, and that agenda has not changed.

REFERENCES

Carden, James. 2016. "Keep Calm and Carry-On: Why the Angst over Brexit?" *The Nation*, June 27. https://www.thenation.com/article/keep-calm-and -carry-on-why-the-angst-over-brexit.

McClintock, Michael. 1991. "American Doctrine and Counterinsurgent State Terror." In *Western State Terrorism*, edited by Alexander George, 121– 54. New York: Routledge

McSherry, J. Patrice. 2005. *Predatory States: Operation Condor and Covert War in Latin America.* New York: Rowman & Littlefield Publishers, Inc.

Rodrik, Dani. 2011. *The Globalization Paradox: Democracy and the Future of the World Economy.* New York: W.W. Norton & Company, Inc.

Rozanski, Carlo. 1998. "Auto de la sala de lo penal de la Audiencia Nacional confirmando la jurisdicción de España para conocer de los crímenes de genocidio y terrorismo cometidos durante la dictadura argentina." Court case, Madrid, November 4. www.derechos.org.

Wolfe, Alan. 1980. "Capitalism Shows Its Face: Giving up on Democracy." In *The Trilateral Commission and Elite Planning for World Management*, edited by Holly Sklar, 295–307. Boston: South End Press.

www.ingramcontent.com/pod-product-compliance
Lightning Source LLC
Chambersburg PA
CBHW052011030426
42334CB00029BA/3178